THE POLITICS OF THE SOUL

THE POLITICS OF THE SOUL

Eric Voegelin on Religious Experience

edited by Glenn Hughes

ROWMAN & LITTLEFIELD PUBLISHERS, INC.
Lanham • Boulder • New York • Oxford

ROWMAN & LITTLEFIELD PUBLISHERS, INC.

Published in the United States of America
by Rowman & Littlefield Publishers, Inc.
4720 Boston Way, Lanham, Maryland 20706

12 Hid's Copse Road
Cumnor Hill, Oxford OX2 9JJ, England

British Library Cataloguing in Publication Information Available

Library of Congress Cataloguing-in-Publication Data

The politics of the soul : Eric Voegelin on religious experience /
edited by Glenn Hughes.
    p.   cm.
    Papers presented at workshops and symposiums at several places
from 1993–1996
    Includes bibliographical references and index.
    ISBN 0-8476-9232-9 (cloth : alk. paper). — ISBN 0-8476-9233-7
(pbk. : alk. paper)
    1. Voegelin, Eric, 1901– .—Contributions in concept of religious
experience. 2. Experience (Religion)   I. Hughes, Glenn, 1951– .
B3354.V884P65   1999
291.4'2'092—dc21   98-37875
                                                             CIP

Printed in the United States of America

∞ ™ The paper used in this publication meets the minimum requirements of
American National Standard for Information Sciences—Permanence of Paper for
Printed Library Materials, ANSI Z39.48–1984.

This book is dedicated to
Robert Luc
with love and gratitude

[The wise man] will rather, I said, keep his eyes fixed on the constitution in his soul, and taking care of and watching unless he disturb anything there either by excess or deficiency of wealth, will steer his course and add to or detract from his wealth on this principle, so far as he can.

Precisely so, he said.

And in the matter of honors and office too this will be his guiding principle. He will gladly take part in and enjoy those which he thinks will make him a better man, but in public and private life he will avoid those that may overthrow the established condition of his soul.

Then, if that is his chief concern, he said, he will not willingly take part in politics.

Yes, by the dog, I said, in his own city he certainly will, yet perhaps not in the city of his birth, unless through some divine good fortune.

I understand, he said. You mean that he will be willing to take part in the politics of the city that we were founding and describing in our discourse. For I don't think that it exists anywhere on earth.

Well, I said, perhaps there is a pattern of it laid up in heaven for him who desires to contemplate it and so beholding to constitute himself its citizen. But it makes no difference whether it exists concretely now or ever. He will practice the politics only of this city and of no other.

Probably so, he said.

—Plato, *Republic*

In the depth the soul experiences its death; from the depth it will rise to life again, with the help of God and his messenger. The depth of existence, the anxiety of the fall from being, is the Hades where the soul must turn toward life or death. It is a terrible hour of decision, for in the night where life and death are confronted they are difficult to distinguish. Arete is free, but wisdom is weak. In its freedom the soul resists death. But the forces of existence, past and present, are strong as well as deceptive; persuasively they pull the soul to accept their death as life. In its freedom the soul is willing to follow the helper. But in order to follow his guidance, it must recognize him as the guide toward life; and life looks strangely like death when it drags the soul up to die to the depth in which it lives. Nevertheless, the struggle itself becomes a source of knowledge. In suffering and resisting the soul discerns the directions from which the pulls come. The darkness engenders the light in which it can distinguish between life and death, between the helper and the enemy. And the growing light of wisdom illuminates the way for the soul to travel.

—Eric Voegelin, *Plato*

Contents

Preface

Early in 1995, the remarkable Ken Whelan—intellectual gadfly, cofoun-
der of the San Quentin Drama Workshop, and diligent reader of Voegelin—encouraged me to organize a panel discussion entitled "Eric Voegelin
and Religious Experience" for the Eric Voegelin Society's annual meeting
with the American Political Science Association. With the support of Ellis
Sandoz, the society's director, the session took place that autumn, and
from the experience came the idea of drawing attention to the value of
Voegelin's contribution to the understanding of religious experience by
publishing a book of significant new essays on the topic.

Most of the colleagues I approached as potential contributors expressed
a readiness to write something, and over a few years the collection attained its present form. It brings together the work of Voegelin scholars
from a variety of disciplines—political science, theology, history, and
philosophy—and of notable expertise: authors of Voegelin monographs
and editors of essay collections on Voegelin's work are represented here.
The contributing authors have been models of patience and goodwill during the long preparation of this manuscript, and to each of them I express
my sincere appreciation.

Without the opportunities for deepening my involvement in the world
of Voegelin scholarship provided by Ellis Sandoz, director of the Eric
Voegelin Institute at Louisiana State University, this book would not have
come into being. I was particularly helped in carrying it through to completion by the lovely generosity and excellent advice of my friends and
colleagues Michael P. Morrissey, Fred Lawrence, and Geoffrey L. Price.
Valuable encouragement was also given along the way by Pat Brown, Paul
Kidder, Paulette Kidder, David Levy, Tom McPartland, Steve Shankman,
and Eugene Webb. I am grateful to Stephen Wrinn and his coworkers at
Rowman & Littlefield Publishers for their receptivity and expertise. Most
of all, I want to acknowledge a happy debt to Paul Caringella, friend and
beneficent guide, upon whose graciousness, knowledge, and wise good
humor I have come to rely.

Acknowledgments

Two chapters in this book have appeared elsewhere in earlier versions. Michael P. Morrissey's "Voegelin, Religious Experience, and Immortality" was presented as a paper at the Lonergan Workshop at Boston College in June 1995, and a version of it appeared in *Lonergan Workshop, Volume 12*, edited by Fred Lawrence (1996). William Petropulos's "The Person as *Imago Dei*: Augustine and Max Scheler in Eric Voegelin's *Herrschaftslehre* and *Political Religions*" is an expansion of a paper presented in German at the Second International Eric Voegelin Symposium, December 9–10, 1993, at the Geschwister-Scholl-Institut für Politische Wissenschaft der Universität München, and an earlier version appeared in the series of occasional papers on Voegelin edited by Peter J. Opitz and Dietmar Herz (Ludwig-Maximilians-Universität, Munich: Eric-Voegelin-Archiv, 1997). Grateful acknowledgment is made to the respective editors for permission to publish these essays here.

I am indebted to Paul Caringella and the Voegelin Literary Trust for permission to quote from the unpublished manuscripts and correspondence in the Voegelin Archives at the Hoover Institution, Stanford University, and from Voegelin's letter to Alfred Schütz of September 17–20, 1943, published in *Faith and Political Philosophy: The Correspondence Between Leo Strauss and Eric Voegelin, 1934–1964*, edited by Peter Emberley and Barry Cooper.

Permission to quote from the following works of Eric Voegelin has been granted by the Louisiana State University Press: *Order and History*, vol. 1, *Israel and Revelation*, copyright 1956, vol. 2, *The World of the Polis*, copyright 1957, vol. 3, *Plato and Aristotle*, copyright 1957, vol. 4, *The Ecumenic Age*, copyright 1974, vol. 5, *In Search of Order*, copyright 1987; *The Collected Works of Eric Voegelin*, vol. 12, *Published Essays, 1966–1985*, copyright 1990, and vol. 28, *"What Is History?" And Other Late Unpublished Writings*, copyright 1990. Material from *Hermetica*, ed. Brian P. Copenhaver (Cambridge: Cambridge University Press, 1992) is reprinted with permission of Cambridge University Press. Quoted material from *Faith and Political Philosophy: The Correspondence Between Leo Strauss and Eric Voegelin, 1934–1964*, trans. and ed. Peter Emberley and Barry Cooper (University Park: Pennsylvania State University Press, 1993), pages 321–347, copyright 1993 by the Pennsylvania State University, is reproduced by permission of the publisher. Excerpts from Max Scheler, *On the Eternal in Man*, trans. Bernard Noble (London: SCM Press, 1960), are reprinted courtesy of SCM Press. The cover photograph (paperback edition) is reprinted from Michel Dillange, *La Sainte-Chapelle*, published by Editions Ouest France, with the kind permission of the photographer and the publisher.

The Earhart Foundation generously provided a summer fellowship in 1996 to Stephen A. McKnight, which enabled him to prepare chapter 8. I wish to express gratitude to the same foundation for financial support while this book was in the final stages of preparation.

Introduction

The crisis of Western culture that has been sending out warning shocks or shaking the foundations for two centuries now is as much as it is anything else a religious crisis, a crisis of fundamental spiritual disorientation. Its genuine philosophical prophets and most astute analysts—Kierkegaard and Dostoevsky, Nietzsche and Heidegger—have all understood this well. But to grasp the decisive character of such a crisis while it still unfolds is an enormously difficult matter, since the very essence of the crisis is the failure of accepted principles of interpretation, of traditional paradigms of order and meaning, to make sense of what is going on and to provide social orientation. The deeper the crisis, then, the more profound must be the reevaluation of historical process, of inherited assumptions, and of the very purpose of society and existence, if the breakdown is to be diagnosed with adequate completeness. Who in our own time has notably surpassed the thinkers just mentioned in rendering intelligible the spiritual crisis of contemporary Western civilization? Few candidates suggest themselves, but there are those who would make such a claim for Eric Voegelin.

Known primarily as a political scientist, Voegelin has produced a large body of work whose centerpiece is the five-volume *Order and History* (1956–1987). Little acquaintance with that work is needed to realize that its scope and ambition go well beyond what is normally understood as political science or even political philosophy. Voegelin's writings comprise a full-scale retheoretization of society, history, and personal existence, a philosophy of history on a grand scale, that reaches back to the earliest civilizations and concerns itself with every major mode of self-interpretation by which human beings have sought to orient themselves in the cosmos: mythological, philosophical, religious, and political. Not unexpectedly, a project of such intent and scope lays many challenges before the reader; and Voegelin's work has indeed developed something of a reputation for difficulty. Truth be told, the intellectual demands

1

placed by Voegelin on his readers are not terribly severe. The truer challenge is the radical manner in which Voegelin questions contemporary assumptions, categories of interpretation, and definitions of terms such as *reason, science, divinity,* and *history,* as he advances his analysis beyond the inadequate horizon of modernity in seeking an understanding of the Western crisis. To appreciate the quality and gauge the success of Voegelin's diagnosis of contemporary disorientation, one must be willing to follow his lead in making certain difficult adjustments to one's inherited horizon of assumed truths. And one of the most important of these adjustments involves Voegelin's insistence on the utter centrality of religious experience to human existence.

Order and disorder in both personal and political life are always, according to Voegelin, rooted in responses to spiritual experiences. This principle is reflected in the theoretical argument for which Voegelin is best known in the intellectual world, his characterization of modern ideologies and mass political movements as "gnostic" in both motivation and outlook. The "gnostic" label, derived from spiritual movements of late antiquity, indicates that for Voegelin such ideologies and movements perform an essentially religious function, and have their genesis in real, if ultimately distorted, spiritual yearnings. As political movements such as fascism and National Socialism stand for Voegelin as the harshest symptoms of our civilizational crisis, their identification as manifestations of spiritual disorder underline his conviction, confirmed by a lifetime of research, that a correct diagnosis of the contemporary crisis depends in part on clearly understanding its roots in underlying religious experiences and impulses.

These assertions suggest that by "religious experience" Voegelin does not mean what most would understand by the phrase: a discrete or isolated sector of human concern, usually institutionally mediated, in which traditional religious practices are engaged in or some kind of distinctly spiritual awareness is sought or achieved. Indeed, Voegelin's notion of religious experience, though it obviously embraces such activities, applies first of all to experiences so basic to human living that they may be said to constitute a structural element of consciousness, one of its permanent dimensions. (Eventually Voegelin became convinced that the phrase "religious experience" was too burdened with misleading connotations to serve his purposes, and it disappears in his later work.) In order to indicate the nature and scope of Voegelin's notion of religious experience, and so the range of phenomena addressed in the following essays, we must consider some aspects of Voegelin's theory of consciousness, a theory developed and refined over decades to provide a solid foundation for his comprehensive philosophy of history.

For Voegelin, human consciousness is initially the awareness of ignorance and a growing desire to understand: a restless questioning, a seeking of meaning. Out of this search for meaning have come the endlessly variegated achievements of human insight, discovery, and invention. But the growth of knowledge also serves to expand the scope of questioning, with new questions pressing on toward what is now known to be unknown; and this process is in principle unending, as there can never be a complete reduction of the unknown into the known. The horizon of the known unknown may recede, but only up to a certain limit, where consciousness recognizes that there are truths that lie beyond the reach of finite human knowing—irreducible mysteries corresponding to our questions about the ultimate whys and wherefores of existence. Consciousness, therefore, is permanently structured as an informed questioning, or, as Voegelin puts it, as a "tension" between absolute ignorance and absolute knowledge.

Now this tension of questioning, which is the essence of every person, desires above all to know about itself: what it derives from, what it is intended for, what it may or may not be. We seek to know the meaning of our own existences, the significance of our parts in the drama of reality. But the meaning any personal existence might have could be known fully only by knowing the meaning of reality as a whole. So every human consciousness by nature seeks an understanding of the ultimate meaning of itself and everything else, of the primary origin and purpose of things, the "ground" of meaning. Consciousness is therefore, in Voegelin's phrase, a "tension toward the ground" of reality.

This description of human consciousness as a "tension toward the ground" is a favorite formulation of Voegelin's in his mature writings, a construct whose intended theoretical sense depends on keeping the following point in mind: The originating "ground" of reality toward which human questioning is by nature oriented is not merely a goal of intended, or hoped for, knowledge. It is also the ontological matrix of conscious existence itself, the something from which consciousness has emerged. The ground of reality is thus not only the goal but also the source and profoundest identity of each person. In sum, we may say that, for Voegelin, human existence is an adventure of discovering what its own existence might mean, through a search for the meanings of things and their ground, being moved to this search by the very ground of which it is in search.

This theoretical account of the basic structure of conscious existence not only provides Voegelin with his core definition of what it is to be human, but also gives him a foundational, and in his view suitably heuristic, notion of the "divine." The notion of the divine for Voegelin refers first of all to the mysterious ground of reality of which consciousness is aware as soon as it is aware that it is not its own ground. This awareness is massive with feeling. The tension of consciousness is not only an intellectual tension but also an emotional and dispositional tension, apprehensive with love and fear, hope and despair, anxiety and trust. To consciousness aware of the mystery toward which its yearning tends, therefore, the ground is not only an ultimate object of inquiry but also the terrifying or comforting, awe-inducing depth of original being, the numinous, fascinating "other" that creates and sustains cosmos and consciousness. Humans symbolize this power in numerous ways: as sacred natural or physical forces, objects, or locations; as intracosmic divine persons, such as Zeus (Greek) or Marduk (Babylonian); as an impersonal transcendent principle, such as *Brahman* (Hindu) or *Tao* (Chinese); as a personal transcendent God. They also rebel against it, ignore it, and declare it unreal. But acknowledged or not, it is, according to Voegelin, universally experienced as the origin and co-constituting partner of human consciousness at all times.

All of these issues are treated in more detail in the essays that follow, but enough has been stated to make it clear how Voegelin can consider "religious experience" to be a basic structural element of conscious living and not simply a matter of prayer and meditation, worship, doctrines, and religious institutions. In his view, human existence is the drama of a person's response to the mysterious and precarious gift of conscious existence from the divine ground. Against the main currents of contemporary intellectual life, therefore, Voegelin reestablishes on a sophisticated philosophical foundation the deeply traditional conclusion that existence is a process of human-divine interaction, and that human history in general is the history of human-divine encounter.

With this view, Voegelin's analyses of order and disorder in history have among their consistent aims a disclosing of the religious stratum of experience in the creation of the symbols that have structured the human world and guided human energies. This is one of the interpretive principles informing the multivolume *Order and History*, and both there and elsewhere in Voegelin's work it yields uncommon explanations. For example, in *The World of the Polis* and *Plato and Aristotle* (both 1957), the second and third volumes of *Order and History*, and in many subsequent essays, Voegelin's examination of the Hellenic philosophers focuses on how central to their discoveries were "experiences of transcendence" and of trust in the divinely ordered intelligibility of both human reason and the world. In fact, Voegelin argues, philosophy in its original sense and practice can be defined as "the love of being through love of divine Being as the source of its order." Again, on the first page of the book that initially brought him widespread attention, *The New Science of Politics* (1952), Voegelin writes of how "the central problem of a theory of politics," the problem of representation, is intrinsically bound up with religious questions insofar as it involves "an exploration of the symbols by which political societies interpret themselves as representatives of a transcendent truth." Or again, it may be noted how, in the lengthy introduction to the same book, Voegelin presents a critique of positivism in which he explains how he was able to "define with precision the technical points of irrationality" in the positivistic outlook only through understanding it to be "a variant of theologizing" and by properly diagnosing its "underlying religious experiences."[1]

In light of such an approach to the sciences of politics and history, it is not surprising that Voegelin's work has excited the interest of more than a few theologians. One of the earliest books of essays to be published on his thought was a collection of theological responses and critiques, *Voegelin and the Theologian: Ten Studies in Interpretation* (1983). Among the finest full-length studies of his writings is Michael P. Morrissey's *Consciousness and Transcendence: The Theology of Eric Voegelin* (1994). Morrissey goes so far as to claim that Voegelin's contribution to political science and philosophy of history involved him in such a profound and successful retheoretization of human existence in spiritual terms that it represents "perhaps the most important contribution to theology on the contemporary scene," and that Voegelin's later writings, such as "The Beginning and the Beyond: A Meditation on Truth" (1977), "Wisdom and the Magic of the Extreme: A Meditation" (1983), and the fifth and final volume of *Order and History, In Search of Order* (1987), "is the kind of work that should properly be called theology."[2] Morrissey (see chapter 1) is principally, though not exclusively, concerned with Voegelin's contribution and challenge to Christian theology, and the same can be said of most other commentators focusing on the religious or spiritual dimension of Voegelin's work. But scholarly interest is growing in its transcultural significance, a significance elaborated to some degree in the following chapters, whose selection intentionally reflects the universality of Voegelin's understanding of religious experience.

The chapters in this collection have been arranged into three groups on the basis of affinities of scope or topic. The first group, under the heading "Religious Experience and the Human Condition," includes three essays that establish the philosophical depth and historical breadth of Voegelin's analysis of the religious dimension. Next, under the heading "The Priority of Meditation," come two essays that focus on Voegelin's view of meditative practice as central to philosophical activity. Finally, under "Spiritual Sources of Order and Disorder," there appear three essays concerned with Voegelin's account of religious experience as a force both for human formation and deformation.

Michael P. Morrissey's "Voegelin, Religious Experience, and Immortality" (chapter 1) is an excellent introduction to Voegelin's analysis of religious experience. Morrissey begins by placing this analysis firmly in the context of Voegelin's vocation as a political scientist, examining how for Voegelin (as for Plato) political order depends on the proper formation of individual psyches through, among other things, the development of specifically spiritual virtues. This requires Morrissey to address Voegelin's portrayal of human existence as a *metaxy*, a reality "in-between" the human and the divine, the temporal and the eternal. With this concept so crucial to Voegelin's later work clarified, the essay settles on its main topic, Voegelin's explication of the symbol *immortality*, and then concludes with a brief note on the challenge that Voegelin's work poses to contemporary theology.

Chapter 2 turns to the sphere of civic life, and to the role of spiritual openness in the constitution of community. In "Grounding Public Discourse: The Contribution of Eric Voegelin," John J. Ranieri assesses Voegelin's work as a contribution to the fostering of public discourse and rational community, focusing in particular on his recovery of the meaning of reason as openness to experiences of transcendence. Ranieri argues that the implications of this theoretical recovery allow us to identify Voegelin as a multiculturalist and religious pluralist, who at the same time is nothing of a moral relativist—and who therefore provides precisely the philosophical underpinning so needed by democratic societies pledged to the values of toleration and acceptance of diversity. A key aspect of the historical background to that commitment is addressed in chapter 3, Geoffrey L. Price's "The Epiphany of Universal Humanity." Price carefully summarizes Voegelin's account of the historical growth of the experience and recognition of universal divine presence in the soul. He begins with a look at Voegelin's brilliant study of an Egyptian poem from roughly 2000 B.C., "Dispute of a Man, Who Contemplates Suicide, With His Soul," then advances to his treatment of the relevant achievements of Socrates and Plato, and proceeds finally to Voegelin's analysis of the Christian epiphany.

The chapters of part II focus on the topic of meditation. In chapter 4, "The Person as *Imago Dei*," William Petropulos investigates a highly significant factor in Voegelin's intellectual development: his reception of Augustine's *Confessions* and of Max Scheler's philosophy of religion. This reception, which is analyzed through close textual reading of the little-studied manuscript of Voegelin's unfinished *Herrschaftslehre* and of his 1938 book *Political Religions*, is assessed by Petropulos in light of Voegelin's portrayal of meditation as the defining act wherein human persons are revealed as created "in the image of God." Petropulos's detailed study is nicely complemented by chapter 5, William M. Thompson's "Philosophy and Meditation: Notes on Eric Voegelin's View." Thompson examines Voegelin's view of meditative practice as the basis of philosophizing, paying particular attention to epistemological questions and religious parallels from various traditions. Thompson emphasizes both the resoluteness and the rich results of Voegelin's own "meditative wandering" through history and reality in his philosophical quest for truth.

Part III begins with Michael Franz's "Brothers Under the Skin" (chapter 6), which analyzes Voegelin's provocative claim that exemplars of well-ordered consciousness such as Plato and St. Paul are closer kin to secular ideologists such as Marx and Comte than one would suppose, by virtue of their sharing a rare sensitivity to core experiences of an essentially spiritual nature. One of the purposes served by Franz's analysis is to show that Voegelin's critique of modern ideologists is not itself an ideological condemnation, and that, despite Voegelin's having often been taken for a political conservative of one sort or another, his classification as a conservative or "rightist" thinker is both mistaken and misleading.

Franz's essay concludes with a brief account of Voegelin's notion of "the balance of consciousness," a notion developed for describing balanced spiritual orientation in the existential tension between the worldly and the divine. My own essay, "Balanced and Imbalanced Consciousness" (chapter 7), is an expanded study of this notion, beginning with a brief explication of what Voegelin indicates are some of the conditions required for attaining "balanced" consciousness. I present a suggestive catalogue of types, or modes, of "imbalanced" consciousness—that is, outlooks or attitudes that reflect in one way or another a distorted understanding of the relation between the worldly and the divine, the immanent and the transcendent.

The final chapter is by historian Stephen A. McKnight. In "Voegelin's Challenge to Modernity's Claim to Be Scientific and Secular," he shows how Voegelin's critique of modernity as "gnostic," and his characterization of "secular" social science as the functional equivalent of an esoteric religion, are confirmed and enriched through an appreciation of the influence of traditions such as Hermeticism on modern utopian movements. His essay fittingly concludes the collection by underscoring the fact that religious experiences lie at the root of the political and cultural visions of modernity.

Together these essays substantiate Voegelin's claim that appreciation of the role of spiritual experiences in personal and social development is one of the keys to understanding the political disasters and cultural malaise of the twentieth century. His philosophy of existence and history goes a long way toward making the present historical situation intelligible, and consequently bearable—and even, on the basis of this heightened understanding, an occasion of some hope. Voegelin would say that this is, after all, one of the first duties of the philosopher: to resist the disorder of the age by struggling to achieve an understanding of its causes, and to allow the insights emerging from this struggle to educate and heal the disoriented soul.

Notes

1. Eric Voegelin, *Order and History*, vol. 1, *Israel and Revelation* (Baton Rouge: Louisiana State University Press, 1956), xiv; *The New Science of Politics: An Introduction* (Chicago: University of Chicago Press, 1952), 1, 25.

2. *Voegelin and the Theologian: Ten Studies in Interpretation*, Toronto Studies in Theology, vol. 10, ed. John Kirby and William M. Thompson (New York: Edwin Mellen Press, 1983); Michael P. Morrissey, *Consciousness and Transcendence: The Theology of Eric Voegelin* (Notre Dame, Ind.: University of Notre Dame Press, 1994), 4.

Part I

Religious Experience
and the Human Condition

1

Voegelin, Religious Experience, and Immortality

Michael P. Morrissey

As a philosopher and political scientist, Voegelin sought to answer the fundamental political questions: What is the source of order in history and society? From what do we take our bearings in fashioning our human existence? To what do we turn in our seeking the right way to live? For Voegelin the answer to these questions is as simple as it is profound: religious experience. That is to say, the fundamental source of order in human existence is rooted in experiences of transcendence, in the attunement to divine reality, in our getting in tune with God. This is the wisdom of the ages that Voegelin has recovered and proclaimed for us in our own time of political and spiritual crisis.

I shall attempt to unpack the profundity of this simple assertion that lies at the heart of Voegelin's thought. But I must warn that one is hard-pressed to find anything simple in Voegelin's very dense and complex works. If only he were a dogmatist or propagandist or sophist, it would be a lot easier to understand his works and to present his thought in an essay. But Voegelin is not a dogmatic thinker; he is a philosopher and thus his works are much more exacting of his reader. One cannot simply extract Voegelinian truths from his writings, because he is not a dispenser of teachings or opinions but rather a lover of wisdom. And so it is a long and arduous task to reach up to the mind of Voegelin the philosopher. I will try to represent his thinking on this matter as clearly and precisely as possible, attempting to be as faithful to Voegelin's thought as Voegelin himself was faithful to the task of philosophy.

Religious Experience as the Ground of Political Order

What exactly does this proclamation mean, that religious experience is the ground of order?[1] First of all, according to Voegelin's analysis, it means that the ultimate foundation of political and social order is not found where most people expect to find it today, such as in ideal political regimes like democratic governments or constitutionalism. It is not found in developing economic structures that maintain social stability through material production or full employment or a viable standard of living. It is not found in peaceful international relations or a balance of military and economic power among nations. And it is not found in any institutions, even the institutions of civil law or family or even "religion" itself. Rather, Voegelin takes his bearings from the Platonic insight that "the city is the soul writ large." This means that the substance of a society is psyche, that social order depends on the order of the individual soul. Therefore, the diagnosis of health and disease in the soul is at the same time a diagnosis of order and disorder in society, for a society's order ultimately rests on the ordered souls of its citizens, on their intellectual, moral, and spiritual virtues, or what today we would call character.

Since Voegelin bases his scholarly studies on this fundamental principle of classical political philosophy that perceives the isomorphism of soul and society, he has not written texts for foreign-policy or domestic-policy decision makers. He is not concerned with "politics" in the topical sense. He is not even concerned with "family values" or school systems or churches and their structure and function. One cannot extract a list of Voegelinian doctrines or propositional truths from his work upon which one could devise pragmatic policies to implement in any of these spheres of contemporary life (to the regret of many of his readers). As a philosopher and a political scientist in the Platonic sense, Voegelin analyzes the problems of political order at a deeper level. He boldly proclaims that the fundamental condition of political order in any culture and in any society is quite simply the attunement of its citizens' souls to the divine ground of their existence. This is the heart of the matter.

But what exactly does this mean for us today? It means that however we choose to live our lives, however we choose to govern our institutions, we must ultimately take our bearings on the ordering of the personal soul to divine Mystery that has been experienced in a normative way by the great prophets, sages, saints, mystics, and philosophers of the past. It means we must hear anew the authoritative words of these individuals who have gone before us, who in expressing their experience of the divine discovered the truth about the order of reality and about their participation in the unfolding drama of history. Such experience is "religious," and, as Voegelin teaches us, it occurs in either one of two ways: by reason, through one's noetic search for the divine, or by revelation, through the divine pull on one's soul. In other words, human order, as personal, social, and political, depends on human beings' existence in "immediacy under God," which necessitates the continuous recovery, on the level of experience, of the great discoveries and the great revelations of God in history. These foundational events are what Voegelin names the "spiritual outbursts," the "theophanies," the "leaps in being," the "noetic and pneumatic differentiations of consciousness." In a characteristically Augustinian vein, Voegelin sees the ordered existence of humans, created in the image of God, as dependent on one's *amor Dei*, while resisting the disordering forces of *amor sui*. To remove the love of God as the ordering force of the soul, as Thomas Hobbes and his epigones did, is to fall into spiritual anarchy. And as the modern age has testified all too well, social and political anarchy will inevitably follow.[2]

The truth of the matter is this: all humans are called by natural inclination as well as by divine grace to partake in this attunement. Moreover, a society's political order depends upon the living of human life in cooperation with God taking shape in the souls of its people. Following the classical philosophers, this attunement, for Voegelin, is primarily dependent on the life of self-transcending reason becoming a dominant force in the formation of individuals in a society. Politically speaking, the core religious experience at the heart of social order is participation in the divine Logos by way of the divine Nous that dwells within us. It is an experience given to all humans insofar as they are human. As Aristotle proclaimed in the opening line of his *Metaphysics*, humans share equally in the life of self-transcending reason, for "all men by nature desire to know." But of course this equality is only potential. We know that humans are empirically unequal in the application or fulfillment of their potentiality.[3] Thus, Voegelin adopts the tenet of classical politics that the good society is one that makes the life of self-transcending reason possible in at least a minority of its members who become a creative force in that society. Such living attunement to the ground is apparently not given to all after all. Why is this? In many societies, restrictions of size and wealth make the life of reason unobtainable, not to speak of the psychic tension that for most people makes the noetic life nearly unbearable.[4] But civilizational order requires that the life of reason and virtue be lived by a select few. In Aristotle's *Politics*, these few mature, virtuous souls are called the *spoudaioi* without whose influence the *plethos*, the masses who are ruled by intemperate passion, come to predominate, leading to social breakdown and political disintegration.

For Voegelin what is needed, then, for social and political order, is an authentic grounding in religious experience, at least by a significant few who live the mature, spiritual life, from whom others in a society can take their bearings. The problem, however, is this: in spite of the host of fervent practitioners of "religion" in all its forms all around us (seen today for example in the rampant spread of evangelical Christianity around the world), even in spite of a plethora of people having "religious experiences" (and a great variety of them, according to William James in his classic study of the phenomenon almost a century ago), the experiences that Voegelin talks about, and their truth, are generally lost to the modern world. We must ask why. The reason is that the real content of a definite class of religious experiences that reveal the true meaning of existence has been lost. The normative experiences of transcendence in history have largely been eclipsed by dogmatic beliefs, by mere excitations of religious feeling, by mindless imitations of the purveyors of "religion," by hypostatized concepts and ideas, by nominalism, or on the other hand, by the cultured despisers of religion, the enlightened secularists who have turned the hermeneutics of suspicion into a creed. The essential problem today, according to Voegelin, given the preponderance of these secondary, derivative mediations of religious meaning, and the atheist revolt against them, is that people have largely lost contact with reality. The symbols that gave life to the ancients no longer speak their truth to moderns. And there are too few people alive today who can imaginatively reenact the original experiences of transcendence in their own consciousnesses.

And here lies the great irony. The fashionable view of modernity is that it is largely constructed on the return to human experience behind dogmatism, as seen for example in the great modern thinkers: Descartes, Kant, Hegel, Husserl, Heidegger, Locke, James, Bergson, and Jaspers, as well as in the rise of empiricism, phenomenology, existentialism, and pragmatism (the sweeping movement in modern thought that has been referred to as "the turn to the subject"). But for Voegelin, the recovery of experience behind dogmatism has actually been accomplished only, and in a rather "backhanded manner," by way of the historical sciences.[5] We moderns have by and large not recovered in any personal, experiential way the originating experiences of religion and philosophy that lie at the origins of Western Civilization. We have lost the immediate encounter with the transcendent, what Voegelin calls "the truth of existence." The weight of Enlightenment secularism and scientism and its instrumental rationality, as well as the ideological undercurrents that pervade the modern mind, have taken their toll, producing the age of "the closed soul." The recovery of the great texts and revelatory events of the past that has been accomplished has for the most part not penetrated to the engendering experiences behind the symbols that mediate their meaning. Accordingly, in the attempt to retrieve an immediate grasp of reality behind dogmatism, the divine ground of existence has been lost. An example of this can be seen in William James's own great work, *The Varieties of Religious Experience*. James obeyed the fundamental principle of American pragmatism, from which Voegelin learned a great deal in his youth, that ideas must be grounded in experiences. But in spite of his illuminating inquiry into a wide variety of mystical experiences, James prescinded from the

classical and Christian formulations of religious experience that established the order of history and society in the West since antiquity. The
same can be said for Max Weber's sociology of religion. A major symptom
of Weber's value-free science was his exclusion of the foundational experiences of order in classical philosophy and early Christianity.[6] We might
call this avoidance the modern conceit: the prohibition of the divine
ground as actually experienced in history, a prohibition against which
Voegelin rebelled and worked to overcome in his early years.

In short, Voegelin is in search of a reality no longer alive, because, in
his judgment, we have lost the experiential core of reality. So the fundamental task of his entire work has been to restore the experiences that led
to the founding of the great philosophies, religions, and cultures in history, to make radiant once again the opaque symbols of the human-divine
relation. As a philosopher Voegelin was determined to return not just to
the original experiences but also to the original analytical vocabulary that
first embodied their insights. As he once remarked to Gregor Sebba in
1933, we must return to the source because that is where the water is
clearest.[7] In this sense there is nothing "original" in Voegelin, who believed that lack of originality was a characteristic of authentic philosophizing. What appear to be obscure neologisms in Voegelin's writings are
actually restored ancient symbols. They are the result of a rescue mission,
a return to simplicity, a recovery of lost insights as originally formulated.
The most important of these rescued symbols is the *metaxy*, a Greek term
meaning "in-between" employed by Plato. In fact, the heart of Voegelin's
restoration project is his articulation of life in the In-Between, the "middle" state of human existence that shapes all our experiences, especially
our religious experiences. The *metaxy* became the chief emblem of Voegelin's philosophizing during the last twenty years of his life. It is a very
simple idea, but its truth is perhaps the most difficult thing to fully com-
prehend in Voegelin.

The *Metaxy*

The *metaxy* is Plato's symbol for the in-between plane of human existence
denoting the "place" of human participation in reality and the domain of
human knowledge. For Voegelin, the discovery of the *metaxy* is a differentiating event in history, an epochal event that divides history into two
periods, giving it a before-and-after structure. The occasion of this historical breakthrough is the experience of the divine in the psyche of Plato,
an experience that was more differentiated than that of the compact myths
that Plato inherited in fifth-century Hellas. The specific discovery that
illuminated this in-between structure of human existence was the ordering

faculty in the psyche that Plato called the *nous*, a term that was originally coined by Parmenides to symbolize the human faculty of ascending to the vision of being. Thus, the classical philosophers understood this "noetic" core of the soul as the divine force of self-transcending Reason that allows one not only to perceive and resist personal and social disorder, but also to seek the true order that is ultimately divine. With the emergence of the noetic consciousness of the *metaxy* in Plato's soul, the age of the people's myth had to yield to the authoritative force of the philosopher. In the wake of this historic event there is no going back, for a marked progression has occurred whereby, argues Voegelin, the process of history has now become luminous for its meaning.[8]

The most resonant expression of the *metaxy* occurs in the *Symposium*, Plato's literary masterpiece on the topic of love.[9] Specifically it occurs in the course of Socrates' climactic speech on Eros delivered to Agathon and others attending the drinking party. Actually, Socrates' speech is not a "speech" presented in direct discourse, but the report of a dialogue that he had with Diotima whereby Socrates lets the truth about love unfold dialectically. Because the truth about Eros is revealed to Socrates from the prophetess Diotima and concerns the quest for immortality, the mythic tale about love that he relates is to be regarded as a revealed truth about salvation, that is, a saving tale that originally appeared noetically in the *metaxy* of Plato's own erotic consciousness. For this reason alone, one might justify the great significance Voegelin gives this symbol of the *metaxy* in his work, unlike most interpreters of Plato who fail to recognize its revelatory import due to its lack of prominence in the whole of Plato's dialogues.[10] The experiential insight of the symbol has been killed with the death of a thousand oversights. We might say that Voegelin has saved the chief symbol of this saving tale, and its revelatory truth, from its own death in the philosophical tradition.[11]

Socrates' speech begins with the proclamation that Eros is not a god, as the previous speakers presupposed, but "a great spirit" (*daimonion*) that plays the role of mediator between mortals and immortals. In other words, love is not purely divine, but exists "in-between" (*metaxy*) the human and the divine (202e). Socrates then relates the myth of Eros's birth. Eros is the son of Poros (wealth, resource) and Penia (poverty, want), conceived when Penia seduces Poros in his state of intoxication while celebrating the birth of Aphrodite. Thus love is conceived on the day the goddess of beauty is born. And as the child of need and fullness, Eros partakes in both while serving divine beauty in all things (203b–204a). For Voegelin, the myth of Eros's descent (by way of the "sad-loving quest" for fullness or perfection, and the penetration of wealth into poverty) reveals Plato's own personal experience, which is universal, for everyone whose soul enters into the philosophical activities of love experiences the quest for fullness, or completion, or perfection, or true goodness and true wisdom, which inevitably follows upon the prior awareness of one's state of ignorance and need.[12] In other words, what one ultimately desires is immortality, for love seeks to possess forever what it does not possess: divine Beauty and Goodness. According to Diotima's tale, immortality is experienced through the procreation of both body and soul, between which the higher virtue belongs to the pregnant soul, for the highest activity of love is the conversation of souls, and not the mere coupling and procreation of bodies, souls possessing a higher beauty more in accord with divine Beauty. Socrates' speech ends with the famous climb up "the ladder of love" where one comes to know divine Beauty itself beyond all beautiful bodies and souls in this world. This sublime ending of his speech is an image of the human quest for immortality where one ultimately comes to be with that which is eternal. In this specific context of Socrates' speech on love in Plato's *Symposium*, we can understand what the *metaxy* is ultimately about for Voegelin. It is about "the philosophical experience as the tension between wisdom (fullness) and ignorance (penury)." It is about "the right relation of man to the divine ground of being; the philosophical tension between time and eternity [that] is recognized as the right order of the soul, which implies the claim of fulfillment for all."[13] And so an explanation of the *metaxy* must now necessarily turn to an analysis of the experience of immortality, which makes the truth of existence in the In-Between truly luminous for its meaning.

Immortality

As an event of participation in reality, human consciousness is structured by experiences in the tensions between birth and death, ignorance and wisdom, immanence and transcendence, imperfection and perfection, time and eternity, mortality and immortality, apeirontic depth and noetic height, creation and salvation, the One and the Many, the Beginning and the Beyond.[14] Life is lived in the tension between all these polar opposites. The place of human experience is in the middle, between them, and nowhere else. For purposes of illustrating the nature of Voegelin's whole project of restoring life in the *metaxy*, I will focus on the set of poles named mortality and immortality, which is intrinsically related to all the other sets of poles. The greatest clarity about the structure of human religious experience may come by considering the erotic tension toward the divine ground that issues in symbols of immortality.

Immortality is what love desires. Of all human experiences we might designate "religious," the quest for immortality is the one most significant, for it designates a peak of spiritual sensitivity toward one's life and death. It is what the Christian doctrine of salvation is ultimately about. Of course it has parallels in every major religious tradition, for the human desire to partake in the eternal divine life is a constant in history and can be traced back as far as the records go, textually at least as far back as the Gilgamesh epic of the late third millennium B.C.,[15] or in our own Judeo-Christian tradition to the story of the Garden of Eden, from which Adam and Eve are banished lest they reach out and eat of the tree of immortality too—what they really want![16] No doubt the quest for eternal divine life is real and universal. However, Voegelin would argue that the popular doctrinaire conception of immortality today, shorn of its experiential ground, is a fantasy involving the notion of an autonomous reality called "afterlife" in which one may believe or not believe. The legitimate mytho-poetic images of afterlife are the product of speculative imagination in-spired by the faith and hope of living toward a perfection beyond the imperfection of this world, that is, in the unknowable mode of divine existence.[17] Inspired by mythic images of salvation codified by theological doctrine, many people believe, mostly on the passions of alienation, piety, and fear, in a realm of immortal deliverance beyond this world granted by God at death. But they do not themselves participate in the living experiences of an immortalizing life. When such belief becomes hyposta-tized as an objective realm of existence beyond the existence of this world—that is, existence in another world beyond the created world of Genesis 1—the result is a cosmic dualism, as well as the spiritual harden-ing and deadening of the psyche.

Voegelin argues that such doctrine, in whatever culture it is found, is largely derived from the compact symbols of cosmological myth (be they ancient Hellenic, Egyptian, or Israelite, or Plato's philosophical myths of salvation,[18] or Dante's very vivid Christian images of Hell, Purgatory, and Paradise), and not in the living process of what Aristotle called *athanatiz-ein*, immortalization, or the engendering experience that yields such imaginative depictions of afterlife in the first place. This is why in his 1965 essay "Immortality: Experience and Symbol,"[19] Voegelin never discusses the imaginative symbols of afterlife, though at its conclusion he antici-pates the disheartened response of his readers who inevitably feel let down by his analysis and want something more than the "anemic immor-tality" he offers. But Voegelin is not forthcoming. To give his readers something more would be to submit to Whitehead's "fallacy of misplaced concreteness," to erect symbols into entities and then discourse on the entities divorced from their experiential ground. To embark on such spec-ulative constructions would be to repudiate the philosophical anthropol-ogy that Voegelin learned from Schelling: "Anthropology is now system-atically made the key to speculation; nothing must enter into the content of speculation that cannot be found in human nature, in its depth as well as in its heights, in the limitations of its existence as well as in its openness toward transcendent reality."[20] As always, Voegelin never strays from the ground. And his analysis never departs from the *metaxy* to discuss the pre- or postexistence of an immaterial soul in eternity beyond the *metaxy*. The soul (*psyche*) is simply the name of that place in existence where humanity has an experience of eternal being; it is the sensorium of transcendence, of the movements and countermovements in the tensions of being. It is not a subject about which one can give predications in philosophical propositions. The soul not an object of sense experience, but is rather a reality that becomes noetically illuminated by the one who suffers its movement toward the transcendent Beyond in his or her consciousness.

To put it simply, according to Voegelin, "there is no 'transcendent reality' other than the Beyond experienced in the 'rise' [of the soul]. If it is torn out of the experiential context, it suffers the intentionalist reduction to an object in whose existence one can believe or not; the experienced *fides*, we may say, leaves a fideistic belief as its sediment."[21] The problem occurs in our use of language that separates "the transcendent" from the experience of transcendence and transforms it into a fideistic object that exists apart from the soul's movement toward its goal in the *metaxy*. No doubt because Plato was aware of this problem too, that is, the penchant to hypostatize, to abolish the *metaxy* by hauling the Beyond into this world, he has Socrates' speech in the *Symposium* end on an ambiguous note. Just like Voegelin's essay "Immortality," it too appears "anemic" to those who wish for something more. But Socrates' only resolve about the one who has successfully climbed "the ladder of love" is that "by giving birth to true virtue and nourishing it, he would be able to become a friend of the gods, and if any human being could become immortal, he would" (*Symposium* 212a). The matter is entirely provisional; no doctrinaire belief in immortality as an objective state of existence in an afterlife is proposed. After hearing this speech one is left not in a state of certain knowledge about the matter, but in a state of faith concerning "the activities of love," which promise a mysterious union with divine Wisdom at the end of the erotic quest in the In-Between. Eros is that great spirit (*daimon*) that mediates the human-divine relation and initiates the movement. Whoever is possessed by Eros grows above the status of a mortal and becomes a "spiritual being" (*daimonios aner*).[22] The real truth of the matter is revealed in the experience of love; to separate the symbols from the experience they illuminate is to deform and falsify them. We must return again and again to the in-between state of experience, to the movement of love itself in order to understand the truth of symbols of immortality as well as the order of human existence in society and history. I might say in passing here that Voegelin, in his later years, would sometimes speak of the "order of love" as the foundation of political order.[23] Through Plato he saw the philosophical experience of the order of reality as an experience of the order of love. The love of the divinity beyond the cosmos is the formative principle of the cosmos. The *parousia* (presence) of that divinity maintains the soul in order (*kosmos*). When that love is not present in reality there is disorder (*akosmia*).[24]

But we must be careful not to misconstrue Voegelin here. His seemingly iconoclastic skepticism about afterlife does not mean that he advocates discarding its popular mythic images and beliefs. However, as a philosopher he does seek to avoid what he called in his last work "imaginative oblivion," the willful forgetting of the structure of existence in tension toward the Beyond through allowing the imagination to imagine the non-imaginable.[25] When the imagination through its creative powers transforms a non-thing reality—that is, transcendent reality—into an imaginable thing—that is, an "afterlife"—it destroys the metaleptic tension of human participation in reality. The attempt to gain power over reality by imaginatively creating its image is the initial human vice that leads to the deformation of consciousness, to projection psychologies, to the inversion of consciousness into unconsciousness, all contributing to the history of disorder. In our quest to know reality and to believe in its truth, we easily forget that we humans reside in the *metaxy*, not beyond it. We do not create the world; we participate in it.

Nevertheless, following Plato (in his *Epinomis*), Voegelin argues that the traditional myth and its images should not be simply abandoned under the differentiating pressures of a more adequate experience and symbolization, for then people whose faith has been lost through the debunking of myth will become spiritually disoriented and fall into a worse chaos, since they are not inclined to become philosophers able to explore the truth of the matter on the level of noetic reflection.[26] The simple fact is that there has never been a society whose self-constitution was noetic, that is, a society ordered by Reason. Every known society in history has expressed its experience of order through symbols that are mythical, revelatory, apocalyptic, gnostic, theocratic, or ideological, but not exclusively noetic, for noetic truth once it emerges cannot simply replace non-noetic truth. It can only serve as a corrective or addition alongside less differentiated symbolisms that provide a sense of order for most people, everywhere, most of the time.[27] The persistence of non-noetic interpretations of reality, even after the rise of noetic ones, is what causes the fundamental tension in the field of political reality. The clash between noetic and non-noetic knowledge of social order is what leads to the fate of philosophers who are punished or exiled or even killed. The same phenomenon occurs with prophetism when the one who speaks the pneumatic word of

God is slandered, mocked, and put to death for being an iconoclastic subverter of the political-religious status quo. As Plato's famous parable tells us, the ascent from the darkness of the cave to the light of truth is liberating, but the descent from the light back down to the cave is fraught with peril and persecution. Of course, this was Socrates' own fate, and we all know what happened to Jesus.

Voegelin reminds us that the symbols of immortality are not informative; they are evocative. They are not descriptive but exegetic, for they refer not to entities in the external word but rather to the movement of the soul within the *metaxy*. They are not concepts with an external referent but indices of language arising from the religious experience of the eternal as consciousness becomes aware of its movement toward the ground. Their meaning can only be understood if they evoke in the listener or reader the corresponding movement of participatory consciousness as experienced by their original authors, that is, in the experience of the loving quest for the divine Beyond.[28] But as I have said, Voegelin argues that this religious experience of immortality, or, more properly speaking (to use Aristotle's language), the practice of immortalizing, is largely lost to believers and nonbelievers alike who have inherited the hypostatized symbols of afterlife mistakenly thought to refer to a spatio-temporal object or place. Or worse, it has been completely deformed by the utopian dreamers who offer an imaginary immortality by promising salvation in this world, primarily on the order of a Nietzschean project of self-salvation, or the enlightened activist and progressivist projects of political mass movements fomented by the mood of anxiety and alienation that constitutes the modern age. In either case, there is the escapist refusal to accept the tension of existence between imperfection and perfection. One way of escape is simply to deny the tension and to withdraw into one's own self-suffering, as Nietzsche did a century ago, glorifying it by letting the inflated ego play the games of the will to power. The more insidious escape attempts to overcome the tension through activist revolt, through the transfiguring of imperfect existence into an immanent state of perfection, by way of what Voegelin calls "magical politics," the stuff of modern gnosticism that bears the brunt of his critique.[29] In either case there ensues the "existential deformation that becomes manifest in the God-is-dead syndrome, together with the major misconstructions of reality it entails."[30] In this respect we can perhaps begin to understand just what Voegelin means by what he calls "the postulate of balance" that must always be maintained, for once achieved it is never permanent.[31] Once the balance of consciousness is lost it leads to the extreme of madness, like the magician's dream that moved Shakespeare in Sonnet 129, reflecting on the disturbance of reality he experienced due to the erotic passion in his own soul, to conclude that

> All this the world well knows yet none knows well,
> To shun the heaven that leads men to this hell.[32]

The seeking of heaven can lead to the establishment of hell once balance in the *metaxy* is lost, as it is lost, beyond the personal sphere of the erotic, in violent political mass movements, in bowing to the spell of magical language in political propaganda, in sophistic intellectual trickery (such as in deconstructionism today[33]), in religious fundamentalism and sectarian movements, and in apocalyptic pronouncements of the New Age. As our century has revealed by way of insidious ersatz religions, the death of God is only a prelude to the death of humans, which the magical constructions of the superman and the will to power have actually brought about, culminating in what Voegelin calls "the murderous grotesque of our time."[34]

What are the classical and Christian roots of a balanced consciousness and a balanced symbolism?

For Aristotle the ground of immortality was the virtue of developing the highest, most divine element within human nature, the immortal Nous, promising the fulfillment of human nature in the direction of transcendence.[35] But here lies the problem, for however the fulfillment of human nature is to be understood, one cannot legitimately objectify transcendence or transcendent fulfillment, which our consciousness, which *intends* things even when it seeks to know something that is not a thing, tends to do. Our very language in discussing this issue is disorienting because humans are neither "mortal" nor "immortal," these terms describing in a predifferentiated sense the "objects" of cosmological existence (in the compact Homeric sense of mortal humans and immortal gods).[36] It is better to say, as Voegelin does, that consciousness exists in the *metaxy* between the "mortal" and "immortal" poles of existence. What we can say is that life lived in the *metaxy* is spiritual life, the mutual participation of the human in the divine and the divine in the human. For Aristotle the very employment of reason (philosophy) is the practice of death that will let the soul, in death, arrive at some immortal, divine truth. Thus, following Aristotle, Voegelin says that "the unfolding of noetic consciousness is experienced as a process of immortalizing"; one "is immortal in his present existence inasmuch as by his noetic psyche he participates in the Beyond."[37] Thus the noetic quest is a process of transfiguration. The psyche's own self-reflective action is a response to the appeal from the Beyond whereby it discovers its own "theomorphic nature."[38] With this discovery the classic philosophers understood human being to be more than mortal Homeric being, and moving to a perfection of life in death. The life to be gained is not a given: it requires human cooperation with the source of immortal life. Personal attunement with the revelation of divine presence is a prerequisite.

For Plato, immortality comes by way of cultivating a love of knowledge and true wisdom, as in the *Timaeus* (90a–c); or by engaging in erotic friendship, as in the *Phaedrus* (256a–c); or by "the activities of love" (*eros*) by which one climbs "the ladder of love," as in the *Symposium* (201d); or by conversion of the prisoner in the cave who is forced to turn around (*periagoge*) by the mysterious spark of divine grace and ascend to the divine Agathon, as in the *Republic* (514c–e); or finally by "the practice of death" (*thanatos*) that will let the soul in death arrive at its divine, immortal status in truth, as in the *Phaedo* (81a). With his frequent citations of these Platonic texts, Voegelin reminds us that there is no Transcendent Beyond lying around somewhere to be included as part of someone's system of belief; there is only, if anything, an experience of its immortalizing presence, such as in a philosopher's act of meditation or reflection.[39]

In Christianity, the experience of immortality, though equivalent to the Greek experience, takes a different turn. As symbolized in the New Testament the human relation to the immortalizing presence of God is less noetic and more pneumatic.[40] That is, the stress falls not on the *structure* of the movement in the *metaxy* but on the *movement itself*—not on the immortalizing search for the divine, but on the assurance of transfiguration through the overwhelming irruption of divine presence in the soul. In St. Paul's experience, the focus is on the process of transfiguration in the life of those who, like himself, behold and believe in the vision of the resurrected Christ. It is the personal experience of moving toward an *eschaton*, and thus is an experience revealing the eschatological direction of history. In the spiritual vision of resurrected life, Voegelin says, "the accent shifts from man's participation in divine immortality to God's participation in human mortality." From this analysis Voegelin argues that Christ is neither a man nor a god (that is, a mortal or an immortal), but the historical event of the fullness of divine presence in a man, revealing the suffering presence of God in everyone drawing them to divine, immortal life.[41] Christ represents the pleromatic *metaxy* in history, the fullness of mutual divine-human participation. Therefore, the gospel is a saving tale that saves to the degree that it successfully invites the reader or listener, by the power of its revelatory word about the life, death, and resurrection of the Christ, to partake in a similar movement of transfiguration, just as Jesus invited his disciples into the same saving love of God by his full mediation of that love. In other words, to put it simply (but profoundly), Jesus saves because Jesus was really "in tune." He was in tune with the Father drawing his disciples into the same, though not complete, attunement with the divine ground of their existence. This truth is best seen in Matthew 16 (the story of Peter's confession), which Voegelin calls "the perfect analysis of the existential tendency in relation to God, just as the fullness of Christ is."[42]

The same metaxic truth is also captured in Augustine's restless soul seeking ultimate rest in the love of God, a movement that reaches a noetic peak in his neo-Platonic vision of God in *Confessions*, Book VII. It is likewise seen in Anselm's noetic quest for God in the *Proslogion*. Anselm's *fides quarens intellectum*, the meditative and prayerful search for the God of his Christian faith, reaches the equivalent experience of illumination as Augustine's. The soul's movement toward the divine light meets the light of divine perfection, which falls into the soul revealing human existence as a state of imperfection seeking perfection. In this Anselmian experience, says Voegelin, is contained the promise of perfection and fulfillment, "[f]or in order to express the experience of illumination he [Anselm] quotes John 16:24: 'Ask, and you will receive, that your joy may be full.' The Johannine words of the Christ, and of the Spirit that counsels in his name," says Voegelin, "express the divine movement to which Anselm responds with the joyful countermovement of his quest."[43] So, we may conclude, whether by a philosopher, a theologian, or a political scientist, in the end the quest for order turns out to be the quest for God.

The disturbing fact for many who forget these classical and Christian insights, and in various ways seek to transcend death, is that there is no direct experience of immortality per se, nor can there be, since there is no escape from the *metaxy*. There is no immortality in this world, only the movement toward immortality (i.e., *athanatizein*, or Christian sanctification). Because human existence is structured by birth and death, coming into being and going out of being, there is only the movement *toward* a life that transcends death, toward "the joy that is full." After all, humans are indeed mortal, living a life structured by birth and death. But that is certainly not the whole story. Spiritual existence in this mortal world is structured by the movement between time and the timeless. In experiences of transcendence, the eternal does not become an object in time, nor is our temporal existence ever transposed into eternity; but human existence is nonetheless a movement in the tension of the In-Between of the human-divine *metaxy*. So, life is indeed more than that structured by birth and death. We participate in timeless meaning insofar as our life is lived in the flow of presence that is more than human.[44]

But if the poles of the tension are hypostatized as independent entities—if the partners to the encounter are torn asunder and converted into subjects and objects of experience that exist apart from the experiential relation—then the true understanding of reality is lost and the vision of our humanity deformed. Once the poles of the tension are detached from the experience of participation in reality, and faith and hope in a mystery beyond this world become a basis for the ersatz knowledge of objects, the result is spiritual disorder.[45]

This then is the existential core of political and social order according to Voegelin's analysis: the movement of the soul in religious experience, best seen in the tale of immortality. It is no accident that Plato ends the *Republic*, his greatest dialogue on political order, with the myth of immortality, the myth of Er. It is the tale saved from death that Socrates makes the true word of persuasion, the saving tale that if accepted will truly save by preserving us from "all extremes of good and evil" and by making us "beloved to ourselves and to the gods" (*Republic* 621c).

In conclusion, taking his philosophical bearings from the *Republic*, Plato's greatest myth of order, Voegelin proposes a transpolitical solution to the problems of political society: the core of political and social order in history is found in theomorphic humanity, a notion richly and succinctly expressed in the following summary statement:

> Man thus can be the model of paradigmatic order in society only when he himself has been ordered by divine being, when as a consequence he partakes of divine substance, when he has become theomorphic. The theomorphism of the soul, we may say, is the supreme principle of the conception of order that originates in the experience of transcendence and leads to the discovery of history.[46]

To the extent that persons and nations continue to violate the First Commandment, from which all the others flow, by remaining in rebellion against God, as well as against theomorphic human nature lived in the *metaxy*, the politics of disorder will continue into the next century and beyond. It is incumbent upon us then to heed the clarion call of Voegelin whose work has shown us how order can be restored first and fundamentally by our "attunement to the ground," by our experiencing the ordering love of God.

Three Exigencies for Theology

Three exigencies for theologians result from Voegelin's recovery and analysis of experience in the *metaxy*:

1. *Expansion of the historical and spiritual horizon.* A first expansion occurred during the "ecumenic age." Today a further expansion is called for. The experience of *fides* is not confined to the Christian; the data of theological inquiry must include all human experience. Voegelin's vision of divine presence in history is truly catholic, a universal horizon. The Spirit listeth where it will. Voegelin states that the expansion is necessary given "the enormous enlargement of the historical horizon, spatially cov-

ering the global ecumene and temporally extending into the archaeological millennia, that has occurred in the present century. . . ."[47] Philosophy and theology has today only begun to attend to the realm of phenomena to be explored in its global breadth and its temporal depth. The theoretical activity of the scholar must be based on all relevant empirical data, which today is so vast as to be virtually indigestible. But if theology is to be a true science, no relevant data can be dismissed wherever they appear.

2. *Christology.* The process of theophanic incarnation cannot be confined to Jesus or the Christian orbit; it is the universal presence of the divine in the human, of the word of God in the word of humans. Though the presence of Christ in Jesus may be the most fully differentiated and fully embodied presence of God in human history, it is not the only; the divine is revealed in a process of history with nodal points, not once and for all at any one point. Nonetheless, Voegelin sees in the Christian visions (particularly Paul's vision of the resurrected) a "pleromatic *metaxy*," which locates in the story of Jesus' life, death, and resurrection the fullness of divine presence. "History is Christ written large."[48] As Thomas Altizer has observed, reflecting on this most poignant of utterances, this means that for Voegelin there can be no ultimacy or finality for any historical event, no "absolute sacredness for a particular or contingent event."[49] History is open, not closed. To identify an ultimate truth in history would abolish the tension of existence and lead to the metastasis of humanity.[50]

3. *Myth.* Voegelin often cited Aristotle's return to the myth in his old age because, like Aristotle, he was a "philomyther" as well as a philosopher.[51] Voegelin did the same in his return to the cosmogonic myth in Plato's *Timaeus.* Saying as early as 1957 that "[t]he soul as the creator of the myth, and the myth as the symbolism of the soul, is the center of the philosophy of order. That center, the philosophy of the myth, is reached by Plato in *Timaeus* and *Critias*," Voegelin returned to the *Timaeus* in his last days, as seen in the last pages of his last volume, *In Search of Order.*[52]

But it wasn't merely his love of myths that Voegelin discovered late in life. He saw that there can be no escape from the myth. Myth has always been and will always continue to be the principal vehicle by which societies develop and maintain their collective identity. The mythic vision is what establishes order in a sea of chaos. This is as true for Christians with their saving tale of the gospel as it was for ancient Babylonians, Egyptians, and Israelites in their mythic constructions of human and divine order. Given the persistence of cosmological symbolism in the ordering of societies, myth can never be eliminated. In spite of the differentiating events that are the spiritual outbursts in history, the cosmos still remains. Since the primordial experience of the cosmos still remains, so cosmogonic myths, which tell the story of the divine-cosmic beginnings, must remain too.[53] There is no differentiating advance in history beyond the myth as the symbolic form of cosmic order, not even with the scientific advances of modern physics and cosmology.[54]

Myth preserves the luminosity of consciousness—the awareness of participating in and from a divine beyond—over against the intentional mode of consciousness, whose purview is the world of things. But the beyond of things is the transcendent realm of divinity, the ultimate source of order that grounds all things within reality. It is what is lasting in reality. Myth serves as the vehicle of attunement to what is lasting in being. The loss of myth is thus the loss of the divine.

Notes

1. "Religious experience" is not a technical term for Voegelin, although one finds it frequently in his writings up through *The New Science of Politics* and the first volumes of *Order and History*. In his later work he ceases to use the term "religion," concluding that it is too vague and confuses the nature of real experiences with the problems of dogma and doctrine. His analysis of the Latin term *religio* with regard to the distinction between "experiential" and "doctrinal" truth appears in Eric Voegelin, *Order and History*, vol. 4, *The Ecumenic Age* (Baton Rouge: Louisiana State University Press, 1974), 43–48; see also Eric Voegelin, *Autobiographical Reflections*, ed. Ellis Sandoz (Baton Rouge: Louisiana State University Press, 1989), 51. Voegelin instead uses such terms as "experiences of transcendence," "theophanies," and especially "noetic and pneumatic differentiations of consciousness." This last phrase is based on historical references to the foundational spiritual events in human history that occurred in the context of the clash of ethnic societies during what Voegelin calls the "ecumenic age" of empires (roughly 600 B.C.–600 A.D.). Karl Jaspers identified the period between 800–200 B.C. as the "axis-age" of world history when these great foundational events occurred, but Voegelin regards Jaspers's parameters of the "axial" period as too narrow; to include the whole sweep of "spiritual outbursts," Voegelin suggests a period from the thirteenth century B.C. to the tenth century A.D. The major outbursts Voegelin identifies are philosophy in Hellas, prophetism in Israel, Buddhism in India, Confucianism and Taoism in China, and Zoroastrianism in Persia. The first two locate the settings of the most differentiated religious experiences. See Eric Voegelin, "Configurations of History," in *The Collected Works of Eric Voegelin*, vol. 12, *Published Essays, 1966–1985*, ed. Ellis Sandoz (Baton Rouge: Louisiana State University Press, 1990), 100–101.

2. On the Augustinian ordering of the soul and the Hobbesian revolt, see Eric Voegelin, *The New Science of Politics: An Introduction* (Chicago: University of Chicago Press, 1952), 184–87.

3. The truncation of the unrestricted desire to know is a result of cultural conditioning, egoism, bias, ideology, and scotosis. For a discussion of these forces see Bernard Lonergan, *Insight: An Essay in Human Understanding* (New York: Harper and Row, 1957), 191–92; 218–42. Lonergan states that "[i]f everyone has

28   *Michael P. Morrissey*

some acquaintance with the spirit of inquiry and reflection, few think of making
it the effective centre of their lives; and of that few, still fewer make sufficient
progress to be able to withstand other attractions and persevere in their high
purpose" (225).

4. See Voegelin's essay "Industrial Society in Search of Reason," in *World
Technology and Human Destiny*, ed. Raymond Aron (Ann Arbor: University of
Michigan Press, 1963), 31–46, at 34–36. Though Voegelin was by profession a
political scientist throughout his life, his later work prescinds from any discussion
of the optimal governmental regimes or constitutional forms a society might take,
suggesting perhaps that the only true requirement for sound political order is the
personal order of the individual soul to divine reality that a society must both
reflect and serve. On this see Ellis Sandoz's comment in his introduction to *Published Essays, 1966–1985*, xxi.

5. "Immortality: Experience and Symbol," in *Published Essays, 1966–1985*,
57.

6. *Autobiographical Reflections*, 12. On Weber's "value-free" science, see *The
New Science of Politics*, 13–22.

7. Gregor Sebba, "Prelude and Variations on the Theme of Eric Voegelin,"
Southern Review, n.s., 13 (1977): 658n.

8. *The Ecumenic Age*, 187.

9. It also features in an important passage in the *Philebus* (16c–17a), where
Plato symbolizes the mystery of being as existence intermediate between (*metaxy*)
the One (*hen*) and the Unlimited (*apeiron*), denoting the In-Between status of
things; see *The Ecumenic Age*, 184–85.

10. For a rare exception see Steven Shankman, *In Search of the Classic* (University Park: Pennsylvania State University Press, 1994), 21–26.

11. Voegelin first introduced and analyzed this symbol in his 1964 essay "Eternal Being in Time," published in Eric Voegelin, *Anamnesis*, trans. and ed. Gerhart
Niemeyer (Notre Dame: University of Notre Dame Press, 1978), 116–46. His
treatment of it in its Platonic context appears in Section II: "Philosophy as a
Constituent of History." Voegelin continued his exegesis of this element in the
Symposium in *The Ecumenic Age*, 185–87, where in a very trenchant analysis he
emphasized the truth of the *metaxy* as revelatory.

12. *Anamnesis*, 128.

13. *Anamnesis*, 129, 130.

14. Voegelin's fullest catalogue of the tensions in existence is found in his
"Equivalences of Experience and Symbolization in History," in *Published Essays,
1966–1985*, 119–20.

15. *The Epic of Gilgamesh* is not a text that Voegelin analyzes anywhere.
Rather an anonymous Egyptian text, circa 2000 B.C., called "Dispute of a Man,
Who Contemplates Suicide, With His Soul," serves his analysis of an early historical experience of life, death, alienation, and immortality that has remained a constant in consciousness. See "Immortality," 58–64.

16. For a penetrating interpretation of the story of the Garden of Eden, not as
a story of a Fall but rather as a quest for immortality, see James Barr, *The Garden
of Eden and the Hope of Immortality* (Minneapolis: Fortress Press, 1992).

17. I put "afterlife" in quotation marks to remind the reader that it is not a term used by Voegelin, most likely because he saw it as a hypostatized concept of the immortal beyond. I take the following statement of Voegelin to suggest that images and symbols of a personal or collective "afterlife" are not themselves unbalancing of consciousness, but become so when they are divorced from the experiences of the beyond that they symbolize and are distorted into representations of immanentized reality: "All 'eristic phantasies' which try to convert the limits of the *metaxy*, be it the noetic height or the apeirontic depth, into a phenomenon within the *metaxy* are to be excluded as false. This rule does not affect genuine eschatological or apocalyptic symbolisms which imaginatively express the experience of a movement within reality toward a Beyond of the *metaxy*, such as the experiences of mortality and immortality" ("Reason: The Classic Experience," in *Published Essays, 1966–1985*, 290).

18. Such as to be found in the *Phaedrus*, the *Gorgias*, and the *Republic*. For Voegelin's last reflections on the *Phaedrus* myth of the immortal soul, see "The Beginning and the Beyond: A Meditation on Truth," in *The Collected Works of Eric Voegelin*, vol. 28, *What Is History? And Other Late Unpublished Writings*, eds. Thomas Hollweck and Paul Caringella (Baton Rouge: Louisiana State University Press, 1990), 212–17; and "Quod Deus Dicitur," in *Published Essays, 1966–1985*, 384.

19. Delivered as the Ingersoll Lecture on Immortality at Harvard Divinity School on January 14, 1965; see "Immortality," 52–94.

20. Voegelin, "Last Orientation," unpublished ms., 179–80; quoted in Jurgen Gebhardt, "Toward the Process of Universal Mankind: The Formation of Voegelin's Philosophy of History," in *Eric Voegelin's Thought: A Critical Appraisal*, ed. Ellis Sandoz (Durham, N.C.: Duke University Press, 1982), 68.

21. "The Beginning and the Beyond," 218.

22. See "Eternal Being in Time," in *Anamnesis*, 128.

23. See, for example, "Wisdom and the Magic of the Extreme: A Meditation," in *Published Essays, 1966–1985*, 335.

24. See Eric Voegelin, *Order and History*, vol. 3, *Plato and Aristotle* (Baton Rouge: Louisiana State University Press, 1957), 36.

25. On the role of imagination and its deformation see Eric Voegelin, *Order and History*, vol. 5, *In Search of Order* (Baton Rouge: Louisiana State University Press, 1987), 37–41 and 61–62.

26. "Immortality," 93; "What Is History?," in *What Is History?*, 30. Elsewhere, speaking on how the nature of faith in the "exodus" journey toward "the heavenly Jerusalem" gets objectified by the various escapes from history (gnostic and apocalyptic), Voegelin remarks on this very problem: "People do not ordinarily live with this tension, yet they still want to immigrate into the kingdom of God. This pole of the tension will be objectified by various imageries into a kingdom of God, depicted in very definite colors and incidents" ("Configurations of History," 106).

27. See "What Is Political Reality?," in *Anamnesis*, 144, 145, 185.

28. "Wisdom and the Magic of the Extreme," 344. Elsewhere in discussing his method of "reflective inquiry," Voegelin says that "[w]hile the original symbols

contain a rational structure that can be further articulated through reflection, the reflective acts of cognition can be true only if they participate in the divine reality that participated in the emergence of the symbols. The reflection, thus, assumes a reality engaged in becoming cognitively luminous" ("The Beginning and the Beyond," 189).

29. On the utopian dream of perfection, see the first part of Voegelin's essay, "Wisdom and the Magic of the Extreme," 316–26.

30. "The Beginning and the Beyond," 190.

31. On the "balance of consciousness," see *The Ecumenic Age*, 227–38.

32. For Voegelin's analysis of this sonnet, see "Wisdom and the Magic of the Extreme," 328–29.

33. Shankman's *In Search of the Classic* is a penetrating Voegelinian critique of postmodernism by a philosophically trained literary critic.

34. "Reason: The Classic Experience," 278. On the "grotesque" see, for example, *Anamnesis*, 161–62ff.

35. "Such a life, however, is more than merely human; it cannot be lived by man qua man but only by virtue of the divine that is in him. . . . If then the Nous is divine compared with man, so is the noetic life divine compared with human life" (*Nicomachean Ethics*, 1177b26–31).

36. On the deforming split of the *metaxy* into "mortal" and "immortal," and Plato's comprehensive vision of the Whole, see "Wisdom and the Magic of the Extreme," 358–65.

37. "Reason: The Classic Experience," 279; "The Beginning and the Beyond," 225.

38. "The Beginning and the Beyond," 226.

39. "The Beginning and the Beyond," 221.

40. Under the Christian orbit the symbolism equivalent to immortality is of course "resurrection."

41. "Wisdom and the Magic of the Extreme," 369.

42. "Philosophies of History: An Interview with Eric Voegelin," *New Orleans Review* 2 (1973): 135–39, at 137. This text from Matthew, like Plato's treatment of *opsis* (vision) in the *Republic* and the *Laws*, is used by Voegelin to illustrate the distinction between revelation and information.

43. "Quod Deus Dicitur," 383–84 (in a misprint, the text in *Published Essays, 1966–1985* locates the quoted Gospel passage as John 6:24). One should be mindful of the fact that these words of Voegelin come from his deathbed meditation.

44. "Immortality," 91.

45. See "What Is Political Reality?," in *Anamnesis*, 173, and "The Beginning and the Beyond," 230.

46. "Anxiety and Reason," in *What Is History?*, 22.

47. "Remembrance of Things Past," in *Published Essays, 1966–1985*, 309.

48. "Wisdom and the Magic of the Extreme," 369–70; "Immortality," 78.

49. Thomas J. J. Altizer, "The Theological Conflict Between Strauss and Voegelin," in *Faith and Political Philosophy: The Correspondence Between Leo Strauss and Eric Voegelin, 1934–1964*, trans. and ed. Peter Emberley and Barry Cooper (University Park: Pennsylvania State University Press, 1993), 275.

50. See "Equivalences of Experience and Symbolization in History," 129.

51. In his *Metaphysics*, Aristotle remarked how the *"philomythos* is in a sense a *philosophos*, for the myth is composed of wonders" (982b18–19); and in an extant fragment of a letter from his last years, he wrote, "The more solitary and retired I become, the more I love the myth" (*philomytheros*). Voegelin discusses these passages in "What Is Political Reality?," in *Anamnesis*, 158, and in *The Ecumenic Age*, 191–92. See also "Equivalences of Experience and Symbolization in History," 126, and *Autobiographical Reflections*, 108.

52. *Plato and Aristotle*, 170; *In Search of Order*, 91–107.

53. See *The Ecumenic Age*, 10. In his personal correspondence, Voegelin once said in response to the question of the two intentionalities of consciousness—one in the direction of revelation and the other in the direction of the external world (or what he later came to call luminosity and intentionality)—that "one must consider it possible, therefore, that the unity of the two intentions is not [to] be found on the level of differentiated consciousness at all, but rather in the cosmo-logical myth, in the imaginative tale of a reality that still includes the divine" (Eric Voegelin to David Walsh, December 21, 1974, Eric Voegelin Papers, Hoover Institution Archives, Stanford University, Box 40, Folder 2).

54. See Voegelin's essay "The Moving Soul," in *What Is History?*, 163–72. In this "thought experiment," Voegelin argues that the image of a physical cosmos cannot be constructed simply on the basis of theoretical physics. The construct of a spatiotemporal "universe" as assumed and presented by modern physics is a modern mytho-speculative "symbolism" of the cosmos as an intelligible whole. Thus it is a demythologized equivalent to cosmological myths, such as the "look at the Heaven" of Xenophanes, and equally based on the "primary experience of the cosmos," which is a constant and pragmatic human experience in history (xxv, 170–72).

2

Grounding Public Discourse: The Contribution of Eric Voegelin

John J. Ranieri

Amid current debates concerning multiculturalism, pluralism, the place of religion in public life, and the overall state and future of American democracy, one seldom hears the name of Eric Voegelin. This, I believe, is unfortunate. Voegelin's thought has much to recommend it as a serious attempt to deal with issues such as these. Indeed, if we take Voegelin at his word, it was the social and political crisis of his time, the perceived loss of rationality in public discourse, and the replacement of such discourse with ideological posturing that served as the catalyst for his work.[1] And if this were not reason enough to view his work as possibly relevant to our present situation, there is the further fact that in Voegelin we have a thinker who is a multiculturalist, a religious pluralist, and, at the same time, a nonrelativist in matters having to do with the human good. In what follows, I will offer reasons to support this interpretation of Voegelin's philosophy. In three sections I (1) give a brief account of some of the issues affecting public life in contemporary American society; (2) examine Voegelin's understanding of reason, publicness, and the ways in which he believed genuine public discourse could be fostered; and (3) show how Voegelin's thought is relevant to some of the questions that have been raised concerning reason and public life.

The Present Situation

The pluralism found in contemporary liberal democratic societies is an inescapable reality. Regardless of one's attitude toward this situation, it surely poses a challenge. The question arises with increasing frequency as to whether it is possible to sustain democracy without at least some acknowledgment of commonality. On what ground can people of widely diverging religious, moral, and cultural perspectives possibly meet? Is it possible to go beyond identities based on gender, race, or ethnicity to encounter one another at a level shareable by all human beings? Or are these differences irreducible? If so, this implies that the bond among citizens consists of little more than a responsibility to recognize the other as different and to do no harm, either out of fear of punishment for doing otherwise or, more positively, out of regard for the other as an autonomous agent like oneself.

The problem is particularly acute for liberal democracy, because by its very nature it is committed to the equal representation of all. But what does it mean to be recognized as equal within a pluralistic society, and from what perspective are competing claims for recognition to be judged? The very commitments that constitute liberal democracy give rise to the challenge of somehow encompassing widely ranging understandings of the good life within a single polity. Increasingly, in the view of many who reflect seriously on democracy, the "politics of recognition" has become a "politics of difference," in which "[t]he language of opposition now appears as a cascading series of manifestos that tell us that we cannot live together; we cannot work together; we are not in this together; we are not Americans who have something in common, but racial, ethnic, gender, or sexually identified clans who demand to be 'recognized' only or exclusively as 'different.'"[2] The notion of a public realm in which people engage one another in spirited, often heated debate has given way to "culture wars," a term that at times comes close to being more than a metaphor.

An important way in which this tension has played itself out centers around the issue of multiculturalism. In academia, battles over college core curricula have pitted those who view the introduction of non-Western works as an abandonment of the cultural heritage that sustains democracy and as a dangerous slide toward relativism against those who see in the inclusion of previously excluded voices the fulfillment of the democratic commitment to equality and the end of an oppressive, demeaning Eurocentrism. Multiculturalism poses acute challenges for the political realm as well. Charles Taylor has noted that if human life is inherently dialogical, then the need for recognition is not only a matter of equal rights but is rather constitutive of our individual and communal identities.[3]

Questions concerning pluralism, multiculturalism, the role of religion in society, and the future of liberal democracy are inseparable from questions about the nature of publicness and the possibility of public discourse. In a pluralistic democracy it is crucial that there be some means for people of widely diverging beliefs and practices to discuss matters that affect them all as citizens. One need not romanticize either the traditions of the American founding or the public life of the ancient Greek polis "in order to realize that a public discussion of polity issues appealing to all intelligent, reasonable and responsible persons is a necessity, not a luxury, for any humane polity."[4] It seems necessary that some notion of rationality, however rudimentary, be presupposed in discussions about how best to order our lives together as citizens.

Yet to recognize the need for some sort of appeal to reason in the public realm is merely to state the problem; it can hardly be said to have resolved it. For how can we speak of a public role for reason, when the very nature and efficacy of reason in the public realm is called into question? Without a shared understanding of reason how can we speak of a public realm at all? In addition, underlying much contemporary thought is the acknowledgment that reason itself has a history, thus undermining its claims to universality and objectivity. If reason is itself the product of particular social-cultural-historical conditions, then how can it serve as the ground for public discourse, especially in diverse and pluralistic societies? Might it be that the only role left for reason is as an instrumental means to achieve predominantly technological ends, since rational agreement on more substantive issues such as what constitutes a good life has been abandoned as futile in light of the historically and culturally conditioned character of rationality?[5]

Voegelin gave a good deal of attention to questions such as these. Reflecting upon his life as a philosopher, Voegelin was quite explicit in stating that while his work culminated in a philosophy of history, it was still to be understood as arising in response to the political situation.[6] He decried the loss of rational discussion in contemporary society, and he sought, in all his efforts, to recover the life of reason in the present situation. For Voegelin, communication was the "*modus procendi* through which a society exists." That being the case, he worried about the tendency of communication in modern society to be understood solely in terms of "pragmatic communication," that is, communication as a technique by which to induce behavior in conformity with the communicator's wishes. In similar fashion, Voegelin feared that the prevalent modern conception of rationality as coordination of means and ends threatened to lose sight of those goods that were the source of rational order. The alienation of citizens from public life, and the withdrawal of more and more people into private worlds centered around trivial distractions geared to the alleviation of emptiness and boredom, were, in Voegelin's view, threats to democracy, "because the human beings whose personality is formed, or rather deformed, by the mass media of communication are the voters whose wishes must be satisfied by the elected representatives."[7] Throughout his life, he was concerned with the revitalization of the public realm.

Voegelin on Reason and Public Life

For Voegelin, reason is nothing other than the openness of human beings toward the ground of existence.[8] The experience articulated in the symbol of "the ground" has to do with the human awareness that

> Man is not a self-created, autonomous being carrying the origin and meaning of his existence within himself. He is not a divine *causa sui*; from the experience of his life in precarious existence within the limits of birth and death there rather rises the wondering question about the ultimate ground, the *aitia* or *prote arche*, of all reality and specifically his own. The question is inherent in the experience from which it rises; the *zoon noun echon* that experiences itself as a living being is at the same time conscious of the questionable character attaching to this status. Man, when he experiences himself as existent, discovers his specific humanity as that of the questioner for the wherefrom and the whereto, for the ground and the sense of his existence.

There is no detached, Archimedean point from which humans might coolly ask questions about the ground of existence as if they somehow stood apart from it all: "The ground is not a spatially distant thing but a divine presence that becomes manifest in the experience of unrest and the desire to know." Reason encompasses a person's self-reflective awareness of his or her orientation toward the ground, that dimension of the person by which one is conscious of such an orientation, and the ground itself as the source and goal of our questioning unrest. Reason is present whenever people experience themselves as following the dynamism of their questioning unrest and as being moved by wonder. It emerges from the *metaxy*, the "in-between," of divine and human, that "place" where our very humanity is constituted. While reason is always present as the constituent of humanity, its differentiation and articulation is a historical event, the great achievement of the Greek philosophers.[9] For Voegelin, to speak of humans as rational creatures is to recognize this shared openness toward the ground as constitutive of our specifically human nature. It is also to recognize that "[r]ational discussion on order in the existence of humanity and society is possible only when accompanied by knowledge of transcendental fulfillment."[10]

This notion that reason is inseparable from our orientation to a transcendent end needs to be properly understood. It would be a serious misconstrual of Voegelin's thought to imagine that in speaking of "transcendental fulfillment" he means that one cannot be rational unless one "believes in God." While Voegelin freely employs religious terms such as "transcendental," "divine ground," and "God," these must always be understood to arise from the experience of being drawn or moved by a reality that is somehow "beyond" the cosmos. As such, these terms represent that dimension of reality recognized as the divine "pole" within the experience, rather than entities whose existence one could ascertain and about which one would speak as if they were objects in the external world. In employing these terms in this fashion, Voegelin's point is to reinforce the notion that they refer to a reality that, while never encompassed by human questioning and not ever completely knowable, remains the background, goal, and source of all human wonder. One does not have to "believe in God" to be rational; but each of us is called upon to respond to the normative exigencies of our capacity to wonder, and in doing so questions of the ultimate meaning and intelligibility of reality arise spontaneously. The *question* of God lies within our horizon. The rejection of such questions—the refusal, in Voegelin's words, "to be drawn into the realms of the transcendental"—means that one has chosen an intellectual and spiritual obscurantism; it is certainly not being rational.

In order to capture something of its broad and protean character, Voegelin refers to "reason" as a symbol; a symbol arising from experiences of participation in reality, experiences of openness, of seeking, and of being drawn. I do not think it is possible to overemphasize the importance Voegelin places on this experiential dimension of reason. By grounding rationality in experience, Voegelin felt that he had properly situated reason at its deepest source. While one could talk about experiences of openness and even develop a language with which to do so, the experiences themselves are not reducible to any other reality and do not, therefore, admit of "proof." The experience rendered by the symbol "reason" is basic and foundational. For Voegelin:

> Either the openness is a reality and then you can't prove it—you can't prove reality; you can only point to it—or it isn't. Well it is. We know—we have documents of the experiences, they are in existence: the dialogues of Plato, the meditations of St. Augustine on time and space, or the thornbush episode in *Exodus*. Here are the documents of the openness towards transcendence. You can't have more. There's nothing you can prove or disprove.[11]

While aware of the possible objection that these experiences might be merely "subjective," Voegelin would point out that the experiences articulated in classic documents (like those cited in the previous quotation), while varying widely in expression, all reveal a common openness to reality, and he would turn the question back on his interlocutor by asking the person to account for the apparent similarity in basic structure among experiences cutting across the most varied and otherwise dissimilar cultures, societies, and historical epochs. This means that while symbols may have emerged from apparently incommensurable cultures, it is possible, by means of "meditative exegesis," to recognize an equivalence among the symbols and the experiences expressed by those symbols. To speak of equivalence is not to suggest that the multiplicity of experiences and symbols discovered in the course of history all reflect a constant identifiable "core" experience; for to claim that one has formulated the core experience is to succumb to the temptation to absolutize one's formulation. There is no common core experience to be reached behind the symbols; what there is is a mystery experienced and articulated through symbols. There is equivalence of symbols because widely divergent symbols testify to the constitutively human experience of participation, of wonder, and of being moved or drawn by the reality of which we are a part. There is equivalence of experiences because the mystery of participation cannot be definitively described.[12]

In what I believe is one of the more important statements Voegelin made about his method of procedure and the criteria by which to evaluate documents concerning experience, he stated that, "The test of truth, to put it pointedly, will be the lack of originality in the propositions."[13] The truth of symbols emerges from within the context of other symbols drawn from the wider cultural-historical field. Symbols or accounts of experience that, upon analysis, are found to be recognizably equivalent to other classic symbolizations within this field can be understood as testifying to the common human experience of participation in reality.

By tracing reason to its experiential origins, Voegelin made clear the *empirical* nature of his work. Voegelin would claim that his notion of reason was neither a theory nor an idea; it was a symbolic expression of well-attested experiences in the history of humanity. He was quite conscious of empirically grounding his philosophical language. This is why throughout his work we find him returning again and again to the data: symbols, myths, religious and literary texts, works of art, and any other expressions of the human spirit. His was a radical empiricism that went beyond the symbols and texts to recapture the experiences underlying these expressions. The more data he could amass from the study of comparative religion, archaeology, anthropology, ancient civilizations, and elsewhere, the more empirically verified would be his interpretations of the originating experiences. Nor was this a matter of Voegelin imposing his own preconceived ideas on the data. Anyone familiar with his thought knows that Voegelin was quite capable of changing his mind and altering his interpretation in light of new evidence, even if it involved a major reorientation of his work.[14] This point needs to be emphasized, since for Voegelin any philosophical language that is not somehow empirically grounded, that is, that does not reflect the structure of human existence in the *metaxy* by remaining close to experience, easily degenerates into an ideology that obscures the experiential basis of reason and thereby makes rational discussion impossible.

Voegelin's attention to the experience of openness as the core of rationality was an attempt to discover a common ground for rational discussion that would not be bound to the definition of reason as formulated in any particular cultural, religious, or philosophical tradition, while at the same time remaining recognizably equivalent to the same experience as witnessed to by each tradition. His focus on experience was a response to a situation marked by what he described as a "noisy struggle among the possessors of dogmatic truth—theological, or metaphysical, or ideological." Adding to the confusion was a recognition that "[t]he search for the constants of human order in society and history is, at present, uncertain of its language."[15] Voegelin realized that the meaning of *reason* itself had become problematic; like so many other symbols it had become disengaged from its engendering experiences. His was a conscious effort to recapture reason by moving to a deeper level of commonality, the level of experience and its symbolization. While Voegelin's attempt to restore the life of reason to society is a concern he shares with a number of his contemporaries, his unique contribution lies in the way he has searched for the common ground of rationality by focusing on the experiences underlying humanity's symbolizations. If reason was to serve as the basis for public discourse, it had to be rooted in experiences accessible and familiar to all. At this level, even those who belong to apparently incompatible cultural or religious traditions may be able to engage in genuine conversation.[16]

It is not difficult to understand why reason, understood in this broad fashion, is also the source of publicness. To be rational is to be in a relationship of openness to the ground. While this relationship may be (and often is) obscured, it is nonetheless true that all are potentially capable of rational discourse, for all people share in "the existential tension toward the ground, and the ground is for all men the one and only divine ground of being." It is this shared openness toward the divine ground that Heraclitus described as *xynon*, the "common," and Aristotle referred to as the source of *homonoia* or "like-mindedness." To speak of *xynon* and *homonoia* is to recognize a shared, constitutive orientation to reality as making possible human understanding, conversation, and community. As such, this orientation is the ground of publicness and the source of social cohesiveness, whether differentiated explicitly, as it was by Plato and Aristotle, or remaining compactly expressed as in earlier, prephilosophical modes of symbolization. Refusal to acknowledge what is common is to imagine that one's consciousness is private, and by so blocking reality one "becomes thereby a private man, or in the language of Heraclitus, an *idiotes*." Where there is no acknowledgment of the "common," where openness to the ground is lacking, rational discussion would be impossible, and reason cannot become the source of a lasting public order.[17]

Where this life of reason is absent, a society cannot properly be called either good or political.[18] Where openness to the ground is lacking, we can speak of "masses" but not of political society. Ignorance of the ground effectively puts an end to the possibility of the rational discussion that is at the heart of authentic political life. Bereft of reason, the nonpolitical "subject" is left with the alternatives of "tradition-conscious subordination or antitraditional opposition."[19] Every society consists of people at various levels of attunement; thus each society will embody a unique configuration of tensions ranging from those genuinely attuned to the divine ground to those in whom reality has been eclipsed. If, as is often the case, those in whom this eclipse has taken place come to dominate a society, the public life of that society will suffer, for those estranged from reality are estranged from the common experience that makes public life possible at all. In such situations it is the *idiotes*, the person characterized by spiritual vacuity and radical individualism, that becomes the socially dominant figure.

So long as there exists a dominant "substantial public" (where "substantial" connotes openness to the ground), a strong governmental authority, or enough cultural capital remaining from those traditions in which reason as existential openness has not been eclipsed, the disturbances of public order caused by deformed consciousness will be kept to a minimum. However, as institutions such as universities and the media, under the influence of educators and commentators suffering from an atrophy of reason, continue to destroy people's consciousness of the ground, there emerges an ever-growing mass of people who have been educated to nonpublic existence. This comes about because where the ground has been eclipsed in consciousness, reason is lost, and the loss of reason means the erosion of *homonoia*, without which *philia politike* cannot exist. In place of social responsibility rooted in the acknowledgment of a common participation in reality and a common regard for the other as reasonable, we find instead a narcissistic and apolitical emphasis on individual development, self-expression, and originality, due to the fact that where the ground of reality has been denied it will likely be replaced by the notion that the individual is the ground of his or her own existence. When those trained in this way attain a critical mass within a society, a climate is created in which social movements of estrangement can assume power.[20]

Faced with such a situation, what can be done? Voegelin holds out little hope that a large number of people will be attracted to the life of reason. Potentially, all are equal in this regard, "but empirically (for whatever reason) they are unequal in the application of their potentiality." "The psychic tension of the life of reason is difficult for the majority of the members of a society to bear"; and because of this, "any society in which

the life of reason has reached a high degree of differentiation has a tendency to develop, along with the life of reason, a 'mass belief.'" The
growth of such mass belief "may reduce the life of reason to socially
meaningless enclaves or even forcefully suppress it."[21] While Voegelin believes that rational discussion remains a possibility in contemporary society, he would also maintain that such discussion cannot be conducted
with those in whom the life of reason has atrophied. Unfortunately, such
people have come to dominate the "climate of opinion" that determines
the present age.[22]

Confronted with such prospects, how is one to proceed in making reason socially effective, and what are the resources at one's disposal? As a
first step, what is required is both a "careful analysis of the noetic structure of existence" and a critical clarification of the structure and sources
of the present disorder. The recovery of reason is an arduous task, one
that involves a painstaking reconstruction of "the fundamental categories
of existence, experience, consciousness, and reality," along with the development of "the concepts by which existential deformation and its symbolic expression can be categorized." Following this analysis, there is the
need to foster "the formation of the psyche by encouraging participation
in transcendent reason."[23] What this means is nothing less than the creation of a "community of language" able to criticize ideologies without
itself falling into ideological language.[24]

Those who have committed themselves to this task are not to engage in
revolutionary action or even take an active role in formulating specific
economic, legislative, and social policies. Their task is to aid in the recovery of reason through careful study, research, reflective analysis, and discussion of those experiences of the ground as manifested in every culture,
and to communicate as well as possible the types of conduct that would
be appropriate in light of such experiences.[25] Explication of experience is
not a matter of discovering universal principles and applying them in concrete instances. Voegelin's focus is always on the permeability of the
human person to the presence of the divine ground, not on the apprehension of eternal truths. In openness toward the ground one becomes capable of rational discussion and ethical behavior.[26]

The communities of language envisioned by Voegelin are not to withdraw into themselves. He does not advocate religious-contemplative apol-
iticism in the face of social disorder. Those in whom reality has not been
eclipsed have a responsibility to both communicate and point toward their
experience in the hope that others will come to share it as well. The ultimate goal of Voegelin's project is persuasion with an eye toward social
transformation. For Voegelin, "the purpose of the analysis is to per-
suade—to have its own insights, if possible, supplant the opinions in social reality."[27] Persuasion is not manipulation; it is always an offer, an

invitation, and a process "in which the substantive order of a community is created and maintained." Where reason is understood primarily as instrumental and communication is conceived only as pragmatic in purpose, they "cannot function as persuasion in the Platonic sense at all, but only induce conformist states of mind and conforming behavior. . . . Communication, once it has become essentially pragmatic, can no longer rely on the persuasiveness of the reason it has decapitated."[28] Of course, the creation and reinforcement of a "substantial public," that is, a public guided by the life of reason, becomes especially difficult when the socially dominant public is estranged from reality, but one must still try to create communities of language with sufficient persuasive and exemplary power to shift social dominance from those suffering from estrangement to those in whom reason as openness has not been eclipsed. Such communities may, in time, achieve some degree of social effectiveness. If this were to occur, public opinion would compel reform.[29] It is to the public that one must appeal, because those in positions of leadership are not likely to respond favorably to calls for reform, imprisoned as they are by their interest in preserving their own positions. While Voegelin did not hold out a great deal of hope that persuasion would prove to be especially efficacious in the short term, it remained his conviction that, since the tension toward the ground is never completely extinguished in the human person, a rational social order remains a possibility.

Concretely, Voegelin sees a pivotal role for universities in helping to form people in the life of reason. Unfortunately, these institutions have too often abdicated their responsibility.[30] The university, from Voegelin's perspective, does not exist to indoctrinate; indeed Voegelin believes that doctrine in any form is frequently part of the problem. What the university can do, however, is foster students' questioning unrest, and help them appropriate themselves as rational men and women through serious engagement with texts that give voice to experiences of openness. Voegelin finds the possibility of exposure to such texts becoming increasingly frequent with the contemporary revival and expansion of those disciplines that study humanity and its symbols, for example, classical, patristic, and scholastic philosophy, classical philology, and comparative religion.[31]

Voegelin is not suggesting that a course in the Great Books is the key to restoring public discourse. What he is calling for is careful reflection on classics from all historical-cultural traditions; a reflection that takes them seriously, not as books that must be read in order to be considered "cultured" or in order to fulfill a diversity requirement, but as avenues to those experiences of reality that underpin and provide meaning to our shared lives. The role of the university, then, is to create a context in which people may recover an openness to reality through an encounter with experiences of transcendence as these experiences are mediated in the classics of every culture. People so transformed will not easily succumb to the lure of ideologies. At the heart of social transformation, then, is mystagogy.[32]

The Relevance of Voegelin's Thought in the Present Context

Those looking for specific technical solutions to resolve particular social problems may well be disappointed by Voegelin's suggestions. Nonetheless, the health and survival of democracy would seem to depend on a vibrant public realm in which it is possible for people of various cultural and religious perspectives to meet and deliberate about common concerns. This would seem to imply the need for an understanding of reason that is wide and deep enough to encompass a variety of widely ranging perspectives. And here I believe that Voegelin has a valuable contribution to make.

There is, first of all, Voegelin's broad understanding of reason. He challenges the hegemony of reason conceived in an instrumental or technical fashion, and in doing so he joins the ranks of those philosophers who believe that a crucial factor in renewing public discussion is the recovery of earlier understandings of *praxis* and *phronesis*.[33] Voegelin's contribution to this enterprise consists in tracing reason to its source in experiences of transcendence.

By showing the connection between reason and these kinds of experience, Voegelin has provided a basis for public discourse that avoids some of the problems associated with certain Enlightenment notions of reason still influential in Western democracies. Charles Taylor has recently reminded us of a tendency in some strains of liberal thought to imagine that its language is neutral with regard to conflicting conceptions of the human good and universal in its applicability. He has also shown how this universal perspective enters into tension with the "politics of recognition." A universalism blind to differences supports a strong commitment to equality; but this very commitment to equality fosters a situation in which those wishing to be recognized as equal insist that their *particular* identities be acknowledged, respected, and preserved. The charge leveled by some of those seeking greater recognition is that the supposed universal, difference-blind principles are themselves the reflection of a particular liberal, Enlightenment culture, "a particularism masquerading as a universal."[34] This criticism would apply as well to any notion of reason that claims to have discovered universally applicable principles, rights, and immunities.

Voegelin was sympathetic to this criticism of universalism and its claims to have discovered permanent and timeless principles. Throughout his ca-

44 *John J. Ranieri*

reer he was deeply suspicious of any "universal" principles that could not be traced to experiences of openness to transcendence. Voegelin was particularly wary of a tendency within the Anglo-American political tradition to attribute universal significance to those political doctrines that contributed to its historical, economic, and political success.[35] He comments ironically in his essay "The Oxford Political Philosophers" that the philosophers in question "are willing to accept the mystery of incarnation: that the principles of right political order have become historical flesh more perfectly in England than anywhere else at any time," and he fears that the "institutional symbolism of the English polity has become accepted as the language of political discourse."[36] Voegelin expressed similar reservations about liberalism as a whole, and its tendency to forget that "it is not a body of timelessly valid scientific propositions about political reality, but rather a series of political opinions and attitudes which have their optimal truth in the situation which motivates them. . . ."[37] Underlying Voegelin's concern is the question of whether the rights and freedoms so important to Anglo-American, liberal democracy are actually timeless "principles" or rather "prudential measures that will, under given historical circumstances, create the best possible environment for the attainment of the highest good." Voegelin is certainly not against such freedoms; but he perceives a danger in substituting the "useful" for the rational, and elevating whatever "works" into principles that become "inalienable, eternal, and ultimate." Too often in the West, Voegelin finds "a strong tendency to forget, both in theory and practice, that 'goodness' is the quality of a society and not of a governmental form."[38] For Voegelin, the genuine "principles" needed to support public discourse and social order can only be derived from a philosophical anthropology which finds "the ordering centre of human personality in the experience of man's relation to transcendent reality."[39]

If it is the case, though, that the universalist presuppositions with which we operate reflect only one possible model for rationality and the ordering of the public sphere, then it would seem that we are forever locked in an unbridgeable ethnocentrism. Once again Charles Taylor has characterized the situation well. After commenting how "supposedly independent and culture-transcendent theories of politics turn out to be heavily dependent on certain parochial Western forms of political culture," he wonders if the only other alternative is to understand each culture only in its own terms. If so, then each culture is interpretively self-enclosed, and there is no way of making any kind of evaluative judgments between cultures, including cross-cultural judgments of rationality. Complicating the problem is the fact that the practices, activities, and ways of life of various cultures are often not simply different but incommensurable, that is, incompatible in principle. A liberal polity can handle with relative ease practices, activities, and so on, that are merely "different," that are simply variations on common, already accepted, existing practices. But "incommensurable ways of life seem to raise the question insistently of who is right." Taylor believes, however, that cross-cultural judgments can be made; what is needed is a "language of perspicuous contrast," which would be "a language in which we could formulate both their way of life and ours as alternative possibilities in relation to some human constants at work in both." This language would bring to light areas in which every culture falls short in its attentiveness to the normative exigencies of rationality and understanding.[40]

There are a number of ways in which Voegelin's thought addresses these very issues. The search for a language of "constants" with which to speak of experiences of reality was a central part of Voegelin's work.[41] To recall a point made earlier, Voegelin was quite conscious that reason had to be grounded on a level at which the most disparate cultures could meet in dialogue. His exegesis of experience, his theory of equivalences, and his identification of reason with openness to the ground was an attempt to do this. The constants developed through meditative exegesis emerge from a careful comparison of symbols that tries to remain close to the underlying experiences. The normative and empirical nature of such an approach stems from the fact that it constantly returns to the data; symbolizations are always understood within the context of a vast variety of other symbols and "tested" against them.[42] No particular culture is privileged with regard to its symbols or its formulation of experience; and if, through the efforts of the historical sciences, further relevant data shed new light on the structure and meaning of the tension toward the ground, it may be necessary to call into question the assumptions underpinning one's cultural horizon. One is able to make such judgments because what emerges from the historical field of symbols are patterns and configurations of meaning that reveal the normativity of reason as residing in the openness of experiences of transcendence. Voegelin does not claim to offer a neutral, universal perspective that transcends all cultures while belonging to none; this was precisely part of the problem he identified in Western parochialism. Instead, what he offers is an approach that is sensitive to the historical emergence of reason as it manifests itself in every culture, while at the same time recognizing the constancy, throughout history, of the openness that constitutes the core of rationality.[43]

In this way, Voegelin's understanding of reason is wide enough to serve as a bridge between cultures that, in Taylor's terminology, would be considered incommensurable. Voegelin's sensitivity to the historical differentiation of reason enables him to recognize the presence of reason in cultures that might otherwise be incomprehensible to each other. From Voegelin's perspective, a cosmological culture in which the compactness of myth predominates is essentially no less rational than a culture in which reason has more clearly differentiated. Like Taylor, however, Voegelin would say that certain differentiations can be recognized as advances, and to the extent that reason has been more fully differentiated, "theoretical" cultures may be judged superior, at least in some areas. Both philosophers appear to locate this superiority in the fact that where the differentiation of reason has freed the political, technological, and economic realms from the dominance of myth, whole new possibilities have opened for human life, possibilities that are not of interest only to those in the modern West but for all who wish to act effectively in the world.[44] Neither Taylor nor Voegelin, however, would argue that a judgment of superiority in certain areas should be extended to the entire way of life found in theoretical cultures. Indeed both men have raised serious questions as to the adequacy of modern culture in expressing the richness and fullness of authentically human life.

Voegelin's conception of reason is also relevant to contemporary discussions about multiculturalism and pluralism. His thought reveals a deep appreciation of how reason, as the tension toward the ground, is present in seemingly disparate cultures throughout history. In this regard, Voegelin's perspective reminds one of the work done by David Tracy on the nature and role of the "classic."[45] Whereas argument (understood as publicly defending one's assertions by means of "evidence, warrants, and backings appropriate to the concrete subject-matter under discussion") may be the primary candidate for publicness in a liberal democracy, the disclosive and transformative truth of the classic produces its effect by engaging us at the level of imaginative possibility—a more elusive but no less public and important function. While certainly not downplaying or ignoring the role of argument in matters of publicness, both Tracy and Voegelin would maintain that the strength of the classic in fostering publicness lies in its ability to "manifest disclosive and transformative truths in a manner that is not reducible to the structure of our more usual arguments." Rather than argument, the model operative here is that of *conversation* with the classic; an interaction, which, precisely as conversation, is shareable, public, and a possible source of consensus in the public realm.[46]

The power of the classic lies in its paradoxical ability to be both particular and public. This insight animates much of Voegelin's analysis. Characteristically, Voegelin maintained that the life of reason could be found in such diverse sources as Siberian shamanism, Coptic papyri, the petroglyphs in the caves of the Ile-de-France, and the symbolisms of African tribes.[47] And while he remained committed to the belief that the optimal differentiation of reason had occurred in ancient Hellas, this did not lead him into Eurocentrism or into embracing a Western canon as the fixed standard by which other cultures should be judged. If anything, there is in his later works an increased emphasis on the inability of any given tradition to permanently embody the truth.[48] This humility with regard to the symbolizations of other cultures, along with the careful attention he gives to the structurally similar experiences expressed in these symbols, lends a refreshing balance to Voegelin's treatment of multiculturalism.

Some might object that in much of his work Voegelin does indeed accord a privileged status to Greek philosophy, especially Plato. There is no question that Voegelin believed that the differentiation of reason (as the *articulate and self-conscious* awareness of the structure of openness to reality) took place among the Greek philosophers. But Voegelin was equally careful in pointing out the need to go beyond Plato and Greek philosophy, and that while the differentiation of reason may have occurred within the particular historical setting of the Greek polis, it was necessary for philosophy to free itself from the "mortgage of the polis."[49] Voegelin admired the Platonic-Aristotelian achievement because these philosophers had developed a language, a "noetic theology," which because it so clearly articulated the structure and tension of existence was able to serve as a framework for recognizing and evaluating other accounts of the human experience of reality. The issue is not whether one accepts Plato's language; it is more important to recognize that historically, a particularly important articulation of the structure of reality and the human response to this reality occurred in the person of Plato. That articulation was an important advance for humanity as a whole, because in the Greek philosophers reason had become conscious of itself and its structure. To use an analogy: while we speak of Newtonian science, we do not thereby consider Newton's insights to be applicable or relevant only to the culture of seventeenth- and eighteenth-century England, even if his achievement is not explicable apart from the historical cultural context in which it arose. Just as Newton's work was a permanent advance in our understanding of the physical world, so, Voegelin would argue, the Greek achievement was a permanent gain in our *human* understanding of reason and its relationship to experience.

This last point can serve as a reminder that, while Voegelin is immensely respectful of diverse cultural and religious traditions, his stance is not uncritical. He would, I think, have little patience with those whose demand for cultural recognition is accompanied by a demand that a judgment of equal worth be rendered with regard to that culture's customs and creations. Nor would he subscribe to the idea that all judgments of worth in these matters are merely reflective of the present structure of power. In principle, all cultures may reveal something of the life of reason and ought to be respected as such. But Voegelin was also quite clear that the basic criterion for rational discourse and for being able to describe a society as "good" was the presence of a vibrant life of reason, understood as existential openness. Where such openness was lacking, Voegelin did not hesitate to render a sharply negative judgment on the culture or society in question. This accounts for some of his rather trenchant comments concerning the pluralistic character of Western democracies.[50]

A good part of Voegelin's hesitancy in wholeheartedly embracing pluralism as it existed in liberal democracies was due to his concern that below the surface of "that pluralism of opinion which supposedly is the guaranty of peaceful advances toward truth" there lie the unresolved religious and ideological wars of preceding centuries. This insight led Voegelin to the following conclusion:

[The] rich diversification of socially entrenched and violently vociferous opinion is what we call our pluralistic society. It has received its structure through wars, and these wars are still going on. The genteel picture of a search for truth in which humankind is engaged with the means of peaceful persuasion, in dignified communication and correction of opinions, is utterly at variance with the facts.[51]

A statement such as this ought to dispel any notion that Voegelin's approach to the problems confronting contemporary society was naive. In his view it was the superficial pluralism of the liberal polity that masked the profound tensions underlying the uneasy peace of the present situation. The increasing difficulty with which liberal societies attempt to placate groups of people of widely divergent horizons, and the polarization of citizens around certain seemingly intractable social problems, would be evidence to Voegelin of pluralism's inadequacy in providing a lasting basis for genuine peace. It is not pluralism per se that draws Voegelin's criticism, but a lack of seriousness concerning the very difficult challenges involved in seeking real understanding, and the avoidance of the persistent questions as to what it means to lead an authentically human life. For Voegelin, the "peaceful persuasion" on which pluralistic democracies pride themselves is only salutary when reason is recognized as having its origins in experiences of transcendence; hence the urgent need for the type of persuasion of which Voegelin has spoken so eloquently. In Voegelin's view, contemporary emphasis on pluralism was often little more than a masquerade for indifference to genuine conversation.

Voegelin's recognition of the wars underlying the tenuous stability of pluralistic societies can help us to understand the crucial, but rarely emphasized, role that the value of toleration plays in his thought. Because of the attention given to his philosophy of consciousness and history, it is easy to overlook the importance he placed on toleration. Voegelin stated clearly that animating his philosophical analysis was a profound aversion to murder and his horror at finding people shooting one another for no reason. Throughout his writings one finds words of praise for those whose awareness of the limits to any humanly discerned verity leads them to the generous conclusion that "every myth has its truth."[52] Deeply attentive to experience, Voegelin remained decidedly ambiguous with regard to the conceptual formulation of that experience in religion, metaphysics, and theology.[53] Whether or not one considers his criticism of doctrine and dogma to be valid, his reservations stem in large part from the fear that too often such formulations took on a life of their own, becoming "truths" used to justify the persecution of the unenlightened and the recalcitrant. Voegelin's struggle to devise a language with which to speak of experience was an attempt to find a level of discourse that could encompass the quite valid insights of religion, theology, and metaphysics, while at the same time transcending their tendencies toward dogmatism. Is it any wonder that he looked to Plato for inspiration, especially the Plato whose toleration of "unseemly symbolizations" Voegelin so admired?

It is important, however, to distinguish Voegelin's position concerning toleration from what could be described as a liberal stance. Historically, liberal toleration has sprung from a concern to end the destruction wrought by religious wars. But philosophically, the grounding of this toleration has coincided with an epistemological agnosticism in regard to knowledge of the transcendent. In general, liberalism is skeptical of any language that appeals to a transcendent "hypergood"[54] as a criterion by which to ground or throw light on the types of social goods that ought to be pursued. If truth in religion and metaphysics is unattainable, it makes little sense to argue over such matters, as they admit of no defense or justification beyond personal conviction.

Voegelin shares with liberalism a profound concern to limit the social effectiveness of intolerance, whether ideological or religious. There is even a sense in which Voegelin's refusal to endorse as definitive any particular tradition's account of truth makes his thought congenial to liberalism's epistemological grounding of toleration. However, there remain profound differences as well. Voegelin agrees that liberalism arose as a sensible reaction to a historical context marked by wars of religion. For Voegelin, though, the very fact that liberalism was a response to particular historical circumstances meant that the liberal demand for toleration was not to be enshrined as a universal truth, but as a sensible, historically contingent response to the situation at hand. Commenting on the selective toleration advocated by Locke, Voegelin wonders whether "behind the formulae of freedom and toleration hides the orthodoxy of a liberal, semi-secularized Protestant church-state." The uncritical embrace of a liberal model "that is so manifestly historically contingent must lead unavoidably to difficulties, and cause severe damage when it is dogmatized into a world view and its elements are raised to articles of faith." The example of National

Socialism's manipulation of the democratic process in order to gain power led Voegelin to conclude that liberal principles such as toleration must not be taken so absolutely that they allow the unscrupulous to destroy the very order these principles were meant to sustain.[55]

If, however, the liberal justification of toleration is found wanting, how is society to defend what is still a value of great importance? Not surprisingly, Voegelin locates the source of toleration in humanity's constitutive orientation to the transcendent ground. It is this, and not any historically conditioned prudential measures (however appropriate they may be at the time), that constitutes the basis for genuine toleration. Commenting on Bodin's *Colloquium Heptaplomeres*, Voegelin understands the essence of toleration to be found in a "balance between silence and the expression of a reality of knowledge" (where "reality of knowledge" is another formulation of Voegelin's understanding of reason as "existential transcending toward the ground"). Toleration, thus understood, is the fruit of an awareness of a reality "transcending incomprehensibly everything that we experience in participation," accompanied by the realization that any and every language we use is ultimately inadequate in describing this reality.[56] The true source of tolerance is to be found in *conversio*: "a being-carried in by love" by allowing oneself to be moved by the divine ground. A person thus converted understands that symbols and doctrines are attempts to articulate their experience; they are not final truths that would justify intolerance and violence.

No doubt there are some who would dismiss this account of the source of toleration as little more than pious romanticism. They might point to the history of religious intolerance to further support their position that religion is a source of the problem, not part of the solution. One need not dispute the fact that atrocities have been committed in the name of religion. At the same time, to argue from these unfortunate facts to the conclusion that all religion is inherently intolerant bespeaks a profound lack of knowledge concerning the experiences at the heart of religion, and how these experiences, far from being a source of division, exhibit a remarkable unity.[57] Voegelin knew well the damage done by the doctrinaire throughout history, and he was quite conscious that little or no practical good could come from so-called dialogues in which each party simply repeats its own orthodoxy. Nor was he especially sanguine about the possibility of reaching authentic dialogue. He remained convinced, though, that the unity necessary for genuine conversation had its basis in experiences of transcendence. Public order and public discourse would best be safeguarded by encouraging as many people as possible to recover these experiences in themselves.

Thus the surface similarities between Voegelin's antidogmatism and that of liberalism are found to mask crucial differences. From Voegelin's perspective, the problem with liberal toleration is that it is the product of an epistemological context in which the experience of reason as openness to the ground has been lost. Within this context, liberal thinkers observe the destruction induced by wars of religion and seek to blunt the influence of religion by relegating its claims to the status of private, epistemologically uncertain opinion. Understood in this fashion, religion comes to be contrasted with reason, a reason that has come to be conceived as an instrument of pragmatic effectiveness and technological control. Voegelin is well aware of the problems caused by the intolerance of dogmatism, but he traces these problems to the historical development of a situation in which the originating experiences have been lost. What is needed is a personal and communal recovery of those experiences that fosters conversion of mind and heart; not the obstruction of access to such experiences through a philosophical position that reduces questions concerning the ground to a matter of private opinion. From Voegelin's perspective, the problem with liberal society was that it tried to provide lasting foundations for rational discourse and public order by employing an impoverished language that had become disengaged from its experiential roots.

Views such as these sometimes led Voegelin into disagreements with those with whom he otherwise shared a common concern for the restoration of reason in contemporary society. An example of this is the exchange of correspondence between Voegelin and Hannah Arendt concerning his review of her book *The Origins of Totalitarianism*. Briefly summarized, Voegelin believed that Arendt failed to perceive the essential similarities between liberalism and totalitarianism, that is, their common indifference if not hostility toward the divine ground of reason. In response, Arendt, arguing on the basis of historical events, thought that Voegelin had treated the "phenomenal differences," which to her "as differences of factuality are all-important," as "minor outgrowths of some 'essential sameness'. . . ." She concluded her reply with the observation that *in fact*, liberals were obviously not the same as totalitarians. Voegelin remained unconvinced, and while he acknowledged that analysis had to begin with the social-political phenomena at hand, he also insisted that

the question of theoretically justifiable units in political science cannot be solved by accepting the units thrown up in the stream of history at their face-value. What a unit is will emerge when the principles furnished by philosophical anthropology are applied to historical materials. It then may happen that political movements, which on the scene of history are bitterly opposed to one another, will prove to be closely related on the level of essence.[58]

Voegelin believed that external differences on the level of history could mask a more profound identity, an identity that could be discovered only through an analysis of the underlying experiences of reality.

At a certain level, Arendt's criticisms of Voegelin have some merit. He does exhibit a tendency, at times, to treat the "phenomenal" level of social and political reality as secondary in relation to what occurs on the level of "essence" or experience. In addition, Voegelin's recognition of cross-cultural, transhistorical equivalences of experience leads him, on occasion, to point out similarities where none actually exist.[59] It may well be the case that, in pushing beyond phenomenal differences to the level of equivalences of experience, Voegelin did not always give phenomenal differences the attention they deserved. After all, liberals are *not* totalitarians.

However true this may be, one still wonders if Arendt has fully appreciated the strength of Voegelin's argument. Her point that a liberal is not a totalitarian is well taken, but it is not really an answer to Voegelin's criticism. He maintained that the "true dividing line in the contemporary crisis does not run between liberals and totalitarians, but between the religious and philosophical transcendentalists on the one side, and the liberal and totalitarian immanentist sectarians on the other side."[60] Voegelin's language is strong; but if he is correct in his understanding of humanity as constituted by its relationship to the divine ground, then does not liberalism's agnosticism on such questions of ultimate ends express a view of humanity as impoverished as that of totalitarianism, which, over time, will exact an equally terrible price? Voegelin felt that Arendt, in her analysis, stopped short of this level and avoided the deeper question concerning the ground of reason and public life.

For Voegelin, then, it was a matter of paramount importance whether one grounds toleration and the other values needed to sustain a public order on a liberal basis or in that profound existential openness to transcendence that is the "life of reason." From his perspective the question came to this: Is society better off when its members seek to order their lives in accordance with the structure of reality or when they exist in a state of alienation from that structure? What perplexed Voegelin about some modern responses to this question was that the question itself was considered unanswerable and irrelevant to matters of the public good. While a great admirer of the liberal tradition's ability to deal effectively with public affairs on a pragmatic level, he also saw clearly the limitations of the tradition with regard to sustaining the life of reason essential to a good society. In the short term, it may make little differerence whether one grounds the principle of toleration (as well as the other basic principles of liberal democracy) through an appeal to reason conceived pragmatically, or on the basis of experience (in Voegelin's sense of the word). But the present concern for the state of American society evident in current debates would seem to indicate a growing awareness that in the long term it makes a profound difference.

Voegelin's philosophy, then, is open to a multicultural perspective, deeply concerned with and supportive of the toleration necessary to sustain a pluralistic society, and, at the same time, unafraid of making normative judgments. Where Voegelin differs from philosophical liberalism is in his claim that the more one seriously analyzes and "gets behind" the symbols that articulate a society's experience of reality, the more one becomes capable of developing a language by which to judge the authenticity of personal and social order. In this regard he represents a nonliberal approach that is open to cultural diversity and sensitive to the varieties of religious experience, while at the same time not being afraid to raise and address questions of cultural, moral, and religious authenticity. The normativity of which Voegelin writes is not tied to an acceptance of any particular cultural worldview; it is discovered through careful attention to those experiences of participation in which humanity's constitutive orientation to the ground is made manifest. Access to these experiences may be gained through the literary, artistic, philosophical, and religious "classics" of every culture. The key to the restoration of genuine public discourse lies not in the imposition or acceptance of one particular community's cultural language, but in an openness to the classics of every culture, classics that speak of what is common to all.

A number of Voegelin's critics (including some who are quite sympathetic to his project) fail to appreciate this dimension of his thought and attribute to him an attempt to ground philosophy in religious faith, and specifically in Christian faith. For example, Stanley Rosen speaks of Voegelin's identification of the transcendent source of order with the "Christian God" and believes that Voegelin evaluates the Greek philosophers "in terms of their anticipation of, approach to, or withdrawal from this God." Voegelin's "extreme piety" is said to "trivialize philosophy" by judging the Greeks from the perspective of his "anti-rational, christianized, existentialism." As far as offering proof for the experiences of transcendence to which he accords so much importance, "Voegelin points implicitly to his faith, and explicitly to the faith of others, which he calls their historical experience." Nearly forty years later, Rosen was more nuanced in his treatment of Voegelin's work, but he still noted the Christian orientation of Voegelin's political thought. Rosen held up Leo Strauss as the "spokesman for Platonic-Aristotelian *science*" against Voegelin, the defender of the "metaphysics that descends from the Judeo-Christian tradition."[61] Writing from a similar (but more sympathetic) perspective, Thomas L. Pangle raises the following questions about Voegelin's philosophy:

What is the precise nature and foundation of the normative standpoint from which Voegelin issues evaluations and judgments—the standpoint from which, indeed, he takes the bearings for his whole existence? The superiority of the Christian conception or symbolization of the soul and its experiences, in general—but even more in the specific, historicized, way in which the Christian conception is understood by Voegelin—does not seem to be *demonstrated* by Voegelin. It does not seem to be arrived at by reasoning from premises that are necessary, that are compelling, for all of us, or for all thinking human beings in all times and places. If Voegelin's Christian conception is an undemonstrated or indemonstrable presupposition of faith, what, if anything, makes it persuasive to those who do not share this faith? What ranks it above, or gives it more validity than, other faiths or interpretations of faith, Christian and non-Christian—with their often diametrically opposed moral and political commands? . . . Surely Voegelin intends his Christian conception to be something more than a subjective presupposition of personal faith. But precisely how does Voegelin escape what Strauss refers to as "the desert of Kierkegaard's subjectivism?"[62]

Volumes could, and I hope will, be written on the relationship of Voegelin's thought to that of Leo Strauss and his followers. This, however, is not the place to enter into an extended discussion concerning the accuracy of Strauss's or Voegelin's interpretation of Greek philosophy or the relationship between reason and revelation in their work. Instead, I will limit my concern to the charge that Voegelin's philosophy is rooted in Christian faith. It is a serious charge; because if it is true that Voegelin's philosophical framework is inseparable from a confessional commitment, then it is hard to understand how his thought could serve as a basis for grounding public discourse in a pluralistic society that, at least in principle, accords no preference to any particular religious tradition.

In order to respond to this charge, certain distinctions need to be made. Voegelin did indeed believe that Christianity represented an important differentiation of consciousness. This, however, implies nothing about whether Voegelin was an adherent of Christianity.[63] In a letter to Alfred Schütz (who voiced objections similar to those of Rosen and Pangle), Voegelin was quite clear that "[e]ssentially my concern with Christianity has no religious grounds at all." Voegelin's concern was with philosophy, understood as the "interpretation of experiences of transcendence"; and as it was evident that such experiences had occurred outside the Christian orbit, it was quite possible to "philosophize without Christianity." He added one important qualification, though:

> There are degrees of differentiation in experiences. I would take it as a principle of philosophizing that the philosopher must include in his interpretation the maximally differentiated experiences and that, so long as he is operating

rationally, he therefore does not have a right to base his interpretation on the more compact types of experience while ignoring differentiation, no matter for what reason. . . . Now with Christianity a decisive differentiation has occurred. . . .

Thus, he states in the letter, "[w]hatever one may think of Christianity, it cannot be treated as negligible."[64] Voegelin's point is that Christianity had to be taken seriously as an event in the process of the differentiation of experience. This had nothing to do with sectarian religious commitment; it was simply a matter of being rational. In similar fashion, Voegelin also recognized important differentiations as taking place in ancient Israel and Greece; yet few would think to label him a Jewish or Greek philosopher. For Voegelin, the Christian insight into the tension of existence occupied an important but not a privileged place in human history; while constituting an important advance it was neither the final answer nor an absolute truth. It would be a serious mistake to interpret Voegelin's discussion of Christianity as pointing to any type of confessional adherence on his part or as indicating that one must profess a particular religious faith in order to be a true philosopher.

Might it not be the case that implicit in the criticisms of Voegelin by Pangle and Rosen there exists the Enlightenment prejudice that a decision for Jerusalem (or Rome, or for any positive religion for that matter) is inherently sectarian and particularistic? Pangle is puzzled, because while he is sure that Voegelin does not mean to ground philosophy in a "subjective presupposition of personal faith," he finds it difficult to avoid this conclusion in light of Voegelin's alleged Christian standpoint. Perhaps what is missing on Pangle's part is the previously mentioned insight that while a classic (or in this case, a religious tradition) may be particular in its origins, it may still be public in its effects.[65] Applying this insight to Voegelin's work, one could say that, in this case, the particularity of Christianity need not prevent us from appreciating how the experiences it recounts are of relevance to all human beings.

Pangle is quite right in his claim that the experiences to which Voegelin appeals are not *demonstrated*. They are not "arrived at by reasoning from premises that are necessary, that are compelling, for all of us, or for all thinking human beings in all times and places." But this objection leaves little room for a notion of rationality that is more than a matter of deducing conclusions from necessary principles. While not discounting or denigrating this notion of rationality, Voegelin would insist that "reason" needs to be understood more broadly so as to encompass those foundational experiences that help constitute our fundamental horizon in such a way that we become *capable* of being appealed to on the level of demonstration and argument. Voegelin realizes that a person suffering from an "eclipse of reality" will not be moved by demonstrations from necessary premises; what is required is a profound change in orientation before rational dialogue at this level is even possible. The type of change called for here is the result of allowing oneself to be moved by engagement and conversation with the "classics" and symbols through which these constitutive experiences are mediated.

One wonders, then, in light of our earlier discussion of Western tendencies to identify a particular understanding of reason as universal, whether it is Voegelin's notion of reason, rather than Pangle's, that could better serve as a common basis for "all thinking human beings in all times and places." Pangle implies that since Voegelin's position cannot be demonstrated from necessary premises, it therefore must be based on "faith," where faith is understood as personal and privately subjective. This seems to be Rosen's objection as well, in that he reads Voegelin's position as being dependent on his own faith as well as the faith of others "which he [Voegelin] calls their historical experience." Rosen rightly grasps Voegelin's appeal to experience, but both he and Pangle tend to view this appeal as individual, private, and not at all capable of grounding a genuine philosophical science. In this regard, these critics seem not to have appreciated what was noted earlier about the nature of Voegelin's method and its empirical character; that is, how Voegelin's appeal to experience is constantly referred back to and tested against the widest possible variety of "classic" expressions of experience. The normative standpoint from which he speaks emerges from a careful meditative exegesis of symbols understood within the context of as many other symbols as possible. One verifies one's own similar experiences with reference to this wider field of equivalences. For one who is attentive and open-minded there is nothing "subjective" about such a method at all. The question, then, is not whether Voegelin's "faith," or that to which he appeals in the historical experience of others, is subjective; rather it is whether one is willing to declare *all* such experiences to be private and subjective. But if one wishes to make this assertion in the face of myriad examples of equivalent experiences attested to throughout history, on what rational basis does one do so? This is not a matter of sharing Voegelin's (or anyone else's) faith; it is a matter of being open, in the sense of allowing oneself to be challenged and addressed by experiences amply witnessed to in human history.

Voegelin's harshest criticism is directed not at those who refuse to accept Christian doctrine, but at those who have closed themselves or allowed themselves to be closed to the experiences that find their expression in Christianity and any other tradition that acknowledges the possibility that people can come to know what is true by means other than argument. It is on this point that the real issue is joined, that is, whether or not one is willing to admit that the "classic" that we encounter may serve to mediate an experience in which a truth may be disclosed that eludes formulation in propositional terms. It is not a question of adopting any particular creed; rather, it is a matter of dealing seriously with the claims posed by the constitutive expressions of meaning drawn from many cultures, and being willing to at least contend with the "question of truth" implied in their abiding permanence. Liberalism's agnosticism on these sorts of questions drew Voegelin's ire not because of its indifference to the claims of Christianity, but because it refused to reflect deeply enough upon the primal sources of reason and community. Such a refusal would, he believed, eventually undermine the ground of public discourse upon which democracy depends. Voegelin understood his task as in some way to restore the basis of rational discussion through a return to its deepest origins.

In his later writings, Voegelin turned more and more toward a "meditative exegesis" of experience as his method in doing philosophy. Of course one might be tempted to regard this movement as a turning away from the explicitly public-political concerns of his earlier writings. I believe, however, that such a view is mistaken. Voegelin advocates neither social quietism nor a withdrawal from public life. His goal is therapeutic: to recapture reality, in the hope that such an enterprise will bear fruit in the creation of communities of discourse that may one day render the life of reason socially effective. Voegelin has appreciated that the key to the restoration of a vibrant public life lies in the transformation and conversion of human subjects, and that authentic subjectivity is a function of one's openness to the divine ground. Thus he has tried, in his writings, to reappropriate experiences of reality so that they might then be communicated to others; not as one passes on information, but by helping others to turn toward reality through the fostering of the innate sense of wonder, and by pointing toward those transcultural, transhistorical experiences of participation that provide the basis for what is "common" to all.

No doubt, some will question the practicality of Voegelin's contribution to the grounding of public discourse. But if to be practical has anything to do with attunement to reality, then Voegelin's critics have their answer. For Voegelin, the enterprise in which the philosopher engages is eminently practical—to foster the life of reason and to restore an awareness of reality within whatever context the philosopher finds himself or herself. Voegelin was well aware that his contribution to public life lay not in offering specific solutions to social and political problems, but in the recovery of those foundational experiences of reality in which authentic humanity is grounded. From the standpoint of pragmatic, instrumental reason, this approach may seem misguided and irrelevant. Taking a broader view, might not Voegelin's project contain the very key to practicality?

Notes

1. Eric Voegelin, *Autobiographical Reflections*, ed. Ellis Sandoz (Baton Rouge: Louisiana State University Press, 1989), 93.

2. Jean Bethke Elshtain, *Democracy on Trial* (New York: Basic Books, 1995), xii.

3. Charles Taylor, *Multiculturalism*, ed. Amy Gutmann (Princeton: Princeton University Press, 1994), 43.

4. David Tracy, *The Analogical Imagination* (New York: Crossroad, 1981), 9.

5. David Tracy, "Particular Classics, Public Religion, and the American Tradition," in *Religion and American Public Life*, ed. Robin W. Lovin (New York: Paulist Press, 1986), 115–16.

6. *Autobiographical Reflections*, 93.

7. Eric Voegelin, "Necessary Moral Bases for Communication in a Democracy," in *Problems of Communication in a Pluralistic Society* (Milwaukee: Marquette University Press, 1956), 53, 56, 58. Voegelin distinguished pragmatic communication from both the "substantive" communication aimed at the formation of character and the "intoxicant" communication of the mass media geared toward entertainment and diversion (54).

8. Eric Voegelin, *Conversations with Eric Voegelin*, ed. R. Eric O'Connor (Montreal: Thomas More Institute, 1980), 11. This understanding of reason includes: (1) "the consciousness of existing from a Ground," (2) "the creative Ground of existence which attracts man to itself," (3) "the sensorium whereby man understands himself to exist from a Ground," (4) "the constituent of man through his participation in (the reason of) the Ground; or the constituent force in man *qua* human through participation in the divine *Nous* which is his specific essence"; see *Faith and Political Philosophy: The Correspondence Between Leo Strauss and Eric Voegelin, 1934–1964*, trans. and ed. Peter Emberley and Barry Cooper (University Park: Pennsylvania State University Press, 1993), 308–9. See also Eric Voegelin, "Anxiety and Reason," in *The Collected Works of Eric Voegelin*, vol. 28, *What Is History? And Other Late Unpublished Writings*, ed. Thomas A. Hollweck and Paul Caringella (Baton Rouge: Louisiana State University Press, 1990), 88–89; Eric Voegelin, "On Readiness to Rational Discussion," in *Freedom and Serfdom*, ed. Albert Hunold (Dordrecht: D. Reidel, 1961), 269–84; and Eric Voegelin, "Industrial Society in Search of Reason," in *World Technology and Human Destiny*, ed. Raymond Aron (Detroit: University of Michigan Press, 1963), 31–46.

9. Eric Voegelin, "Reason: The Classic Experience," in *The Collected Works of Eric Voegelin*, vol. 12, *Published Essays, 1966–1985*, ed. Ellis Sandoz (Baton Rouge: Louisiana State University Press, 1990), 268–69, 271. In Voegelin's thought, "experience" is inseparable from the reality in which we participate and the consciousness by which we participate in reality; the experience of reality is located in neither subject nor object but in the immediacy embracing both. "Experience" thus includes a subject's sensory apprehension and knowledge of physical, existing things, but also his or her consciousness of participating in a nonphysical divine presence of ultimate origins; Voegelin prefers to say that expe-

rience of the ground is an experience of a "non-existent" reality. From his study of Plato and Aristotle, Voegelin came to appreciate that at the heart of all experience was a dynamic movement and tension toward the divine ground. Experience is essentially "metaleptic": an overlapping of divine appeal and human questing. Experience is thus an event occurring in the "In-Between." The term "In-Between," or *metaxy*, borrowed from Plato, occupies a prominent place in Voegelin's thought—human existence is always existence in the *metaxy*. See *Autobiographical Reflections*, 72–73; "Reason: The Classic Experience," 279; and "Immortality: Experience and Symbol," in *Published Essays, 1966–1985*, 52–54.

10. "On Readiness," 278.

11. *Conversations*, 23–24. See also his "Immortality," 67–70, for his response to the proposition, "The experience is an illusion." Voegelin argues that, technically, an experience as experience can never be an illusion—no matter what is going on, the person in question is having an "experience" of some sort. The problem, then, must consist in the fact that the one having the experience is mistaken about the "content" of the experience. Here there are two possibilities: either (1) the experienced object does not really exist, or (2) the object exists, but is different from what is experienced. In either case, "the judgment of illusion rests on control experiences of the potentially or actually existent object outside the experience" (67–68). This is problematic, though, for "a judgment of illusion can pertain only to experiences of existent objects, not to experiences of participation in nonexistent reality" (68). Voegelin's point would seem to be that the "control experiences" that would be necessary to arrive at the judgment, "The experience of the nonexistent (i.e., transcendent) ground is an illusion," presuppose a split between subject and object in which one could somehow examine the "content" of the experience. But this is already to have lost the experience, which as an experience of participating in the immediacy of divine presence ontologically precedes any articulation of subject and object.

12. See "Equivalences of Experience and Symbolization in History," in *Published Essays, 1966–1985*, 115–33.

13. "Equivalences," 122. The section immediately preceding this reads as follows: "The validity can and must be tested by placing the propositions in the historical field of experiences and their symbolizations. . . . The validating question will have to be: Do we have to ignore and eclipse a major part of the historical field in order to maintain the truth of the propositions . . . or are the propositions recognizably equivalent with the symbols created by our predecessors in the search of truth about human existence?"

14. Two such shifts were those that marked Voegelin's abandonment of his *History of Political Ideas* and, later, the revision of the plan for *Order and History* after the third volume. See Eric Voegelin, "Autobiographical Statement at Age Eighty-Two," in *The Beginning and the Beyond: Papers from the Gadamer and Voegelin Conferences*, ed. Fred Lawrence (Chico, Calif.: Scholar's Press, 1984), 116–19, and Eric Voegelin, *Order and History*, vol. 4, *The Ecumenic Age* (Baton Rouge: Louisiana State University Press, 1974), 1–58.

15. "Equivalences," 117, 115.

16. "There is no longer a common rational culture. The question is, what do

we do now? We cannot proceed like Thomas; we cannot wave the *Contra Paganos* in our hands and start a debate, because nobody believes in the classic formulations, including most of our Western university personnel in philosophy. So if there is no common basis of intellect, how *do* we talk? The only thing one can do now is to go back of the rational formulations of classic and medieval philosophy, abandon also (for the dialogic purpose) the Old and New Testaments because these are not sources of common belief, and go back of the formulated positions to the experiences which engender symbols" (*Conversations*, 39–40).

17. Eric Voegelin, "What Is Political Reality?," in *Anamnesis*, ed. and trans. Gerhart Niemeyer (Notre Dame: University of Notre Dame Press, 1978), 179; and "The German University and the Order of German Society: A Reconsideration of the Nazi Era," in *Published Essays, 1966–1985*, 7. See also *Faith and Political Philosophy*, 309, and "On Readiness," 278.

18. "Industrial Society," 34, 42. See also Eric Voegelin, *The New Science of Politics: An Introduction* (Chicago: University of Chicago Press, 1952), 27, 49; and Gregor Sebba, "Prelude and Variations on the Theme of Eric Voegelin," in *Eric Voegelin's Thought: A Critical Appraisal*, ed. Ellis Sandoz (Durham, N.C.: Duke University Press, 1982), 21.

19. "German University," 26.

20. "German University," 27; see 7, 18–28. Voegelin believes that it is wrong to speak of National Socialism as a national movement, "since in order for a political nation to exist, there must be a substantial public of sufficient social dominance, and it was just this which was missing in the German case" (27). What Hitler brought to power was instead "the masses of existential subjects with national-conservative mentalities . . ." (27).

21. "Industrial Society," 34–35.

22. "On Readiness," 283–84.

23. "On Debate and Existence," in *Published Essays, 1966–1985*, 51; *Autobiographical Reflections*, 96; "Industrial Society," 45.

24. *Autobiographical Reflections*, 93.

25. See Eric Voegelin, "The Nature of the Law," in *The Collected Works of Eric Voegelin*, vol. 27, *The Nature of the Law and Related Legal Writings*, ed. Robert Anthony Pascal, James Lee Babin, and John William Corrington (Baton Rouge: Louisiana State University Press, 1991), 53–55.

26. See "Necessary Moral Bases," 67.

27. Eric Voegelin, *Science, Politics, and Gnosticism* (Chicago: Henry Regnery, 1968), 19. Such persuasion, if it is to be genuinely effective, must be the fruit of meditation. Without meditation upon the formative "experiences" at the core of every social-political order, those who would restore rationality to public discourse will have nothing of substance to offer. It is for this reason that much of Voegelin's later work was taken up with the "meditative exegesis" of a series of wide-ranging, cross-cultural, transhistorical experiences. For Voegelin, this shift did not signify a movement away from public matters, but rather a deeper probing of their source.

28. "Necessary Moral Bases," 55, 67–68.

29. See "German University," 35.

30. See "German University," 18–35.

31. See *Autobiographical Reflections*, 95–96, and "Immortality," 57.

32. On the recovery of experiences of mysticism as a component in education, see "Autobiographical Statement," 105–6.

33. For example, Gadamer, Arendt, and Habermas. On these issues, see Richard Bernstein, "The Meaning of Public Life," in *Religion and American Public Life*, ed. Robin W. Lovin (New York: Paulist Press, 1986), 29–52. See also "Industrial Society," 42–43.

34. Taylor, *Multiculturalism*, 38–39, 43–44.

35. Voegelin also maintained that it was within the Anglo-American orbit that the classical-Christian tradition had best survived. In particular, the influence of Scottish commonsense philosophy had been a great help in preserving a vibrant tradition of practical rationality. See *The New Science of Politics*, 188–89, and *Conversations*, 65–66. However, while this commonsense tradition was beneficial in fostering the rationality necessary to engage in the activities of day to day life, it was not really up to the task of meeting ideologies at their level of philosophical depth and sophistication. To meet this challenge, the reappropriation of reason as openness to transcendent reality was indispensable. See "What Is Political Reality?," in *Anamnesis*, 212–13.

36. Eric Voegelin, "The Oxford Political Philosophers," *Philosophical Quarterly* 3 (April 1953): 100, 107.

37. Eric Voegelin, "Liberalism and Its History," *Review of Politics* 36 (1974): 506.

38. "The Oxford Political Philosophers," 103; "Necessary Moral Bases," 65–66; "Industrial Society," 41.

39. "The Oxford Political Philosophers," 103. In later works, of course, the terms "principle" and "philosophical anthropology" would be replaced by the language of "consciousness," "experience," and "equivalence." With this terminology Voegelin found a language that could sustain a public realm in a way that went beyond the particularism of any given tradition, even when a particular tradition (such as the Anglo-American liberal tradition) understood its constitutive principles as universally applicable.

40. Charles Taylor, "Understanding and Ethnocentricity" and "Rationality," in *Philosophy and the Human Sciences* (Cambridge: Cambridge University Press, 1985), 123–33, 144–51. See also Charles Taylor, "Comparison, History, Truth," in *Myth and Philosophy*, ed. Frank E. Reynolds and David Tracy (Albany: State University of New York Press, 1990), 37–56. Concerning the questions raised by incommensurable cultures, Taylor writes, "For incommensurable activities are rivals; their constitutive rules prescribe in contradiction to each other. Only where two activities are simply different is there no question of judging one to be an inferior version of the other. . . . That is what is tempting to the anti-imperialist liberal conscience, wary of ethnocentrism. . . . It takes the heat off; we no longer have to judge whose way of life is superior" ("Rationality," 145–46).

41. While Taylor speaks of the need for such a language, he does not seem to have carefully delineated what the "human constants" underlying it might be, in the way that Voegelin has done. I think that Taylor is sympathetic to those

philosophical traditions that relate reason to a transcendent source, but he seems
more hesitant than Voegelin in taking a definite stand based on the analysis of
symbol and experience in the Voegelinian sense.

42. Voegelin recognized that it is quite possible to be a master of such comparative symbols without bothering to raise questions about the very experiences to
which they testify. He wrote: "One of the reasons for this odd state of things will
become apparent from an incident, a few years ago, at a conference on comparative religion: One of the participants broke the great taboo and flatly put it to his
confreres that the subject matter they were treating was irrelevant by the standards
of opinion to which most of them seemed to adhere; sooner or later they would
have to make up their mind whether the science of comparative religion was an
occupational therapy for persons otherwise unemployable, or whether it was a
pursuit of the truth of existence which its subject matter substantively contained;
one could not forever explore 'religious phenomena,' and pretend to their importance, without unreservedly professing that man's search for the divine ground of
his existence, as well as the revelatory presence of God in the motivation of the
search, constituted his humanity; in brief, he confronted them with the question
of truth implied in their admirable achievements as historians. Not everybody
present was pleased by such tactlessness" ("On Classical Studies," *Published Essays, 1966–1985*, 263).

43. In some places it seems as if Voegelin raises questions as to the rationality
of non-Western traditions and therefore the possibility of engaging in rational
discussion with adherents of those traditions (*Conversations*, 39, 58–59, 64, 67,
70; "Industrial Society," 43–45). While in some sense this may be so, I would
understand Voegelin's position to be that although reason had differentiated
within Western (in particular, Greek) civilization, it was always present in other
more compact styles of symbolization such as myth. Reason was present (however
compactly) wherever there was reflection on human experience of openness
toward the ground. Hence, one might advance from myth to philosophy but not
from myth to reason ("Anxiety and Reason," 90–92). With regard, then, to the
possibility of rational discussion with cultures that remained bound by more
compact symbolizations, Voegelin's attitude would appear to be that while it
would certainly be preferable if all conversation partners employed the language
of differentiated reason, this was not likely to happen in the present context. This,
I believe, is why he increasingly devoted himself to the recovery of a common
ground for dialogue rooted in the experiences that constituted reason in both its
compact and differentiated forms.

44. Taylor argues that those who live in pretheoretical societies were just as
interested in dealing effectively with the concrete world in which they lived, and
that contemporary notions that view them as somehow interested only in the
"symbolic" dimension of existence project modern Western distinctions between
the symbolic and the practical onto cultures for whom such distinctions would
not have made sense. Taylor's point is that to the extent that scientific knowledge
"extends and supersedes our ordinary understanding of things, it is impossible to
see how it could fail to yield further and more far-reaching recipes for action"
("Rationality," 148). If this is true, then theoretical cultures pose a challenge to

nontheoretical ones, and the rationality of the theoretical culture may be judged superior, at least with regard to the study of the physical universe. Voegelin, likewise, though he clearly affirmed the rationality of societies that remained bound by the primary experience of the cosmos, also maintained that cultures in which reason had not differentiated could suffer from serious difficulties on the pragmatic level. Where myth predominated, belief in the divinity of natural phenomena might seriously impair human efforts to deal effectively with the environment. See *Conversations*, 70, 72–73, and "Industrial Society," 44–45.

45. For Tracy, a classic is "a phenomenon whose excess and permanence of meaning resists definitive interpretation." While particular in origin, in its effects the classic provides "disclosive and transformative possibilities for all persons." Responses to the classic may be wide ranging, from a "tentative sense of resonance" to the "shock of recognition"; but in every case, "some disclosure-transformation, and thereby some truth, is in fact present—and present as communicable, shareable, public." David Tracy, "Catholic Classics in American Liberal Culture," in *Catholicism and Liberalism*, ed. R. Bruce Douglass and David Hollenbach (Cambridge: Cambridge University Press, 1994), 206; "Particular Classics, Public Religion," 119–20.

46. Tracy, "Particular Classics, Public Religion," 123, 124.

47. "On Classical Studies," 262.

48. For example, see Eric Voegelin, "The Meditative Origin of the Philosophical Knowledge of Order," in *The Beginning and the Beyond*, 43–52; and "The Beginning and the Beyond: A Meditation on Truth," in *What Is History?*, 173–232. Voegelin's refusal to embrace the language of any particular tradition as definitive has led some commentators to point out the possibly radical implications of his thought. Louis Dupre cautions those who would simply label Voegelin as a conservative thinker, "[f]or Voegelin quite simply distrusts all political structures" and "[h]is conservative critique of society moves toward a social system conceived on a more radical basis than any of our present ones possess." Fred Dallmayr notes that "Voegelin's stance toward past formulations or traditional teachings might be called 'deconstructive'—although the term would hardly have found his favor." Dallmayr also believes that Voegelin's emphasis on transcendence "sometimes approximates his writing to contemporary counter-discourses stressing rupture, radical decentering, and alterity or heterology." See Louis Dupre, "A Conservative Anarchist: Eric Voegelin, 1901–1985," *CLIO* 14 (1985): 430–31, and Fred Dallmayr, "Voegelin's Search for Order," in *Margins of Political Discourse* (Albany: State University of New York Press, 1989), 84, 86.

49. On the "mortgage" of the polis, see Eric Voegelin, *Order and History*, vol. 2, *The World of the Polis* (Baton Rouge: Louisiana State University Press, 1957), 168–70, and *Order and History*, vol. 3, *Plato and Aristotle* (Baton Rouge: Louisiana State University Press, 1957), 90. For other comments on the need to go beyond the Greeks, see *The New Science of Politics*, 2–3; "The Oxford Political Philosophers," 109; "Industrial Society," 34–39; *Plato and Aristotle*, 225–27; *Anamnesis*, 34; and *The Ecumenic Age*, 249–50.

50. "The right to be ignorant of the reality and truth of common experience has become, in the twentieth century, the most remarkable and characteristic in-

stitution of Western societies. The institution is firmly established and recognized, has entered public consciousness, and has even been elevated to something like a principle of social order by the self-interpretation of Western societies as 'pluralistic societies' " ("The Eclipse of Reality," in *What Is History?*, 155. See also "Industrial Society," 46, and "Necessary Moral Bases," 58–59, 60–61, 67).

51. "Necessary Moral Bases," 59, 62. Some recent, influential books and articles have also called attention to the deep cultural clashes playing themselves out in the social-political arena. See, for example, James Davison Hunter, *Culture Wars* (New York: Basic Books, 1991), and Samuel P. Huntington, "The Clash of Civilizations," *Foreign Affairs* 72 (Summer 1993): 22–49.

52. Eric Voegelin, *Order and History*, vol. 1, *Israel and Revelation* (Baton Rouge: Louisiana State University Press, 1956), 11; see 9–11.

53. See "Immortality," 52–57, and "The Gospel and Culture," in *Published Essays, 1966–1985*, 172–79.

54. See Charles Taylor, *Sources of the Self: The Making of the Modern Identity* (Cambridge, Mass.: Harvard University Press, 1989), 63–73.

55. "The Oxford Political Philosophers," 106; "Liberalism," 516.

56. "What Is Political Reality?," in *Anamnesis*, 183, 197, 198.

57. See Friedrich Heiler, "The History of Religions as a Preparation for the Co-operation of Religions," in *The History of Religions*, ed. Mircea Eliade and Joseph M. Kitagawa (Chicago: University of Chicago Press, 1959), 132–60.

58. Eric Voegelin, "The Origins of Totalitarianism," *Review of Politics* 15 (1953): 80, 85.

59. See chapters 7 and 8 in John J. Ranieri, *Eric Voegelin and the Good Society* (Columbia: University of Missouri Press, 1995). On Voegelin's doubtful claims of equivalences, see Pheme Perkins's criticism of Voegelin's tendency to attribute the same characteristics to both modern and early Christian gnosticism; Pheme Perkins, "Gnosis and the Life of the Spirit: The Price of Pneumatic Order," in *Voegelin and the Theologian*, ed. John Kirby and William M. Thompson (New York: Edwin Mellen Press, 1983), 222–52.

60. "Origins of Totalitarianism," 75.

61. Stanley Rosen, "Order and History," *Review of Metaphysics* 12 (1958), 257, 260, 262, 267; Stanley Rosen, "Politics or Transcendence? Responding to Historicism," in *Faith and Political Philosophy*, 264.

62. Thomas L. Pangle, "Platonic Political Science in Strauss and Voegelin," in *Faith and Political Philosophy*, 325–26.

63. Voegelin's own religious faith has been the object of some debate. At the very least this would suggest that his Christian commitment or lack thereof was far less obvious than Rosen and Pangle seem to assume. For a recent discussion, see Gerhart Niemeyer, "Christian Faith, and Religion, in Eric Voegelin's Work," *Review of Politics* 57 (1995): 91–104.

64. Eric Voegelin, "On Christianity" (Letter to Alfred Schütz, January 1, 1953), in *The Philosophy of Order: Essays on History, Consciousness, and Politics*, ed. Peter J. Opitz and Gregor Sebba (Stuttgart: Klett-Cotta, 1981), 449–50.

65. See Tracy, "Particular Classics, Public Religion," 119.

3

The Epiphany of Universal Humanity

Geoffrey L. Price

Confrontation with Decline

Through his historical inquiries into the sources of contemporary civilizational disorder presented in his *History of Political Ideas*, Eric Voegelin was driven to extremely grave conclusions. The common spiritual order of Western humanity had become almost irreparably fragmented, at first through changes that remained hidden, and then in outward decline. When the shell of the Western Christian empire had eventually broken—in the schism of the Church and the Thirty Years War—the consequence had been to bring into existence a plurality of churches as well as a plurality of sovereign states. Moreover,

> With the elimination of Church and Empire as public powers, the new community-substances tended to substitute for the dissolving substance of Christian mankind. Within the sovereign national states, the intensity of national consciousness increased; the English revolution of the seventeenth century revealed for the first time the faith in the nation as the chosen people, as well as the universalist claim that the parochial civilization represents Civilization writ large.[1]

As the Christian representation of existence had increasingly lost its hold on the self-understanding of Western humanity, new forces had taken their place. Although nationalism had been a force for centuries, by the late seventeenth century it had unfolded as a spiritual force, claiming the authority that was previously the prerogative of imperial Christianity.

In the same centuries—as evidenced in Clarke's defense of the Newtonian absolutization of space and time against Leibniz—philosophy had lost its spiritual bearings. At the conclusion of his 1948 paper "The Origins of Scientism," Voegelin declared that in the resulting situation, the critical thinker who sensed the loss of spiritual substance was completely hemmed in.

> That in the end, through Einstein, the foundations of physics were revised in conformance with the position of Leibniz, is an important event in the history of science, but it has, for the moment at least, no visible social or political importance. The damage of scientism is done. As a philosophical friend aptly phrased it, the insane have succeeded in locking the sane in the asylum.[2]

How, under these circumstances, could the vision of philosophy be restored?

In 1956, eight years after his study of scientism had appeared, writing at the conclusion of his study of Egyptian order in the first volume of *Order and History*, Voegelin gave close attention to the anonymous "Dispute of a Man, Who Contemplates Suicide, With His Soul," a text from the period of social disorder and upheaval at the end of the Sixth Egyptian Dynasty.[3] In 1965, in his Ingersoll Lecture at Harvard University, "Immortality: Experience and Symbol," in which he confronted again the phenomena of contemporary spiritual and philosophical disorientation, Voegelin again chose the text of the "Dispute" to illustrate his argument.[4] In 1967 he addressed the poem for a third time, in his Candler Lectures at Emory College, "The Drama of Humanity."[5]

The significance that the poem held for Voegelin was indicated in 1967 in the "Immortality" lecture. He declared that the situation experienced by the Man of the poem was comparable to that posed by the state of contemporary civilizational decline.

> The Western philosopher in the twentieth century A.D. finds himself in substantially the same position as the Egyptian thinker in the twentieth century B.C.: both the philosopher and the author of the "Dispute" are disturbed by the disorder of the age, they both are in search of a reality no longer alive in the surrounding images, and they both want to recover the meaning of symbols from their misuse in everyday debate. The contemporary quarrel between doctrinaire beliefs and equally doctrinaire objections is the counterpart of the first, argumentative part of the "Dispute"; and today's philosopher has to wind his way in search of truth through the very type of imagery and argument that has been recognized as expressing a deficient mode of existence by his predecessor of four thousand years ago.[6]

There was now greater prospect of success in this endeavor. Modern scholarship had opened up our understanding of myth in the history of the Ancient Near East, of the Old and New Testaments, of comparative religion, Assyriology, Egyptology, and classical philology, and with this had come renewed knowledge of primary material that concerned the experiences of transcendence upon which order in personal and social existence depends. In this way, a back route had been opened up that had made it possible once again to recapture the experiences from which the symbolism of immortality stemmed. Thus when Voegelin turned again in 1965 to the "Dispute," it was to indicate how an ancient text could once again illuminate the field of philosophy.

In this chapter, I examine the way in which the choices evinced by the Man in this poem underlie Voegelin's understanding of the possibilities for the recovery of philosophy.

The Epiphany of Man

In the "Dispute," the Man, dejected by the misery of social decay, wants to end his life, for it has become senseless.

> To whom can I speak today?
> One's fellows are evil;
> The friends of today do not love.
> . . .
> To whom can I speak today?
> The sin that afflicts the land,
> It has no end.

He is locked in furious argument with his soul, which first urges him not to violate piety and morality by such an act. When the Man responds that suicide can be justified in the extreme circumstances that surround him, the soul changes its argument: now it urges him to forget despair, and to take the pleasure of the days as they come. The Man is revolted by such counsel, and presents his final case for ending his life: death will in fact be a salvation from the evil that surrounds him.

> Death faces me today
> Like the recovery of a sick man,
> Like going out into the open after a confinement.
> . . .
> Death faces me today
> Like the longing of a man to see his home again,
> After many years that he was held in captivity.

The death he contemplates would not merely be his own escape from an unbearable situation, but would open the way to the beyond in which the

gods dwell. There, the Man would be able to strengthen again the divine
rule, assisting the gods in their work of punishing evildoers, restoring
worship in the temples, and himself functioning as a sage adviser in their
presence.

> Why surely, he who is yonder
> Will be a living god,
> Punishing the sin of him who commits it.

> Why surely, he who is yonder
> Will stand in the barque of the sun,
> Causing the choicest therein to be given to the temples.

> Why surely, he who is yonder
> Will be a sage, not hindered
> From appealing to Re when he speaks.[7]

The Man, rejecting the advice of the Soul, grounds his judgment in his
desire to reestablish the mediation of right order from the gods to society.
The life of those living around him who have committed moral suicide is
but a disease; death offers healing from it. No effective resymbolization
of political order through the reestablishment of stable rule through a
Pharaoh is in sight. Therefore, knowing that he alone could be no substitute for such rule, the Man chose to join the living gods, whose substance
could pervade society more effectively than a person in his solitude.[8]

Latent within this decision was a step of great significance. The Egyptian poet lived in a time that had fallen into disorder, because the Phara-
onic dynasty was failing in its function. The traditional expectation was
that the situation could only be repaired by the epiphany of a new Pharaoh who would once again channel the divine-cosmic order of the gods
to society. That the poem should present the Man as considering suicide
as a way, under the current extremities, to join the gods, was a radical
break with those expectations.

> [T]he "Dispute" must be considered an extraordinary, if not a revolution-
> ary, event in the history of empire, inasmuch as it offers a substitute for the
> mediating function of the Pharaoh. . . . The living god Man will shoulder the
> burden of the living god Pharaoh who has failed. There can be no doubt, we
> are witnessing a spiritual outbreak, bursting the primary experience of the
> cosmos and moving in the direction of a personal experience of transcen-
> dence. The author is on the verge of the insight that Man's order, both per-
> sonal and social, will have to depend on Man's existence in immediacy under
> God.[9]

In principle, the Man is choosing to remove himself from life and to enter
the barque of the Sun-God, thus placing himself in the position of the

Pharaoh. By implication, the center of order is understood to be the Man and not the ruler. Nevertheless, the circumstances are such that the insight has no possibility of crystallizing into a new intellectual or spiritual movement; therefore the Egyptian poet can only contemplate suicide.

In the decision of the Egyptian poet, the "epiphany of man" was only latent. Although he faced a situation where the actual renewal of social order was inconceivable, in later situations, where the inherited power of imperial institutions was not so strong as to supplant individual activity entirely, it became possible for single thinkers to initiate and inspire a new movement.

> Now the single individual in the shape of a wise man, a sage like Confucius, or an enlightened person like the Buddha, or of a philosopher like Xenophanes or Parmenides, becomes a centre of the formation of communities, in which the humanity, the peculiar character of man in his relation to all other entities in the cosmos is understood and can form now a rival community to the existing political institutions that was still unthinkable in the Egyptian or in the Sumerian context. . . .[10]

In this way, it proved that the stance of the Man of the "Dispute" could become a real choice in life. Thus the "epiphany of man" became actual: for the time had come for the transfer of authority from rulers of cosmological societies to the prophet, sage, or philosopher as the ruler of a new communal order. "[T]he decisive point [sc. in the philosophical schools] is that man experiences himself here in his immediacy under God. What gives him his autonomy is that he is under God without mediation. We might say the new understanding of man, his new view of his own humanity, is that of his immediate relation to divinity."[11]

Philosophy in the Presence of Death

This argument is incomplete on its own, however. The philosopher may experience himself in his immediacy under God; but he will hardly go unchallenged. The voices represented by the Soul will be present in his fellows. How can the voice of the philosopher be established as authoritative?

In Voegelin's reading, this question is crucial to the resolution of the dialogue in the *Gorgias* of Plato.[12] The voice of Socrates speaks as if echoing the Man in a second "Dispute," conducted this time against the competing voices of Polus and Callicles, the representatives of power and competition in the crisis of Athenian democracy. The confrontation is fierce. Polus is infuriated at having to concede to Socrates the admisssion that a person who does evil does not do what is truly willed: and blusters back that anyone will engage in foul deeds given a chance to get away with it (*Gorgias* 468e).[13] Socrates presses Polus further, to the admission that doing injustice is worse than suffering injustice, and that doing injustice without suffering punishment is the worst of all (479d-e). Polus, intellectually beaten, retires to indifferentism and absurdity. Callicles is roused by this outcome, to vigorous protest. Why?

The whole of human life would be turned upside down, Callicles realizes, if the positions that Socrates maintains were to be followed. People should be doing the very opposite of what they are doing (481c). Callicles does not want to shift his judgment that the city is where his loyalties lie (481d-e). Only slowly, under intense inquiry, does he acknowledge the contradictions involved in his belief that strength and goodness coincide, that happiness is to be found in the satisfaction of desires, and that good and bad pleasures are indistinguishable.

The Transfer of Authority

How, though, is it possible for Socrates to hold authority in this debate? Callicles had earlier held that it was of supreme importance to protect oneself against suffering injustice. Socrates had held that the price of doing so is too high (*Gorgias* 511b-c), to which Callicles had barked back that unjust deeds will always be exacted, since those who stand up to evildoers around them will be robbed and killed. Why was Socrates not moved? Extending Voegelin's argument, we may suggest that just as the despairing Egyptian poet was ready for death as the only way to join the gods in diffusing order once again to society, so Socrates lives as one who is equally ready for death. Through the means of dialogue he is able to communicate without fear the grounds of the true order of the gods beyond death. He declares: "For no one who is not utterly irrational and cowardly is afraid of the mere act of dying; it is evil-doing that he fears. For to arrive in the other world with a soul surcharged with many wicked deeds is the worst of all evils. And if you like, I am ready to tell you a tale which will prove that this is so" (522d-e).

The question of authority thus comes to its climax.[14] The dialogue has shown Callicles, representing the Athenian democracy, to be existentially disoriented. Socrates, as we have suggested, speaks with a voice equivalent to that of the Man in the "Dispute." He can stand up to Callicles' threat that the personal consequences for himself will be unpleasant, because he has already chosen to live by the authority that can be sensed across the boundary with death.

> I think that I am one of very few Athenians, not to say the only one, engaged in the true political art, and that of the men of today I alone practice statesmanship. Since therefore when I speak on any occasion it is not with a view

to winning favor, but I aim at what is best, not what is most pleasant, and since I am unwilling to engage in those "dainty devices" that you recommend, I shall have nothing to say for myself when in court. (521d–e)

Socrates' choices do not leave him in the isolation of the Man: he is now the true Statesman for Athens. True authority is his. As Voegelin points out, in reference to Callicles, "The man who stands convicted as the accomplice of tyrannical murderers and as the corruptor of his country, does not represent spiritual order, and nobody is obliged to show respect to his word. The authority of public order lies with Socrates."[15]

The question remains: if Socrates can make the choice to live as in the presence of death, can that choice be made present to others? Can his lack of fear in the face of the sentence that the law courts could pass be communicated to others? If not, do not the choices of Socrates remain as singular as those of the Man of the "Dispute"? We may pursue these issues through the treatment that Voegelin offers of the question of true judgment in the *Gorgias* and the *Republic*.[16]

The law courts of Athens retain the ability to kill a philosopher physically, but Socrates has shown that their sentence has no moral authority. Wherein, then, lies true judgment? At the conclusion of the *Gorgias*, Socrates stands before Callicles, explaining to him the myth of the judgment of the dead, and warning him that it does indeed represent the truth of things (523a). It has changed its form in recent times: no longer are the souls judged while still alive, when their worldly rank can still be seen and mistaken estimates could arise. Now they are judged while they are dead, when all signs of their former status have fallen away. These changes in the mode of judgment are quite recent, and the Sons of Zeus who undertake the judgment are "dead." The judges then are those who—to anticipate the later Christian terminology—have traversed the "dark night." In life, they have already let their souls be penetrated by the experience of death, and are now bound by active desire to the life of the soul rather than being trapped in the deadliness of somatic passions. Having embraced death in life, in their souls the true meaning of life is laid bare; thus they have the clearness of view that enables them to judge the "living."

In this way, a basis for renewed spiritual authority appears: the "epiphany of man" is complete. The old myth, by which Gorgias, Polus, and Callicles live, is evidently dead. Yet the "dead" and the "living" are still bound together: Socrates, however reluctantly, is listened to. And so, in contrast to the situation of the Egyptian poet, the "living" do not need to choose suicide in order to assist the gods in the spiritual renewal of society. Socrates as interlocutor can speak to his contemporaries as if they too are capable of shaking off the obsessions caused by the "fear and frenzy of the body." As Voegelin states, "The judgment of the dead thus is enacted in part in the dialogue itself, concretely, in the attempt of Socrates to pierce through the 'body' of his interlocutors to their naked souls. He tries to make die, and thereby to make live, those who threaten him with death."[17]

But is the dialogue futile? It cannot be enforced. Socrates attempted to regenerate Athens, but he had to die in the attempt, and there was no victory for the justice that he taught. Does the existential situation of the dialogue created by Socrates then end with his death? No, as Voegelin declared; for the issues it raises do not end with life: they continue into the beyond. The dialogue is spoken by one who, beyond death, is the judge of the living and the force for order in those who will hear.

Thanatos and *Eros*: The Two Aspects of Dialogue

Just as the unknown poet of the "Dispute" speaks on the one hand to reject the claims of the Soul, and on the other hand longs to be present with the gods, so the dialogue of Socrates has two aspects. In the first aspect, we find that when the dialogue is conducted against the representatives of the hostile city, the authority of death as revealed through Socrates is presented as curative. In the *Phaedo*, life is compared to a submarine existence with only a glimmer of the world above. Yet the soul is immortal: and therefore, into the dialogue Socrates pours the force of death—not as a destroying but as a healing power, able to recollect the hearers to their true situation.

> [Socrates:] So it appears that when death comes to a man, the mortal part of him dies, but the immortal part retires at the approach of death and escapes unharmed and indestructible.
> [Cebes:] Certainly.
>
> [Socrates:] But there is a further point . . . which deserves your attention. If the soul is immortal, it demands our care not only for that part of time which we call life, but for all time. . . . [S]ince the soul is clearly immortal, it can have no escape or security from evil except by becoming as good and wise as it possibly can. (*Phaedo* 106e; 107c–d)

Similarly, as Voegelin shows, in the Myth of Er at the end of the *Republic* (618b), the souls in judgment are seen to choose their *daemon* according to their character in their earthly existence.[18] And the souls make unpredictable choices: some who have followed a path of virtue all their lives according to habit may in the afterworld be dazzled by the possibilities offered, and make foolish choices. Those who have suffered for the evil they have done in life are likely to have gained the wisdom to enable them to make better choices (*Rep.* 618c-619e). The freedom that the soul will be granted to make choices in the afterlife is of little value if it has not in life learned uprightness and wisdom. Hence it is vital that that wisdom should be learned.

> And there, dear Glaucon, it appears, is the supreme hazard for a man. And this is the chief reason why it should be our main concern that each of us, neglecting all other studies, should seek after and study this thing—if in any way he may be able to learn of and discover the man who will give him the ability and the knowledge to distinguish the life that is good from that which is bad. . . . (*Rep.* 619b–c)

There is one teacher who has traversed the path through the night of Hades to the light of Truth: that is Socrates. As Voegelin points out, Plato speaks of the ascent of the soul from the day that is night, to the true day, and uses the term almost technically as a definition of "true philosophy":[19]

> [Socrates:] Would you, then, have us proceed to consider how such men may be produced in a state and how they may be led upward to the light even as some are fabled to have ascended from Hades to the gods?
> [Glaucon:] Of course I would.
> [Socrates:] So this, it seems, would not be the whirling of the shell in the children's game, but a conversion and turning about of the soul from a day whose light is darkness to the veritable day—that ascension to reality of our parable which we will affirm to be true philosophy. (*Rep.* 521c)

Socrates then, among the living, is the one man who can tell in its entirety the tale of the world beyond and of the judgment that every soul will encounter. Precisely because the struggle of philosophy is a struggle against the darkness of false judgments, such a guide is needed. As Voegelin writes,

> Arete is free, but wisdom is weak. In its freedom the soul resists death. But the forces of existence, past and present, are strong as well as deceptive; persuasively they pull the soul to accept their death as life. In its freedom the soul is willing to follow the helper. . . . In suffering and resisting the soul discerns the directions from which the pulls come. The darkness engenders the light in which it can distinguish between life and death, between the helper and the enemy. And the growing light of wisdom illuminates the way for the soul to travel.[20]

Thus the encounter with Socrates in the dialogues is cathartic. By telling the myths of judgment in the *Gorgias* and the *Republic*, he brings into life the liberating force of death, and in the face of this, his hearers realize that it is their false judgments and choices that keep them imprisoned. "Death is the liberating force. It enables the soul to live free of the denseness of the lower atmosphere; and when the end has come, it brings the reconvalescence from the illness of life."[21]

In the second aspect, when the dialogue is conducted by Socrates among his friends, then the positive force of his soul, its *eros*, streams into the circle. As a guide, he loves, tends, and develops the best in his hearers, awakening in them the echoing desire for the Good. "The Idea of the Good, evoked in the communion of the dialogue, fills the souls of those who participate in the evocative act. And thus it becomes the sacramental bond between them and creates the nucleus of the new society."[22]

Thus Socrates explains to Phaedrus why the living speech of dialogue is superior to the written form; published teachings may get into inappropriate hands, and when ill-treated they cannot defend themselves. The dialectician, by contrast, can choose whom to debate with, and can work to evoke the very best in his hearers.

> The dialectician chooses a proper soul and plants and sows within it discourse accompanied by knowledge—discourse capable of helping itself as well as the man who planted it, which is not barren but produces a seed from which more discourse grows in the character of others. Such discourse makes the seed forever immortal and renders the man who has it as happy as any human being can be. *(Phaedrus 276e–277a)*[23]

The wise man knows that written discourses have at best a secondary function, and that only those lessons on justice and honor and goodness that are expounded in person are genuinely clear, complete, and serious. He understands that when such dialogues occur, their lessons are "truly written in the soul . . . and worth serious attention: Such discourses should be called his own legitimate children, first the discourse he may have discovered already within himself and then its sons and brothers who may have grown naturally in other souls insofar as these are worthy. . . ." *(Phaedrus 278a–b)*.

The Vision of Universal Humanity

Yet we may still ask: how is a stance equivalent to that of the Man of the "Dispute" and that of Socrates to be sustained today, in confronting the contemporary manifestations of unreason and disorder? There are profound differences with the situation confronted today. In particular, the issue of historical experience, which is absent from the Egyptian's field of experience, and which is only emergent in the outlook of Hellas, has for modern existence become an explicit theme. Consequently, the images against which the philosopher struggles today are those constructed by the doctrinaire philosophies of history stemming from Hegel, Comte, and Marx. Is it possible, in face of these contemporary equivalents of the voice of the Soul in the "Dispute," to discover and symbolize anew the decisions of the anonymous Man and of Socrates, that the apparently living are dead, and that true life is grounded in a realm that exists beyond the boundary with death? In order to approach that question, we must first consider the sources of apocalyptic consciousness, and then turn to the Pauline vision of history.

Two Visions of History

The achievements of philosophy in Greece, as those of prophecy in Israel, did not save either society from succumbing to the expansion of empires. Though the Hellenes had held the Persians at bay, they could not sustain their independence before the Macedonians and the Romans. Israel and Judah fell to the Assyrians and Babylonians; on return from exile, the building of a temple was permitted by the Persians and then by the Macedonians, successive masters of their land, but it was finally destroyed by the Romans. "The empires closed in again on the clearing they had left in history for Israel and Hellas to flower. The attempts at ordering society by the truth of existence, be it the revealed word of God or the philosopher's love of wisdom, appeared to have come to their end."[24]

Moreover, the empires of Persia, Macedonia, and Rome were all in competition; each, seeking to establish its own symbolism of world domination, pursued its aims through war and conquest. The populations that endured these endeavors experienced the succession of imperial powers as senseless misery. Pragmatic history, then, seemed to bear no relation to the visions of the Hellenic philosophers, the prophets of Israel, or indeed the other spiritual outbursts that had occurred in Persia through Zoroaster and in India through Gautama Buddha.

> Measured by the criterion of meaningful order in society, the performance was a disappointment; for the succession of empires in pragmatic history all too obviously did not realize the truth of existence revealed by the theophanic events. If "history" consisted of nothing but a sequence of imperial dominations, it was not the field in which the true order of personal existence could expand into the order of society.[25]

Two reactions to this situation are distinguished in Voegelin's study *The Ecumenic Age*. The first leads to the consciousness symbolized in apocalyptic. In Judaism under the Seleucids in the second century B.C., this reaction reached its height, when—finding the succession of empires senseless—the Daniel Apocalypse concluded that to restore meaning a divine intervention was necessary that would put an end to the grotesque disorder by a change in the whole structure of reality, thus ushering in a world-encompassing kingdom of God.[26]

> He [sc. the fourth beast] shall speak words against the Most High, shall wear out the holy ones of the Most High, and shall attempt to change the sacred seasons and the law; and they shall be given into his power for a time, two times, and half a time. Then the court shall sit in judgement and his dominion shall be taken away, to be consumed and totally destroyed. The kingship and dominion and the greatness of the kingdoms under the whole heaven shall be given to the people of the holy ones of the Most High; their kingdom shall be an everlasting kingdom and all dominions shall serve and obey them. (Daniel 7:25–27)[27]

The second reaction is symbolized in the writings of Paul the apostle. In Romans 8, it is as if the strain of existence that to the Man of the Egyptian "Dispute" was transmitted through the breakdown of political order has been still more acutely heightened. Now it is humanity as a whole that has turned away from God. In consequence, not the life of one person alone, as in the "Dispute," but the whole of creation has been placed under a state of futility and senselessness. Groaning in expectation, it awaits the moment when it, and those within it, will be set free. Together with creation, our bodies will eventually be set free from bondage to the fate of perishing, and enter into the freedom and glory of the children of God.[28] That which is expected is nevertheless not seen, but rests on hope, and must be awaited with patience. What sustains this expectation against that radical disappointment that lay at the source of apocalyptic? Voegelin's study recalls that in Romans 5:1–6, the ladder of the steps that sustain hope are expounded in more detail. The first step is joyful acceptance of affliction within time; the next is perseverance; hope is then possible, and it is sustained through the diffusion of divine grace into the hearts of those who wait.

The first steps of this ladder recall the willingness of Socrates to accept suffering rather than commit an injustice. That, as Voegelin writes, is to be expected, "since both the saint and the philosophers articulate the order constituted by man's response to a theophany."[29] Moreover, Plato and Paul are in agreement that existence in time is not meaningless: that it is the realm where humanity responds to the divine call, and where the divine presence evokes the response of human beings. However, the culminating vision of the Pauline ladder has decisively shifted from that of Socrates. It is grounded in Paul's own experience of Christ in the Damascus vision.

Paul's own conviction that the Christ of the vision was the Son of God (Acts 9:20) could be extended to all:

"For all who are moved by the spirit of God, are sons of God" (Rom. 8:14). "If the spirit (*pneuma*) of him who raised Jesus from the dead dwells in you, then the God who raised Jesus Christ from the dead will also give new life to mortal bodies by means of the spirit indwelling in you" (8:11). Faith in Christ means responsive participation in the same divine *pneuma* that was active in the Jesus who appeared in the vision as the Resurrected. "Justified through faith, we are at peace with God through our Lord Jesus Christ" (Rom. 5:1).[30]

We must note how the accent here has decisively shifted: from that noetic (rational) order, grounded in the divine, which the philosopher can encounter in the world, to the divinely pneumatic (spiritual) salvation from the disorder of the world. The philosopher, following Socrates, is the person who is formed by the noetic virtues of good judgment reached through truthful questioning, and by the existential love that grounds living in faithfulness to the true and the beautiful. By contrast, "The Pauline *pneumatikos* is formed by the divine *pneuma*; as a result, he can 'judge all things' ([Rom.] 2:16) and articulate his knowledge 'in words taught by the spirit' (2:13)."[31] The direction in which the vision looks is not, as in the understanding of noetic order, the order of rational existence in the cosmos. Rather, it looks from the point in consciousness at which the divine spirit breaks in, toward transfigured reality.

This vision, Voegelin argues, takes a decisive step beyond the philosopher's experience, lived paradigmatically by Socrates, of *athanatizein:* "dying within life." In the Platonic myth, the divine movement within reality remains limited: the "true story" of God and man in the *Timaeus* did not step beyond the figure of a Demiurge whose efforts were limited by necessity. In Paul's myth, the destiny of human beings was extrapolated beyond the limits of inescapable involvement in time and the unlimited and became "the story of the fall from and return to the imperishable state of creation intended by divine creativity."[32] Thus the Pauline vision moves beyond the horizon of Socrates, where life is lived as in the presence of divine judgment, attuned nevertheless to the order of the cosmos. For Paul, the range of forces ranked against persons is immeasurably enlarged: he confronts not simply the forces of civilizational decline, but rather the disorder of the entire cosmos which, as symbolized in the Adamic myth of Genesis 3, is the consequence of human concupiscence. In face of these forces, Paul realizes that all human beings, by responding in the openness of faith to the risen Christ, can nevertheless become sons of God, free of the constraints of that necessity that rules the cosmos. No longer is the philosopher's life-as-dying the limit of the recovery of order. Therefore, Voegelin writes,

Compared with the more compact types, the Pauline myth is distinguished by its superior degree of differentiation. In the first place, his vision carried

Paul irresistibly beyond the structure of creation to its source in the freedom and love of divine creativity. . . . Paul, furthermore, differentiated fully the experience of the directional movement by articulating its goal, its *teleion*, as the state of *aphtharsia* [unperishing] beyond man's involvement in the Anaximandrian mystery of Apeiron and Time.[33]

Thus, he concludes, the Pauline vision is not in conflict with the Socratic experience of dying-within-life. Rather, in it a still more penetrating vision has unfolded:

The movement in reality, that has become luminous to itself in noetic consciousness, has indeed unfolded its full meaning in the Pauline vision and its exegesis through the myth. The symbolism of the man who can achieve freedom from cosmic Ananke, who can enter into the freedom of God, redeemed by the loving grace of the God who is himself free of the cosmos, consistently differentiates the truth of existence that has become visible in the philosophers' experience of *athanatizein*.[34]

The Second "Epiphany of Man": Abraham

There is yet a still deeper force against which this vision had to contend. Paul's experience of existential anxiety, unlike that of the Man of the Egyptian "Dispute" for whom the path to the gods was in principle unhindered, was heightened by his discovery that the path to the divine presence was blocked by his own inner discordance. The divine law demanded perfect obedience, but Paul found within himself an opposing law, a law to which even his own reason gave approval, which kept him captive in a way of life that rebelled against the divine command (Rom. 7:22–23). The upward search of his soul, he candidly recognized, was paralyzed: "I do not even recognize my action as my own. For I do not do the good I want, but the evil I hate" (7:19).

Conscious of the all-pervasive sense of human failure and sin, Paul had in his extremity recollected the figure of Abraham. Existing before the law had become oppressive, Abraham had lived his whole life in faith and trust to the God who called him to follow. For that, he had been counted righteous (Rom. 4:3). Paul recognized that for those who came after, the deadly sense of being permanently trapped through transgression of the law could be overcome when people in faith opened their existences to the divine grace and love. The promise to Abraham had been that he would be the father of many nations because of his faith (Gen. 15:5; 22:16–18); this promise Paul had interpreted as applying not to his bodily descendants, but to all who shared in his faith. Thus the universal disorder of human willing (which the Socratic dialogues, at the culmination of the first "epiphany of man," had already portrayed through figures such as those of Callicles and Protagoras as a living death) could be healed. The problem of despair in the face of disorder was thus resolved in principle for all human beings. The God in whom Abraham believed was the God who brings the dead to life again. "'For he is the father of us all' who live 'in the presence of the God in whom he believed, who brings the dead to life again, and who calls into being what is not, as he called what is' ([Rom.] 4:9–17)."[35]

At the culmination of the first "epiphany of man," the *eros* of Socrates streamed into the circle of his hearers, as he guided and encouraged them. At the culmination of this second epiphany, which we may call the "epiphany of universal humanity," the divine grace streams through Abraham, the forerunner, into the lives of all people: "Abraham is the prototype of man's existence in truth. His universal humanity through faith in the universal God that made him the father of many nations was continued by Israel's prophets to the nations, and is now consummated by Paul as the apostle to the nations (4:23–25)."[36] In his vision, Paul had grasped a human existence whose moral impotence had been transformed by the divine grace: "The Pauline apostolate, finally, is the consummation of the historical promise that goes back to Abraham, because through the visions of the Resurrected, God has revealed Jesus as his Son who could do what 'the law, weakened by the flesh, could not do': Entering the form of sinful flesh, he could break the power of the flesh by the power of the divine spirit (8:3)."[37]

Universal Humanity

The apocalyptic consciousness had been generated at the fringes of disintegrating empires. The unpredictable succession of political and military upheavals had succeeded in generating the conviction that history was a field of disorder beyond repair by human action, and that only radical divine intervention could produce a newly transformed realm beyond history. In the Pauline vision, the apocalyptic consciousness is turned aside, just as decisively as the voice of the Soul is disregarded in the Egyptian "Dispute" and the falsity of Polus and Callicles was highlighted in the *Gorgias*. As Voegelin's study argues, Paul's understanding of faith implies that within the limits and strains of historical existence, it is open to every person to respond in trust to the moving presence of divine reality in his or her soul. Paul's vision led to the discovery that there is more to existence in history than the disorder experienced in the sequence of imperial orders would suggest. Through it, the gravest of the rifts in consciousness—that suggested by apocalyptic—was thus overcome. "The emergence of the truth is the historical event that constitutes meaning *in* history; the transfiguration is in process in *untransfigured* history. Through the Pauline vision, man's search for order in the time of history becomes luminous as the transfiguring incarnation of divine reality, of the *theotes* of Colossians 2:9, in the reality of this world."[38]

The overturning of apocalyptic consciousness was, in Voegelin's reading, the central achievement of Paul's vision. The apostle himself had not always been immune to the apocalyptic consciousness; the times when he had wavered were those when he had indulged in the expectation of a second appearance of Christ, which would break into the time of the living and bring historical existence to an end. However, these waverings "do not invalidate the insight he gained through his vision of the Resurrected: Meaning in history is constituted through man's response to the immortalizing movement of the divine pneuma in his soul."[39] Undoubtedly—as we have seen in Plato's treatment of the vision of judgment in the *Gorgias* and the *Republic*—within the limits of noetic consciousness, that insight had already been achieved by Plato and Aristotle. However, although Plato and Aristotle had like Paul been the subject of revelatory visions, those visions had been, as Voegelin emphasizes, of a fundamentally intracosmic character. The Platonic "Third God" never became the creator of the world who reveals himself in history; the philosophic analysis of the divine ground as the source of order in reality had never extended to the pneumatic depths of creation and salvation. In Paul's vision, those achievements of philosophy were not negated, but enlarged. Historical existence came into view as the field in which human consciousness became differentiated in response to theophanic experiences, a field with its own inherent movement toward fulfillment. Not the life of the philosopher alone, founded in the life of *athanatizein*, but the whole of human history, is involved in the divine lasting-out-of-time. Mankind thus is found to have a universal basis. All people exist in the flux of the divine presence, and that presence is the constitutive basis of the universality of mankind.[40]

In his Candler Lectures, Voegelin had noted that one of the characteristics of the modern period is that although people—at least in the West—are generally in agreement that we live in one world, there is no agreement on the oneness, the universality, of either human beings or of God. A humankind that is not universal can fall victim to partial ideas of humanity that lay claim to universality; so a notion gains hold that the "true person" is the proletarian, or the adherent of a communist or a fascist ideology, and the further idea develops that those who do not adhere to or agree with the chosen definition must be killed off. Likewise, a divinity that is not universal can be appropriated to one or other parts of the world content: a nation, or a particular race, for example. None of the three notions of universality—of world, of humanity, of God—can stand on its own: all three must be acknowledged in an adequate account of reality.[41]

Nevertheless, each of the three notions functions not as referring to a reality that is tangible in time and space, but as an index of the ultimate direction of reality. As his subsequent study in *The Ecumenic Age* emphasizes, "Universal mankind is not a society existing in the world, but a symbol which indicates man's consciousness of participating, in his earthly existence, in the mystery of a reality that moves toward its transfiguration. Universal mankind is an eschatological index."[42]

The insight compressed in these words is no mean achievement. On the one hand, as with Socrates' battle against the false words of Polus and Callicles, it strikes at the ideas that in the modern historical consciousness generate civilizational decline. It strikes at the notion that, since there is no universal humanity, then the history of human beings has no inherent continuity or contiguity: and therefore that there is no rational impediment to treating people definitively on grounds of their measurable characteristics assessed in biological, physiological, psychological, or sociological terms. It strikes at the idea that because there is no universal agreement on the nature of divinity, then there is no rational impediment to interhuman competition designed to assert the superiority of a single religion over its rivals.[43]

On the other hand, as when Socrates is in dialogue with his friends, Voegelin is himself seeking to move forward an insight that is still not yet fully within our grasp. Least of all should we confuse his inquiries with statements arising within dogmatic Christian theology. As we have noted, the central theme of his Candler Lectures was that the three ideas form a single unit: universal humanity, universal divinity, and universal world. Yet the idea of a universal divinity had in Christianity reached only an "approximately" good expression:

> . . . only approximately, because even Christianity is still burdened with the idea that universal divinity is, so you might say, a privilege of Christians, and everybody born before Christ is more or less relegated to limbo if not to Hell because he was not yet under universal divinity. So the extension of universals to the rest of mankind before Christ, has been consciously formulated as a problem for the first time, I think, with Thomas in the Middle Ages, and that was not very effective. A real philosophy of history based on this problem of this universal divinity, as I'm trying it here for example, has never been done as far as I know. It's an idea very slow in developing. So we have a pre-history of two thousand years before Christ and an after-history of two thousand years after Christ and it still is not, you might say, generally accepted, one still makes exceptions to that universal divinity as the one divine ground of all being.[44]

Writing to Gregor Sebba just after delivering the Candler Lectures, Voegelin said:

The most important part of the Candler Lectures I consider to be the Theory of the Universals. That seems to me the decisive advance over the classic and mediaeval philosophy of universals, as well as over the "clear" or "innate" ideas that still plague Descartes. The Universals of consciousness do not abstract essences from world-immanent things, but indicate the structure of reality (concretely) in the perspective of a differentiated consciousness. I am working on that problem now.[45]

In *The Ecumenic Age*, published seven years later, we have the results of that work. The present essay can only serve as an introduction to the achievement it represents. The task ahead is to appropriate Voegelin's achievements in this field of universals, and thus to carry into wider understanding and vision the "epiphany of universal humanity."

Notes

1. "History of Political Ideas" (unpublished typescript), pt. 8, ch. 1, p. 5.
2. Eric Voegelin, "The Origins of Scientism," *Social Research* 15 (1948): 462–94, at 494.
3. Eric Voegelin, *Order and History*, vol. 1, *Israel and Revelation* (Baton Rouge: Louisiana State University Press, 1956), 98–101.
4. Eric Voegelin, "Immortality: Experience and Symbol," in *The Collected Works of Eric Voegelin*, vol. 12, *Published Essays, 1966–1985*, ed. Ellis Sandoz (Baton Rouge: Louisiana State University Press, 1990), 52–94.
5. Eric Voegelin, "The Drama of Humanity" (unpublished typescript, transcription by Edmund Carroll; Eric Voegelin Papers, Hoover Institution Archives, Stanford University, Box 74, File 1), 23.
6. "Immortality," 64–65.
7. "Dispute of a Man, Who Contemplates Suicide, With His Soul," trans. J. A. Wilson, in *Ancient Near Eastern Texts Relating to the Old Testament,* ed. J. B. Pritchard (Princeton: Princeton University Press, 1950), 405–7.
8. *Israel and Revelation*, 100.
9. "Immortality," 63–64.
10. "The Drama of Humanity," 23.
11. "The Drama of Humanity," 23–24.
12. Eric Voegelin, *Order and History*, vol. 2, *The World of the Polis* (Baton Rouge: Louisiana State University Press, 1957), 24–45; see 24.
13. Translations of *Gorgias, Republic,* and *Phaedo* are from *The Collected Dialogues of Plato*, ed. Edith Hamilton and Huntington Cairns (Princeton: Princeton University Press, 1961).
14. Eric Voegelin, *Order and History*, vol. 3, *Plato and Aristotle* (Baton Rouge: Louisiana State University Press, 1957), 39.
15. *Plato and Aristotle*, 38.
16. *Plato and Aristotle*, 39–45.
17. *Plato and Aristotle*, 44.
18. *Plato and Aristotle*, 54–62.

19. *Plato and Aristotle*, 59.

20. *Plato and Aristotle*, 62.

21. *Plato and Aristotle*, 12.

22. *Plato and Aristotle*, 13.

23. Translations of *Phaedrus* are from *Plato: Complete Works*, ed. John M. Cooper (Indianapolis: Hackett Publishing Company, 1997).

24. Eric Voegelin, *Order and History*, vol. 4, *The Ecumenic Age* (Baton Rouge: Louisiana State University Press, 1974), 115.

25. *The Ecumenic Age*, 301.

26. *The Ecumenic Age*, 26, 71.

27. Translation of Daniel from *Holy Bible: New Revised Standard Version* (London: Collins Publishers, 1989). Copyright 1989, Division of Christian Education of the National Council of the Churches of Christ in the United States of America.

28. Rom. 8:19–21.

29. *The Ecumenic Age*, 241.

30. *The Ecumenic Age*, 242. Translations from the New Testament within quotations in the text are those of Voegelin, from *Novum Testamentum Graece et Latine*, ed. E. Nestlé and D. K. Aland (London: 1969).

31. *The Ecumenic Age*, 246.

32. *The Ecumenic Age*, 250.

33. *The Ecumenic Age*, 250.

34. *The Ecumenic Age*, 251.

35. *The Ecumenic Age*, 257.

36. *The Ecumenic Age*, 257.

37. *The Ecumenic Age*, 257–58 [punctuation slightly amended].

38. *The Ecumenic Age*, 302 [emphasis added].

39. *The Ecumenic Age*, 303.

40. *The Ecumenic Age*, 305.

41. "The Drama of Humanity," 29.

42. *The Ecumenic Age*, 305.

43. See "The Drama of Humanity," 42–56 ("The Revolt of Man").

44. "The Drama of Humanity," 30.

45. Voegelin to Gregor Sebba, April 26, 1967 (Eric Voegelin Papers, Hoover Institution Archives, Stanford University, Box 35, File 5). I owe this reference to a note by Dr. Brendan Purcell.

Part II

The Priority of Meditation

4

The Person as *Imago Dei*: Augustine and Max Scheler in Eric Voegelin's *Herrschaftslehre* and *Political Religions*

William Petropulos

Eric Voegelin and Max Scheler

As far as we know, Eric Voegelin and Max Scheler never met, nor is there evidence that an exchange of letters took place. Voegelin's study of Scheler occurred primarily in the early nineteen-thirties, several years after Scheler's death in 1928 at the age of fifty-four. References to Scheler by Voegelin are few. In the correspondence with Alfred Schütz, he is occasionally mentioned, and in Voegelin's later writings there are a few isolated references. Still, the sparse references to Scheler in Voegelin's works are to issues vital to Voegelin's understanding of human existence.[1]

In the nineteen-thirties Voegelin was concerned with two phases of Max Scheler's philosophy. In *Rasse und Staat* (1933), he focuses on the (at that time in Germany) much discussed theme of "philosophical anthropology." Arguing against the contemporary theories of race, Voegelin points out that they are based on primitive scientistic prejudices that render them incapable of dealing with the spiritual dimension of human existence. In this context he turns to philosophical anthropology as a prophylactic against scientistic primitivism. The principal question concerning the nature of the human being, he asserts, leads beyond the scope of an approach rooted in natural science with its naive assumptions concerning being.

Although Voegelin does not comment on the validity of the various philosophical anthropologies that he briefly touches upon, he expresses his preference for those forms that treat of basic spiritual experiences. He

quotes Scheler on the "person" as the spiritual source of the unity of the
human being, but he does not enter into a discussion of how this center
is organized. Instead he remarks: "Here is not the place to develop a philosophy of spirit" (*Geist*).[2] And indeed one must conclude that Voegelin's
mention of Scheler in *Rasse und Staat* does not constitute an examination
of the latter's philosophical anthropology, for the question of the truth
of Scheler's position is not raised.

In *Rasse und Staat*, Voegelin explicitly refers to only one of Scheler's
works, the small, programmatic work, concluded shortly before his death,
Man's Place in the Cosmos (1928).[3] On the other hand, the unfinished
Herrschaftslehre (titled "Theory of Domination") on which Voegelin
worked between 1930 and 1932 is concerned with issues found in Max
Scheler's "theistic phase."[4] In these writings of Scheler—the important
works are *Der Formalismus in der Ethik und die materiale Wertethik*
(1913–1916), *Vom Umsturz der Werte* (1915), *Vom Ewigen im Menschen*
(1921), and *Vom Wesen der Sympathie* (2d ed. 1923, expanded)—the philosopher explicated the ground of being as a personal God, and humankind as *imago Dei*.[5]

The study of Scheler in the *Herrschaftslehre* takes place in the context
of a philosophical self-reflection on "meditation as the basic form of philosophizing." This primary mode of philosophizing remained of the
greatest importance to Voegelin. On the other hand, philosophical anthropology became less important to him. In this matter he expressed
his judgment conclusively in 1957: "At the border of transcendence the
language of philosophical anthropology must become the language of religious symbolization."[6] A description of humankind expressed in concepts, he concluded, can lead to the false expectation that mere discursive
reason is adequate to describing what a human being "is." The diminished
importance of philosophical anthropology in Voegelin's later view is consistent with the insights communicated in Scheler's philosophy of religion. Scheler held that the human being is at the center an *ens amans* and
that the noetic acts that are subsumed under this term, foremost the *amor
Dei*, cannot be reified into concepts. A spiritual act is only understandable
by one who, in his or her own thought, reenacts the spiritual movement
of that act, thereby performing the act personally. The conditions for
such an understanding are not merely qualities of intellect, but of the
entire person. Thus, according to Scheler, Plato's description of the *ordo
amoris* necessary for noetic understanding remains conclusive for all time:

[W]e may define the nature of the mental attitude which underlies all philosophical thinking as: *a love-determined movement of the inmost personal Self
of a finite being toward participation in the essential reality of all possibles.*
(*E.*, 74)

[The] Platonic requirement that in philosophy the whole man, not only his isolated intellect or isolated sensibility, etc., should seek participation in Reality is . . . a requirement whose basis is neither psychological, nor purely epistemological, but *ontic*. (*E.*, 90–91)

Now, Voegelin's reading of Max Scheler in the *Herrschaftslehre* is intimately involved with his reception of the thought of St. Augustine. Without suggesting that Voegelin was introduced to Augustine's thought by Scheler—there is no evidence for this assumption—there are nevertheless adequate objective reasons why he would examine both Augustine and Scheler in a work that had at its center the presentation of the human person. There were at least two aspects of Voegelin's intellectual development up to 1930 that would make this reception a logical continuation of his thought: (1) his training, under Othmar Spann, in a sociology rooted in the Fichtean reception of Kant's *Critique of Practical Reason*; and (2) his familiarity with the phenomenology of Edmund Husserl and his associates. To these two aspects of his development, and their consequences for Voegelin's reception of Scheler's work, we now turn.

Sociological Training

Voegelin trained as a sociologist under Othmar Spann,[7] who taught that the essence of community is spirituality (*das Geistige*). The "pairing" or "communing" (*Gezweiung*) that is constitutive of such institutions as the family, art, science, commerce, and state, is a process in which individuals, awakened by spiritual acts and responding with their own, deepen and develop together toward personhood. The member of a family, for example, is not a *homo naturalis* who just also happens to find himself or herself in a family; what a parent "is," what a child "is," only exists in the *Gezweiung*, "family."[8]

In Spann's sociology, the various institutions, viewed in themselves, may be seen as "totalities" (*Ganzheiten*), for they are communities in which specific and essential aspects of spirituality can be realized. But they may also be viewed from the comprehensive standpoint of social life as a whole. In this perspective they become "partial-totalities" (*Teilganzen*) and stand in relationship to one another according to the degree and dignity of the spirituality that can be realized in each of them. For example, the institution comprising the totality of economic relations stands lower on the scale of spiritual being than that comprising religious relations. The highest community is found in humankind's relationship to God: "Just as a member of a totality points to the totality of which it is a part, so that totality points in its turn to a higher one. . . . The center of the highest totality points to God."[9]

Voegelin's concern with these issues in the work of Spann engaged him further in the study of Scheler. Scheler's criticism of Kant's ethics in *Der Formalismus* carries forward the earlier critiques of Fichte and Spann to develop an analysis of the human person as "microcosmos" and "microtheos."[10] In Voegelin's only published work devoted entirely to Kant, "Das Sollen im System Kants" (1930), he explicitly acknowledges his debt to Scheler: "The informed reader will easily note the close connection of my analysis with that of others, especially with that of Scheler."[11]

Phenomenological Influences

In post–World War I German philosophy, the investigation of the human relationship to God received strong impulses from the development of phenomenology. As early as 1922, Voegelin's unpublished dissertation revealed that as a twenty-one-year-old sociologist, he had a mature understanding of the achievements of Edmund Husserl. In "Wechselwirkung und Gezweiung" ("Reciprocity and Community"), Voegelin criticized Georg Simmel's sociology for its reduction of social phenomena to psychological relations between individuals, and presented Othmar Spann's theory of the primacy of the spiritual community as the only solid basis upon which to build sociological theory. The epistemological starting point taken by Voegelin for the thesis is the Critical Idealism of Edmund Husserl.[12]

But despite the central importance of Husserl's work, the philosopher most intimately associated with the phenomenological movement and religious philosophy during this period was Max Scheler. August Brunner, in his foreword to the English translation of *Vom Ewigen im Menschen*, states the case succinctly:

> Scheler was not really a pupil of Husserl. He started out from Eucken and his doctrine of the spiritual life as a final reality. But his intuitive inclinations were very soon bound to feel attracted by the new method and to recognize in it a tool suitable for his own interests. The thing that was new in his philosophy was in fact that he used phenomenology for the investigation of spiritual realities. . . . Scheler shows the characteristic quality of that which is religious. It is a particular essence, which cannot be reduced to anything else. It is a sphere that belongs essentially to man; without it he would not be man. . . . This religious sphere is the most essential, the decisive one. It determines man's basic attitude towards reality and thus in a sense the colour, extent and position of all the other human domains in life. (*E.*, 7–8)

The direction that Voegelin's own interests took, toward the meditative study of the relationship of human personhood to the divine, and toward a recovery and renewal for the modern world of Augustine's path of meditation, would have found encouragement in Scheler's application of the phenomenological approach to religion in *The Eternal in Man.* That Scheler himself was convinced that these issues must be pursued is evident from his introduction to this work, which I cite extensively here. He declared that he

> offers to the public for the first time a few fruits of the work on the philosophy of religion which has occupied the author for many years—the underlying bases for the systematic construction of a "natural theology." The author believes these fundamentals, despite all foreseen objections, to be more assured than traditional bases and also of a nature to encounter a deeper understanding and sounder appreciation from the man of today than the traditional systems of religious theory which lean either to Aquinas or to Kant and Schleiermacher. In the same way as what Kant called the "scandal of philosophy," it is a scandal of theology and philosophy *alike* that the questions of natural theology, *i.e.* the very thing designed to *unite* minds irrespective of sectarian differences, should divide minds even more deeply than points of confessional dogma. It is a further scandal that whatever knowledge of God men owe solely to the spontaneous reason in every man, that which should therefore enable us to see the true bounds of tradition and revelation, is for the most part cultivated in purely *traditional* systems of doctrine.
>
> The author is profoundly convinced . . . that natural theology is unable to perform its task of *unification* either on a basis of Thomism or on a basis derived from the philosophical era ushered in by Kant.
>
> This task it can only perform once it has delivered the kernel of Augustinism from the husklike accretions of history, and employed phenomenological philosophy to provide it with a fresh and more deeply rooted foundation. (Phenomenological philosophy is one which undertakes to look on the essential fundamentals of all existence with rinsed eyes, and redeems the bills of exchange which an over-complex civilization has drawn on them in terms of symbol upon symbol.) When this has been done, natural theology will more and more clearly reveal and demonstrate that *immediate* contact of the soul with God which Augustine, from the experience of his great heart, was striving with the apparatus of neo-Platonism to capture and fix in words. Only a theology of the *essential experience of divinity* can open our eyes to the lost truths of Augustine. (*E.*, 12–13)

That Voegelin himself, after Scheler's death in 1928, was to continue the pursuit of these "lost truths of divinity," we shall see as we turn now to a crucial incomplete manuscript of 1931.

Voegelin's *Herrschaftslehre*

The unpublished text, *Herrschaftslehre,* is divided into three chapters.[13] In the second and third chapters, Voegelin discusses theories of domination as presented by Othmar Spann, Max Weber, Max Scheler, Carl Schmitt, Dostoyevsky, Nietzsche, Friedrich Wolters (historian and author of the authorized biography of Stefan George), Helmut Plessner, and others. Following an analysis of Max Weber's views on domination, Voegelin concludes that the elements of "inner domination," as opposed to legal notions of "legitimate rule," have been neglected. Finding that the theme of "spiritual power" is not adequately dealt with (*H.,* III. 1, 7–8), Voegelin turns to Othmar Spann as "the social scientist who has most rigorously examined the nature of man [*Daseinsverfassung des Menschen*]." For Spann, he continues,

> The human is principally not a closed being for whom the world is outside, so that, in the last instance, all spiritual phenomena would have to be led back to the constitution of objects by a consciousness, led back to the modes of appearance of an object for a subject; even if, to a transcendental purified consciousness. . . . Rather the human is a spiritual being [*Geistwesen*] who is open to a super-personal spiritual reality [*überpersönliches geistig Reales*], which we must more closely define.

Voegelin then adds a direct citation from Spann: "The basic ontological fact is that the 'spirit is contained in a higher totality. . . . All the contents of our spirit, and the spirit itself, are linked to and held in a higher [spiritual reality (WP)]' " (*H.,* III. 11).

Voegelin's own intention, to "more closely define" the nature of the spiritual reality of human existence as it had been outlined by Othmar Spann, is carried forward in the first chapter of the *Herrschaftslehre* (*H.,* I. 1). There Voegelin argues that St. Augustine has laid the basis for an understanding of the person in the exercise (*Vollzug*) of a meditation in which the human discovers himself or herself as a person. To explicate the stages of St. Augustine's meditation, Voegelin also discusses Descartes, Edmund Husserl, and Max Scheler.

Our examination of this chapter is hampered by the fact that the surviving text is incomplete, and lacks the pages devoted to Scheler. Nevertheless, through the references to Scheler in extant parts of the text, we can point to the passages in his writings that were relevant to Voegelin's discussion. The references given are to both the general theme of phenomenology—the correlation between intentional act and object—and the specific religious act and its fulfillment (*Erfüllung*) in a godly being. We now turn to these themes.

Meditation in the *Herrschaftslehre*: Antecedents in Scheler

Voegelin's study of human existence in the *Herrschaftslehre* begins with the sentence: "The determination [*Bestimmung*] of that which a person essentially is [*in ihrem Kerne sei*] takes place, when the attempt is made with adequate means, in a basic form of philosophical thinking [*Grundform philosophischen Denkens*] which we will characterize by the name which Descartes gave it, meditation" (*H.*, I. 1). Voegelin indicates that his understanding of meditation takes as its starting point Augustine's meditations on memory and thought as recorded in Books X and XI of the *Confessions*. He acknowledges that "the forms, in which his Christian thought moves, and the formulae which it finds, have remained to the present day the classic examples for investigations into the essence [*Wesen*] of the person and of time" (*H.*, I. 1). Voegelin then points out that there are two principal ways of exploring the essence of the person, one oriented to being, the other to becoming (*H.*, I. 1).

> Both ways, that of being and that of becoming, lead to the same goal, the meditating person to God and therewith the knowing person [*Erkennenden*] to insight into the essence of the human person, who can be characterized by his openness to a transcendent being, by his being a frontier between the world, with its being and becoming, and a super-world [*Über-Welt*]. (*H.*, I. 7)

In what follows, I will review Voegelin's own discussion of the meditation on being, including some references to the meditation on becoming. I will indicate the parallels between this discussion and that undertaken in the writings of Scheler.

Immediately we note that Voegelin's characterization of the human being as a "border" between the world and God is also the view held by Scheler. Scheler writes: "The human being is a between [*Zwischen*], a border [*Grenze*] and a passage, an appearance of God in the current of life and an eternal overcoming of life over itself." The "human" is "the intention and gesture [*Geste*] of Transcendence itself, the human is the being [*Wesen*] which prays and seeks God. . . . It is not that 'the human prays,' but rather that the human being is the prayer of life overcoming itself; he does not seek God—he is the living X which seeks God!" For this reason, Scheler rejects theories that try to explain human spiritual being in terms of a so-called natural being. Rather, he declares, there is a division through the unity of the "human" that is "infinitely greater than that between humans and animals in the naturalistic sense." He writes, "Between those who are 'born again' and the 'old Adam,' between the 'child of God' and the maker of tools and machines ('homo faber') there exists an essential difference that cannot be bridged. On the other hand, between animal and homo faber there is only a difference of degree."[14]

The principal presentation of Scheler's philosophy of the person encompasses more than two hundred pages and cannot be summed up here.[15] However, the following points may be emphasized, in order to indicate the parallels between his argument and Voegelin's characterization of the human being as a "frontier" between the world and the super-world (*H.*, I. 7).

Noetic acts, Scheler holds, are demarcated from psychic functions. Functions take place, acts must be committed. The level of noetic acts (*Geist*) is that of the meaning of experiences, and not of the experiences themselves. Since the person is only found in the meaning of experiences, the person necessarily transcends all experiences as experiences. Therefore, although spiritual meanings can be indexed "in time"—for they are accompanied by the modes of experience of the human whose body and soul are subject to the laws of the space-time continuum—the noetic life itself transcends the physical and psychic realms. Noetic acts are "essentially psycho-physically indifferent."[16]

Scheler points out that since noetic acts cannot be found in time and space, they resist "objectification." The noetic acts of the person can only be understood by other persons reenacting them. The person is not absorbed in his or her acts, but remains the quality-giving-direction in each act. The center of the person is love, understood as a quality that leads to deeper and deeper knowledge of value and therefore of being. There is a hierarchy of lovable qualities and of types of persons and acts corresponding to these qualities. At the height of this hierarchy stand the human beings who have learned to see themselves, their fellow humans, and the world in the light of the person of persons, God. The experience of the spiritual community with God is the model of all community: "all loving, contemplating, thinking and willing is intentionally united *in deo.*"[17]

Having determined the reality of the human person as the in-between (*Zwischen*) between "world" and God, Scheler then attempts to rescue the insights of Augustine through an analysis of the "religious act" as the personal act *sui generis*. In this connection, Scheler emphasizes the importance of meditation. There is a "prejudice," he writes, to the effect that "no mystical 'experimental theology' could ever acquire any kind of consistent universal validity in the sphere of religious experience or for the theory of such experience." The reason for this view lies "in the lack of knowledge and appreciation of psychic techniques as a means not to ethical, practical ends but to an increase in *religious knowledge*. . . ." Scheler adds that his own philosophy of religion will only find its "full elaboration and verification" in "a fundamental treatment . . . of the *technique* appertaining to the mystical experience of divinity and the corresponding living network of procedures and states of mind" (*E.*, 30).

The Direction of Meditation: Voegelin and Scheler

Voegelin begins his own discussion of Augustine's meditation with the observation that

> every meditation requires a direction-determining beginning. For Augustine (*Conf.*, lib. x) the question is: Where does the soul find God, when it seeks Him in order to rest in Him? After much unsuccessful seeking, he must say: "Nor in all these which I thus run over consulting thee, can I find any one safe place to settle my soul in, but in thyself only; into whom let all my scattered pieces be gathered together, nor let anything of mine be turned back from thee" (x. 60). This turn [*Wendung*] is characteristic for the course of this and every genuine meditation, because it clearly expresses the fact that the seeking [*Suchen*] has a direction, but no rational notations [*Merkmale*] which can describe its goal. Augustine does not seek God of whom he has a specific concept [*Begriff*], but that point in the movement of his soul at which his soul finds peace. This point is found when no driving moment [*treibendes Moment*] remains. The meditative course must therefore be understood as the step by step separating out [*allmähliches Ausscheiden*] of all that which is unsettling [*Beunruhigendes*], all that which is merely world immanent [*irdisch*], until the soul stands naked before God [*nackt vor Gott*]. This place [*Ort*] can only be negatively determined as that which is none of those which the meditative course has passed through in the soul's state of unease. It is radically the other place. What it positively is can only be seen by the one who follows the whole movement of the *confessio*, who has himself enacted the confession [*Bekenntnis*] to God. (*H.*, I. 1)

In making these points, Voegelin's study has many points of contact with Scheler's inquiries. First, we find that what Voegelin refers to as the "direction-determining beginning"—the intention of the heart to reach the world-transcending God—corresponds in Scheler to the religious act being "an essential endowment of the human mind and soul" (*E.*, 267). The religious act must leave all the mere "worldly" behind. Therefore, Scheler writes,

> The most conclusive, though merely negative, sign of a religious act, as distinct from all other acts of mind or spirit, is an attendant insight into the fact that *of its essence it cannot be fulfilled* by any finite object belonging to, or itself forming, the "world." In this sense Augustine's dictum, *Inquietum cor nostrum, donec requiescat in te*, is a basic formula for all religious acts. (*E.*, 251)

Scheler then elaborates this insight in the following terms:

The first thing peculiar to any religious act is that not only the things and facts experienced by the person, but also all things of a finite and contingent kind, are gathered together in a single whole, which includes the subject's own person, and are joined in the idea of "the world." Without this preparatory operation a religious act cannot take place. The second thing proper to the religious act is that in its intention this "world" is overlapped or *transcended*. It is not a question of this particular transitory world that "happens" to exist, but a question of everything partaking of the *nature* of "world" in general—that is, a world in which there is somehow or other realized an embodiment of the essences realized in the world which I know. Transcendence in general is a peculiarity of every conscious intention, for in every one there is present an intending-above-and-beyond its own empirical standpoint, together with the simultaneous awareness that the being of the object reaches out beyond the empirical content of the intention. But only where the thing thus transcended is the *world* as a whole (including the subject's own person) are we entitled to speak of a *religious act*. (*E.*, 250–51)

Second, we find parallels in the treatment by Scheler and Voegelin of the act in which meditation finds its completion. For Voegelin, as we have seen, the "other place," where the soul stands "naked before God," can only be seen by one who has himself followed the whole movement of the confession and has enacted the confession to God (*H.* I, 1). Scheler treats this same issue in terms of the difference between metaphysical and religious acts:

The religious act . . . demands an answer, an *act of reciprocity* on the part of that very object to which its intention is directed. And this implies that one may only speak of "religion" where the object bears a *divine personal form* and where revelation (in the widest sense) on the part of this personal object is what fulfils the religious act and its intention. While for metaphysics the personality of the divine forms a never-attainable boundary of cognition, for religion this personality is the alpha and omega. . . . The religious act is unable from its own resources, or with the help of thought, to *construct* what hovers as an objective idea, notion or intuition before the human performer of the act. He must somehow *receive* the truth he "intends," the salvation and felicity he "seeks"—and receive it via the very being he seeks. To that extent he is in his primary intention already disposed for and concerned with a possible *reception*, however much a multifarious internal and external spontaneous *activity* may be a prerequisite of his reaching the threshold where the reception begins. Where the soul does not—however indirectly— touch God, and touch him in knowing and feeling itself touched *by* God, no *religious* relationship can subsist—not even a relation of "natural" religion. (*E.*, 253–54. Compare *E.*, 168f)

Via negationis in Voegelin and Scheler

In the *Herrschaftslehre*, Voegelin points out that in Augustine's meditation,

the *via negationis* . . . the rejection of all empirical levels of being, leads at
last to the highest level of being, that which all world immanent things are
not. The question of Cap. 6 [chapter 6 of Book X, *Confessions*] expresses the
pure form of this elevation:

> "What now do I love, whenas I love thee? Not the beauty of any corpo-
> ral thing; not the order of times, not the brightness of the light which
> we do behold, so gladsome to our eyes: not the pleasant melodies of
> songs of all kinds; nor the fragrant smell of flowers, and ointment, and
> spices: not manna and honey; nor any fair limbs that are so acceptable
> to fleshly embracements. I love none of these things whenas I love my
> God."

At the highpoint of the negation he [Augustine] follows then with *et tamen*
. . . the turn back, that indeed God is none of this, but for the soul it is
nevertheless somehow God. . . . All statements are, at the same time, both
made and negated [*gleich gesetzt und wieder aufgehoben*], in order to deter-
mine that place at which the fullness of being [*Fülle des Seins*] is to be found
and peace attained by overcoming all which is earthly and impure in being
[*Ruhe von allem Irdisch-Unreinen des Seins*].

> "And yet (et tamen) I love a certain kind of light, and a kind of voice,
> and . . . a kind of embracement, whenas I love my God; who is both
> the light and the voice, and the sweet smell, and the meat, and the em-
> bracement of my inner man: where the light shineth into my soul,
> which no place can receive; that voice soundeth, which time deprives
> me not of; and that fragrancy smelleth which no wind scatters; and that
> meat tasteth, which eating devours not; and that embracement clingeth
> to me, which satiety divorceth not. This it is which I love, whenas I
> love my God." (*H.*, I. 1–2)

This *via negationis* is to be found also at the root of Scheler's "phenomenological method." He himself indicated that his method, independent
of the field of its application, owes its origin to the "negative theology"
of Plotinus:

> [The] method of successively peeling away the correlates and contraries that
> are felt to offer progressive indications to the "phenomenon *demonstran-
> dum*," with the consequent laying bare of the phenomenon and its presence
> to the inspecting mind, is the way which leads to the *phenomenological scru-
> tiny of the essence*. The indefinability of the X under investigation (*per genus
> et differentia specifica*) is a sure sign that in this X we have a genuine elemen-
> tary essence which underlies ultimate concepts but is itself "inconceivable."
> For "to conceive" means to reduce the object of a concept in terms of other
> concepts. (*E.*, 170)

Scheler acknowledges that the deepest intentions of this method are not
generally understood:

Many who make use of this method . . . are surprisingly unaware that as a method it is basically none other than that of "negative theology." For the method of "negative theology" itself arose purely from the deep conviction that the *divine* and holy form as such a prime elementary quality which can only be demonstrated by a slow process of elimination and analogy, a quality which must satisfy all concepts of the divine—positive and negative—but itself remains inconceivable. There is no doubt that as an approach and method phenomenology was first employed, in the time of Plotinus, in exactly this theological context. (*E.*, 171)

Scheler's study also touched on the point developed by Voegelin—that the experience of the "fullness of being" is followed by "*et tamen*" (Augustine) in order to see the levels of being (which have been overcome in the meditative assent) for the first time in their relationship to absolute being. First, Scheler acknowledges the absolute distinction between God and the world:

[T]he *immanentia Dei in mundo* belongs to the essence of God. God is in every existent, so far as it *is*. . . . But it is not correct to say also that everything is in him, as is said in pantheism and acosmic pantheism; there is no *immanentia mundi in Deo*. For the world is according to reality distinct from God, and only because God is infinite mind can God notwithstanding be in everything. (*E.*, 193)

Later, however, Scheler points also to the new knowledge of the realm of being that is reached when the meditative ascent has been concluded:

Finally, *knowledge* of all possible truth, which in itself is an absolute value for philosophy and science (in the latter case, within the limitations imposed by technical aims), takes on a new axiological meaning. It is now *subordinated* to the values and final purpose of an *ontic* process, a *becoming*, which far transcends all knowledge, namely to *the* value and end of the projection of human *personality* into God's personality. At the same time it is subsidiary in the cognition of objects to an extension which is to be coeffected in the cognitive act: here I refer to the extrapolation from known things of their ultimate *determination* or destiny, which is an *ontic* participation in God and can be apprehended when we share some part of the *idea* which God has of them. Indeed, at this stage knowledge is *no longer immaterial* for things. We may now say that things are in some way *affected* by the knowledge man acquires of them. Without undergoing a strictly real alteration (such as is possible through volition, re-conception and action) or being in whole or part constructed (Kantian fashion) by the human mind—without deriving their nature and substance via the cognitive act, since these they possess independently of man through God's idea of them—the "determination" and "meaning" of things are here *realized* by man for the very first time in the cognitive act. Things acquire *ontically* the part of their determination and meaning which ideally they already possess: they are led, *raised*, *restored* to God as the root of all things, the underlying concept and con-summation of all essences. (*E.*, 303)

Meminisse Me Memini

Voegelin's understanding of the goal of meditation, like that of Scheler, is firmly rooted in Augustine's presentation of the meditative ascent.

After passing through the levels of being from corpus and sensus, to anima, the next step in Augustine's meditation is named, in a general fashion [*ganz allgemein*], "memoria."

> "I will soar beyond that faculty of mine, by which I am united unto my body, and by which I fill the whole frame of it with life. . . . Still rising by degrees unto him who hath made me and I come into these fields and spacious palaces of my memory."[18]

Within the faculty of memory [*Gedächtnisvermögen*] a series of degrees are distinguished. a) Memory of sensual impressions, b) memory of objects of the nature of mathematical sentences (platonic anamnesis), c) memory of emotions [*Affekte*]. And when all these levels have been mustered:

> "I come to the memory of memory: and I remember myself to have remembered; like as if hereafter I shall call to remembrance that I have been able to remember these things now; it shall be by the force of my memory, that I shall be able to call it to remembrance" (cap. 13).

The memory which remembers itself, the memory of memory, this iterative faculty [*iterierbare Kraft*] of the human is his inmost self, his *animus*. By means of this iterative capacity [*Iterierbarkeit*] the memory is "quasi venter animi" (cap. 14).

> "Great is the power of memory . . . and this thing is the mind, and this thing am I" (cap. 17).

At this, Voegelin stops to note the extent to which Augustine's meditation anticipates that of Descartes.

In its most compact form, this thought appears in a formulation which points to Descartes:

> "It is I myself, that I remember, I the mind";

and in another place:

> "I cannot so much as call myself without it [sc. memory]" (cap. 16).

The meditation finds its temporary [*vorläufige*] end in a definition of the center of the person [*Personkern*] as the iteration of memory: in the successive acts of memory which are directed in their turn to acts of memory, the *ego ipse* constitutes itself. (*H*., I. 2–3)

That the goal of the meditation is the coming-to-rest of the soul in God is, beyond doubt, central to Voegelin's understanding:

> However the center of the person is not the goal, which, from the beginning, was intended in the meditation; the ego is also world-immanent [*diesseitig-irdisch*]; this level of the human spirit [*Geist*] must also be overcome in the transcendent [*das Jenseits*] of the human, in the super-ego [*Über-Ich*]:
>
>> "I will pass even beyond this faculty of mine . . . that I may approach thee, O sweet light" (cap. 17).
>
> The course of the meditation is prescribed by the structure of the world and culminates for the immanent world [*das Diesseits*] in a center, which is defined by means of the self-reflection of the spirit [*Rückwendung des Geistes auf sich selbst*] and ends by more precisely revealing being as that which, after overcoming the predicates and the structures of the immanent world, [is found] to border immediately on the immanent world. The course [of the meditation] leads from body to soul, from the soul to the *ego ipse*, and from the *ego ipse* to God . . . and finds its clear [*eindeutig*] end, when, after exhausting all of that which is predicable, reaches the place which is no longer a place in any palpable sense. (*H*., I. 3)

Up to this point, I have been following Voegelin's presentation of Augustine's meditation on being, and I have commented on some of its aspects with reference to Max Scheler's philosophy of religion. I turn now to Voegelin's summary of what both meditative ways—that of being and that of becoming—achieve in the *Confessions* of Augustine. Here Voegelin identifies the areas of the meditation that remain to be explored.

Meditation Is the Life of the Person

Voegelin indicates aims for his inquiry that may be considered as carrying forward the intention declared by Scheler, of "deliver[ing] the kernel of Augustinism from the husklike accretions of history" (*E*., 13). The meditation of Augustine, Voegelin declares,

> is the basis for all more recent meditations. But it does not achieve everything which the new philosophy of the person [*Personlehre*] needs. For Augustine the problem of the person is not the focus, but is treated obliquely in the problematic of the dualism between creator and creatura. For the modern [*neuzeitliche*] philosophy of the person, the primary focus is that of the difference between person and world; for Augustine it was between God and the world. For him the entire creation is given objectively [*gegenständlich gegeben*] and within it the person. His vision of the world [*Weltbild*] is or-

dered in terms of space; from the bottom, from the corporeal, to the summit
in the soul. The modern philosophy of the person proceeds from the outward, corporeal, as the outside [*Aussen*] of the person, to the most inward
and intimate of the person. But for Augustine the self-possession [*Selbs-
thabe*] of the person, and therewith the process of iteration, is only a periph-
eral theme. The clearest symptom of this objective order [*gegenständliche
Ordnung*] in which, from the standpoint of an observer, even the person is
an object among other objects, can be seen in Augustine's concept of time.
It is not an internal consciousness of time [*Zeitbewusstsein*], not the constituent of the ego, but exactly the opposite, a dissolvent. The *tempora* and
secula are identical with the creatura in the sense of a concrete realization
[*Erfülltheit*] of the objective course of the world [*Weltablauf*], in which the
person, to the extent that he does not hold himself in the *intentio* to God, is
also consumed. (*H.*, I. 8)

The modern meditations, to which Voegelin now turns, are characterized by having their center in the ego ("*Zentrum im Ich*"). In Descartes
it becomes clear, he writes, that

the meditation is the life of the person itself, in which the person attains
certitude concerning his own essence [*Eigenwesen*]. The person is both the
subject and the object of the meditation. In the meditation as a series of acts
the person experiences himself as a person [*der Person wird die Person selbst
gegeben*]—not abstractly, not as the essence of the person qua person [*an
sich*]; but this essence experiences himself as a person in the concrete case of
his own meditation [*dieses Wesen am konkreten Fall der meditierenden und
in ihrer Meditation sich selbst erfassenden Person*]. (*H.*, I. 10)

Discussing Descartes's Third Meditation, Voegelin writes:

In the meditation I experience myself only in the moment of the concrete
cogitare. Beyond this moment and the next to the next and those which
follow in time, I am only maintained by the power [*trägt mich nur die
Macht*] which created me. . . . The act of creation fills not a moment of finite
time, but is the continuously working force which conserves the person's
life in time [*das Leben der Person dauernd erhält*]. (*H.*, I. 13–14)

Noetic being is not "in" time. We have seen this point already in
Scheler; the person is the prayer to God, the "movement" toward God.
The levels below the noetic realm of being, those of the psychic and somatic functions, are organized by the noetic. For this reason Scheler rejected all notions of proceeding from a falsely asssumed "homo naturalis"
in order to "explain" human being and God. One must proceed from the
noetic level of being, which participates in the godly in the most intense

form and which is not of this world, but the *"Zwischen"* between "world" and God, in order to understand what a human person is.[19]

Imago Dei

Continuing his discussion of Descartes, Voegelin now reaches the point where the true identity of the human can be discussed within modern philosophy. He points out that in Descartes's meditation,

> By means of the sceptical suspension a sphere is isolated in which the essence of the person is to be sought. When this sphere is found, a new method of positive description can begin in which the frontiers, or limits [*Grenze*] of the finite person and that which lies beyond the finite person can be brought into focus [*verdeutlicht*]. Here we find considerations of the type which we find in Scheler's discussion of the essence of Thou-evidence [*Du-Evidenz*]. The ego finds empty spaces [*Leerstellen*], which point to a possible fulfilment. From the nature of these empty spaces one has a notion of the nature of the essence [*Wesen*] of the being which could fulfill them, without having concretely experienced this being. Longing, gratitude and acts of love point beyond the ego toward the need for fulfilment in a Thou. In experiences of this type I become aware of my person as a finite person; finite in the specific sense of being both limited [*begrenzt*] and open to other personal substances. (*H.*, I. 12–13)

Such a discussion can be found also in Scheler's descriptions of the relationship between humans and between the human person and God. In these acts, the "ego" itself is left behind as "part of the world." The ego can be objectified, the center of the person cannot (*H.*, I. 8).[20]

The Religious Act and Political Reality

The Ground of Community

Since all persons are rooted *"in deo"* and by means of this relationship enter into spiritual relationships with one another, Scheler's theory of the *"Leerstellen"* has both religious and sociological implications. In order to understand the use that Voegelin later makes of this argument, we need to quote Scheler *in extenso*. "It is impossible," writes Scheler, "to form any judgement about concrete questions of community without touching on the fundamental questions, What is the *nature* of community? To what ends do its essential forms exist?" It is an essential law, and not an empirical fact, he continues, that it is "inherent in the *eternal, ideal nature* of an intelligent person that all its existence and activity as a spirit is *ab origine* just as much an outward-conscious, co-responsible, communal reality as a self-conscious, self-responsible, individual reality." As far as empirical experience is concerned, the realm of contingent being, there have indeed been "Robinson Crusoes." But

> [e]ven a hypothetical spiritual-corporeal being who had never been conscious of his fellows via the senses would ascertain his membership of a community, his "belonging," precisely on account of a positive awareness that a whole class of intentions in his *essential* nature was craving and *not finding fulfilment*—all types of loving (love of God, of one's neighbour, etc.), promising, thanking, entreaty, obedience, serving, ruling and so on. Hence this imaginary being would not say . . . "I am alone in the world, I belong to no community," but he would tell himself: "I do not know the *actual* community to which I know that I belong . . . but I *know* that I do belong to one." . . . *Where there is an "I" there is a "we,"* or "I" *belong* to a "we." (*E.*, 373–74)

The spiritual ground in which the existence of the person is founded is, in Scheler's diagnosis, the basis for membership of universal community:

> Because we have an awareness, as original as the self-awareness with which it is inextricably associated, of our organic membership in a universal community of spiritual beings, one which we cannot disregard, we have at the centre of our souls an urgent need and limitless pressure of spirit to *transcend* in thought, and aspire beyond in loving desire, not only our solitary, naked self but every one of the historically actual and sensually visible communities to which we belong; this implies in effect, when rationally determined, an urge to regard *every* actual community in its turn as the "organ" of a still broader, more comprehensive and higher community of spirits. There is nothing clearer or surer to our hearts and minds than this: *not one* of these earthly communities (family, municipality, State, nation, circle of friends, etc.), would ever quite suffice to satisfy the demands of our reason and hearts, no matter what degree of perfection it might attain in history. But since all communities of this kind are communities not only of spirits but also of *persons*, this (in principle) boundless urge and the demand of reason for ever richer, more universal and higher community find only in *one* idea their possible conclusion and perfect satisfaction—the idea of communion of love and spirit with an infinite spiritual person who at the same time is the origin, founder and sovereign Lord of all possible spiritual communities as of all actual communities on earth. Just as certain kinds of love are implanted in the *nature* of our spiritual existence—kinds differentiated from the outset, before casual experience of their correlative objects, as emotional acts which demand fulfilment (love, for example, of children, parents, home, country)—so there is also a *supreme* kind of love, love of *God*, which we already feel and possess before we have a clear intellectual conception of the supreme being. That is why Pascal can say to God, "I would not seek thee, if thou hadst not already found me."

Scheler makes clear that only such a community can fulfill the true needs of humanity, and that against it all other associations that seek to form substitutes for it must be measured. He continues:

> We are equally clear in heart and mind that their intentions can be entirely fulfilled and satisfied only by this supreme and final union of love and reason in God, and that we are unable to envisage correctly the communities in which we know ourselves involved, unable to see them in a *true* light, until we are conscious of them against the *divine background* of this supreme and final community of all spiritual beings—until we see their shape against the illumination which only community with the personal God projects. In that community alone do peace and rest attend the endless questing of heart and mind beyond all finite visible communities: *Inquietum cor nostrum* (said Augustine) *donec requiescat in te.* It is in and through *God* that for the first time we are truly *bound in spirit* to one another. This is exactly the meaning of the "first" and "greatest" commandment (Mark 12.30–31), which merges self-sanctification and love of one's neighbour in their common root, the love of God. (*E.*, 374–75)

Res Publica

We see then that in Scheler's philosophy, principally (essentially) the human person exists *"in deo"* and through this relationship enters into spiritual relations with other human beings. The *res publica* is therefore a spiritual community under God. And the soundness or unsoundness of the *res publica* will be found in an examination of the God—or the Idol—in which the society and its members find their spiritual reality.

> Since the religious act is an essential endowment of the human mind and soul, there can be no question of whether this or that man performs it. The question can only be of whether he finds its *adequate* object, the correlative idea to which it essentially *belongs*, or whether he envisages an object, acclaiming it as divine, as holy, as the absolute good, while it yet *conflicts* with the nature of the religious act because it belongs to the sphere of finite and contingent goods. (*E.*, 267)

Scheler's firm grasp of this point enabled him to make fundamental criticisms of the underlying direction of European society. In an essay of 1917, he based his argument on the insight that society, having lost its view of human being as *imago Dei*, had placed faith in worldly idols. Under the general term "humanitarianism," Scheler summarized the course of Europe's spiritual errors from the end of the Middle Ages to the catastrophe of the First World War:

> Humanitarianism rebels against the first principle of the Christian commandment of love: "Love God first above all things"—with the immediate

corollary, "Therefore love your neighbour *in* God, and always in reference to the highest good." . . . [It] rebelled against the commandment in successive periods of classical renascence, in the age of "humanism," and with special force during the Enlightenment. All these great movements worked to construct an ethos which *isolates* man from God and often indeed plays man off against God. Even where it leaves Christian values *in situ* there is a change in the emotion and spiritual act called love of man or love of one's neighbour. What is primarily envisaged by the new "love of man" (of man alone) is no longer his invisible spirit, his soul and his salvation, solidarily included in the salvation of all children of God, with his bodily welfare taking an incidental place as a condition of his perfection and happiness. (*E.*, 367)

The Enlightenment, Scheler argued, had completed the process of the establishment of idolatrous substitutes for true community:

[It] needed only to complete a piecemeal demolition of early Protestantism's topheavy structure of supernaturalism with its dangerous abandonment of the task of *inbuilding* God's kingdom into this intractable world; what then remained was pure humanitarianism, the picture of a mankind without a leader or pattern in its basic objectives. Left to the random impulses of its natural instincts, this mankind had lost with its common reference to God the highest warrant of its unity. As Augustine so long ago had seen, this was a theomorphous idea of man. (*E.*, 371)

The consequence of this turn from the ground of order was—Scheler argued—the mass of competing "interests" whose importance was assumed to be central in the ideologies of modernity. In its logical pursuit of the humanitarian ethos, the nineteenth century had gradually

whittled down that idea of the uniformity of rational human nature into which the Enlightenment had gathered all concepts of truth and falsity, good and evil, right and wrong. . . . What else remained? The idea of conflicting groups following their interests or instincts, be they races, nations, states or classes—a picture of fluctuating conflict of every kind, in which only one thing is of deciding importance: the brutal issue. Everything in the nature of an idea or norm, whether it be of morality or justice, which formerly was intended to govern the relationships of men, is now pressed into the service of these interests and instincts as a bludgeon, knife or other weapon: it becomes epiphenomenal, an old mask behind which group-egoisms pharisaically hide. . . . [The] clearest and most accurate expression of this inner condition of Europe was . . . the ideological worlds of Darwin and Marx. (*E.*, 372)

In the social sphere, as in every other, there was, Scheler implied, no middle ground between openness toward God and atheism:

This law stands: every finite spirit believes either in God or in idols. And from it there follows this pedagogic rule of religion: the correct way of dispelling "unbelief" is not that of guiding a man to the idea and reality of God by arguments external to his personal condition (whether by "proofs" or by persuasion), but that of showing him . . . that he has installed a finite good in place of God, *i.e.* that within the objective sphere of the absolute, which he "has" at all events as a sphere, he has, in our sense, "deified" a particular good. . . . In thus bringing a man to *disillusion* with his idol . . . we bring him *of his own accord* to the idea and reality of God. Hence, what I have called the "shattering of idols" is the principal (and only) way to prepare the religious development of the personality. (*E.*, 267–68)

Voegelin's *Political Religions*: The Shattering of the Idols

Voegelin's last book before his enforced emigration from Austria in 1938, *Political Religions*,[21] draws both on Scheler's insight concerning the positive nature of the religious act, and his declaration of the necessity of "shattering" idols as the basis for a religious criticism of National Socialism.

Augustine's "*inquietum cor nostrum, donec requiescat in te,*" which Scheler had made the guiding principle of his philosophy of religion, is also formulated by Voegelin in his sentence: "The human experiences his existence as being that of a creature and therefore questionable [*fragwürdig*]" (*PR.*, 10). The problem of the questioning heart finding peace in God or failing to complete the religious act (undertaking it with inadequate means) and therefore coming to rest in an idol, is expressed in the pair of opposites, the "open" and the "closed" soul.

For one person, the doors of his being are wide open for a view of all levels of being, from inorganic nature up to God. The world opens wide for him, its contents form into a meditative [*durchdachtes*] relationship to one another to form an order of being, in which the order of value of the levels of being are a hierarchical order of being itself; and as answer to the question concerning the ground of being, to an order of creation. A maximum reception of reality combines with a maximum of rationality in ordering and relating and culminates in the dogmatic ordering [*Durchbildung*] of the spiritual-religious experiences in an Idea of God, such as the occident developed in the *analogia entis*. Another has only narrow glimpses into reality, perhaps only one: of nature, of a great man, his *Volk*, humanity—that which he sees becomes the *Realissimum*, the "Most-real" [*Allerwirklichste*]; it takes the place of God, and thereby obscures everything else—also, and most importantly, God. (*PR.*, 12–13)

The question of "shattering the idols" is taken up in the last chapter of *Political Religions*. Here Voegelin gives detailed attention to symbols current in the political world around him, which, he realizes, are the correlatives of, and expression of, an incomplete act of meditation. He writes: "We want to descend . . . to the forces which create the symbolic forms" (*PR.*, 70). For this purpose he chooses the poems of Gerhard Schumann, "*Lieder vom Reich,*" as embodying

> one of the strongest expressions of politico-religious stirrings. They enable us to follow the movements of the soul out of which the symbols and the historical reality of the innerworldly community are built. As religious stirrings they have their roots in the experience of creatureliness; but the *Realissimum* in which they find salvation is not, as it is in the Christian experience, God, but the *Volk* and the brotherhood of sworn comrades, and the ecstasies are not spiritual [*geistig*], but that of instinct and find their outlet in the blood-intoxication of the deed [*Blutrausch der Tat*]. (*PR.*, 70–71)

He finds that the stirrings induced by the feeling of creatureliness are experienced by the poet Schumann as "abandonment" and the loneliness of one locked into himself. The soul breaks out of this cold loneliness to unite with the divine whole. "United in the stream of the brotherly flow of the world [*mit dem Strom brüderlichen Weltfliessens*] the soul flows into the totality of the *Volk* [*das Ganze des Volkes*]: 'I lost myself and found the *Volk*, the *Reich*' " (*PR.*, 71). The Führer has received God's command and carries it to his *Volk* for their salvation:

> ". . . and climbing down
> he carried the torch into the night.
>
> Millions bowed to him in silence,
> Saved. Pale as morning, the heavens flamed.
> The sun grew. And with it grew the *Reich*." (*PR.*, 72)

But, Voegelin points out, despite the political success of the movement, the poet and his sworn brothers find no peace. Their interest lies deeper than the mere attainment of political power. For Schumann now speaks the following prayer:

> "Don't let it happen, that I set up house.
> Don't let it happen, that I be satisfied and call for peace.
> Throw me into every despair and unease of the heart." (*PR.*, 73–74)

It is not, Voegelin points out, the political victory that fulfills the intention of the poet's heart,

> but the deed itself. And the pain dealt to the enemy should fall back on the doer of the deed himself: "And when you strike, strike into your own

heart"; the friend must be destroyed, even as the enemy is destroyed, until complete isolation is reached. . . . The naked, pointless deed and self-destruction are acts of mystical dissolving of the self and communion with the world to the point of letting go in the intoxication of blood: "The deed was good, when you reddened it with blood."

> At night they dream of the Führer.
> "From their steps one hears the judgement of blood.
> In their souls they carry the Grail.
> Servants of the *Führer*, both guardians and avengers.
> It burns in them, and with them grows the *Reich*." (*PR.*, 74–75)

Let us compare this form of religious experience, which Voegelin identifies as central to the intentions of National Socialism, with that of Augustine. Both have the *cor inquietum* as their starting point. But neither the poet Schumann, nor his brothers, nor their leader, seek personhood "*in deo,*" but rather the elimination of unbearable loneliness—first in the loss of self in brotherhood, which, in its turn, seeks both destruction of enemy and friend, and at last self-destruction. The symbolism of Schumann is the exact opposite of the symbolism of the Christian *imago Dei*: the extinction of personhood itself. By examining the idolatrous symbols of the human being who has inadequately completed the spiritual act, one can appeal to those who identify with such symbols to reflect once again. But one can do no more than point to the idols and make this appeal. For every discussion of religion is confined to the "pointing to" function of negative theology, to the attempt to awaken the spirit of one's partner in discourse to "see" for himself or herself. If the spirit does not awaken and begin its own meditative search, nothing can be done. The positive conceptual description of that which the spirit is not prepared to understand falls upon deaf ears.

Review: Augustine and Scheler in Voegelin's Writings, 1930–1938

As we have seen from the study of the *Herrschaftslehre* above, Voegelin in 1930—with Books X and XI of Augustine's *Confessions* as the *terminus ad quo* and Max Scheler's philosophy of religion as the *terminus ad quem*—demonstrated the basic form of philosophical thinking in which the person finds himself or herself, the *amare mundum et deum in deo*. The *imago Dei* has its being in participation, on the part of the human individual, in the spiritual acts of God. This experience takes place in the "*Zwischen*" between finite "world" and infinite God. Although the human actions, due to finite being dwelling in soul and body, may be indexed in space and time, the noetic acts themselves, the personal realm of "meaning," cannot be said to "exist" in the spatiotemporal continuum. Neither spiritual-intellectual acts, nor the person, can be reified and experienced as "objects." Therefore, in order to be understood, a meditation, as a series of spiritual-intellectual acts, must be committed by the individual seeking knowledge of reality. There are no "results" of meditations that can be intersubjectively examined and judged by humans who have not taken the same meditative way. Nor have meditations "results" for the meditating person that can become his or her possession. Meditation is the act in which the spirit attains openness to the ground of being by becoming this openness at the center of the self. This state, the "open soul," can through *superbia* and *amor sui* be lost again.

Crucial then to this state is the opening of the soul: in the center of the spirit, an experience takes place that resists reification into "objects" and that is constitutive for the being of the person. It follows that for Voegelin, a philosophical anthropology that conceptualizes the structure of the world can be of only secondary importance. And it is therefore clear that Voegelin's reception of Scheler's philosophy of religion was a more important element in his own philosophical development than his reception of Scheler's philosophical anthropology. At the border of transcendence, the language of philosophical anthropology must yield to the language of religious symbolization. And, as Voegelin's reception of Augustine and Scheler has demonstrated, the human person is this border (*Grenze*) to transcendent being.

Further, it is evident that this key insight, and the further insight that it is the *unio mystica* with God, which constitutes the primary experience of community in which all other communities are rooted, enables the diagnosis of Voegelin's last work before his emigration, *Political Religions*, to be developed. Meditation as the basic form of philosophizing, and the person as *imago Dei*, remain of fundamental importance throughout Voegelin's philosophical career. The completion of the meditation as laid down by Augustine and explicated by Scheler is the experience that leads to the mode of being that Voegelin terms the "open soul." The open soul is also the dynamic yardstick for measuring the possible derailments that take place in the inadequately performed meditation, as for example the notion of an "immanent" humanity, or the various notions arising from the temptation of humans to see themselves as "gods."

Epilogue: Scheler as a Silent Teacher in Meditation, 1943–1966

More than ten years after writing the *Herrschaftslehre*, in a letter to Alfred Schütz in 1943, Voegelin again spoke of the meditation as the basic form of philosophical thinking.

Descartes's meditation is in principle a Christian meditation in the traditional style; it can even be further classified as a meditation of the Augustinian type, and has been made hundreds of times in the history of the human spirit since Augustine. The anonymous author of the *Cloud of Unknowing* (a meditation of the fourteenth century) has formulated the classic theme of the meditation in the following sentence: "It is needful for thee to bury in a cloud of forgetting all creatures that ever God made, that thou mayest direct thine intent to God Himself." The goal of the meditation is the gradual elimination of the world content, from the bodily world to the animate, in order to attain the point of transcendence, in which the soul can, in Augustinian language, turn itself in the *intentio* toward God. This meditation is primarily a process in the biography of the individual who performs it; and the keeping at the point of transcendence and the *intentio* are an experience of brief duration. Secondarily, the process can be expressed verbally, and this gives rise to the literary form of the meditation. Conversely, the reenactment [*Nachvollzug*] of a meditation that has been put down in words makes possible again an originary meditation in the reader.[22]

It is clear that, in contrast to the position taken in the *Herrschaftslehre*, Voegelin no longer recognized in Edmund Husserl's work a contribution to this basic form of philosophizing. Husserl, Voegelin now held, had failed to penetrate to the deepest level of the Cartesian meditation, the "ego as the *anima animi*, in the Augustinian sense, whose *intentio* does not turn to the *cogitata* but toward transcendence." Instead, Husserl confined himself to criticizing the psychologism in Descartes's concept of the ego and focusing on the transcendental ego in its turn toward the contents of the world. Yet, it is only in the sense of the meditation that Husserl failed to grasp that the problem of philosophy, as opposed to that of mere knowledge of the world, becomes thematic:

[In] the transcendence of the Augustinian *intentio*, [the] "I" is simultaneously certain of itself and of God (not in a dogmatic sense, but in a mystical sense of transcendence in the Ground). And only from *this* assurance can the egological sphere in Husserl's sense be founded, with its *intentio* going in the opposed direction toward the *cogitata*—whatever form this assurance may then receive in metaphysical speculation.[23]

Husserl, Voegelin now writes, "has isolated the egological problem from the Cartesian meditative complex" because Husserl has

never performed an originary meditation in Descartes's sense. . . . He has *historically adopted* the reduction of the world from the cogitating ego and cannot therefore ground his own transcendental philosophical position from an originary bestowing metaphysics. The limit he never gets beyond is the founding subjectivity of the ego: where the ego gets its function of founding the objectivity of the world from subjectivity remains not only unexplained but inevitably is hardly touched on. Instead of the higher founding in the experience of transcendence, there enters the founding in the intramundane particularity of one of the epistemological problematics established by Descartes.[24]

With his soul closed to transcendence, Husserl

> has taken the way out in the immanence of a historical problematic and with the greatest care blocked himself off from the philosophical problem of transcendence—the decisive problem of philosophy. For this reason, then, there come from a philosopher of rank what appear to be the curiosities of interpretations of history through the telos revealed in him; for this reason the justification of his position as functionary of this telos; for this reason the inability to find the Archimedean point, which he could not find for himself, in the philosophy of others; for this reason the apparent inhumanity in the humiliation of his predecessors; and for this reason—I would also believe—the constantly preparatory character of his work.[25]

Following the Second World War, Voegelin spoke of the meditation with reference to Plato and Aristotle. Historically, he went back to a time before Augustine. In this connection, he no longer referred to the relationship of his endeavor to that of Max Scheler. In 1966, as Voegelin prepared his letter of 1943 to Alfred Schütz for publication in *Anamnesis: Zur Theorie der Geschichte und Politik*, he crossed out the sentence of the original in which he had referred to Scheler. It had occurred, as it had in the *Herrschaftslehre*, in a discussion of Descartes's third meditation, with Voegelin pointing out the similarity between elements of the meditation and Scheler's analysis of the religious act:

> Thus the existence of God is not logically concluded, but, in the experience of the finitude of human nature, the infinite is given. (Similar in the problematic is Scheler's interpretation of longing and other related experiences in which a *negativum* is positively given.) God cannot be in doubt, for in the experience of doubt and imperfection, God is implied. In the limit-experience of being finite there is given, along with this side of the limit, the beyond.

In the published *Anamnesis* text, the parenthetical sentence concerning Scheler was dropped.[26]

Nevertheless, although Scheler is no longer referred to in connection with the meditation here, it is clear that certain essential insights made by Scheler, which had been expressed in Voegelin's unpublished *Herrschaftslehre* and then applied in *Political Religions*, remained an integral part of Voegelin's thought. The meditation as the basic form of philosophizing was performed in 1930 in Voegelin's reception of Augustine's *Confessions* and Max Scheler's philosophy of religion.

Notes

1. For example, see Eric Voegelin, "On Debate and Existence" (1967), in *The Collected Works of Eric Voegelin*, vol. 12, *Published Essays, 1966–1985*, ed. Ellis Sandoz (Baton Rouge: Louisiana State University Press, 1990), 36–37, where Voegelin refers to Scheler's distinction between person-peripheral and person-central areas of the human being.

2. Eric Voegelin, *Rasse und Staat* (Tübingen: J. C. B. Mohr [Paul Siebeck], 1933), 33, translation mine. See *The Collected Works of Eric Voegelin*, vol. 2, *Race and State*, trans. Ruth Hein, ed. Klaus Vondung (Baton Rouge: Louisiana State University Press, 1997), 33.

3. Max Scheler, *Gesammelte Werke*, vol. 9, *Die Stellung des Menschen im Kosmos* (Zürich and Munich: Francke Verlag, 1976); English translation, *Man's Place in the Cosmos*, trans. Hans Meyerhoff (New York: Farrar, Straus and Giroux, 1981).

4. For a description of the phases of Max Scheler's philosophy see: I. M. Bochenski, "Max Scheler," *Europäische Philosophie der Gegenwart*, 2d ed. (Munich: Lehnen, 1951), 150–63; English translation, *Contemporary European Philosophy*, trans. Donald Nicholl and Karl Aschenbrenner (Berkeley and Los Angeles: University of California Press, 1956), 161–75.

5. Max Scheler, *Gesammelte Werke*, vol. 2, *Der Formalismus in der Ethik und die materiale Wertethik* (Zürich and Munich: Francke Verlag, 1954); *Gesammelte Werke*, vol. 3, *Vom Umsturz der Werte* (1955); *Gesammelte Werke*, vol. 7, *Vom Wesen der Sympathie* (1957); *Gesammelte Werke*, vol. 5, *Vom Ewigen im Menschen* (1954). Quotations from *Vom Ewigen im Menschen* are from Max Scheler, *On the Eternal in Man*, trans. Bernard Noble (London: SCM Press, 1960), cited in parentheses as *E.*, followed by the page number: e.g., (*E.*, 5).

6. Eric Voegelin, *Order and History*, vol. 3, *Plato and Aristotle* (Baton Rouge: Louisiana State University Press, 1957), 363.

7. In 1934 Voegelin spoke of himself as a "student of Othmar Spann." See Dirk Käsler, *Soziologische Abenteuer: Earle Edward Eubank besucht europäische Soziologen im Sommer 1934* (Opladen: Westdeutscher Verlag, 1985), 142–47.

8. See Othmar Spann, *Gesellschaftslehre* (Leipzig: Quelle und Meyer, 1923), 95–96; *Gesellschaftslehre*, vol. 4, *Othmar Spann Gesamtausgabe*, eds. Walter Heinrich et al. (Graz: Akademische Druck- und Verlagsanstalt, 1969), 136–37.

9. Spann, *Gesellschaftslehre* (1923), 179; *Gesellschaftslehre*, vol. 4, *Gesamtausgabe*, 221.

10. *Der Formalismus*, 406ff.

11. Eric Voegelin, "Das Sollen im System Kants," in *Gesellschaft, Staat und Recht*, ed. Alfred Verdross (Vienna: Verlag Julius Springer, 1931), 136–73, at 137n.

12. Eric Voegelin, "Wechselwirkung und Gezweiung," Doctoral dissertation; Wien, Universität zu Wien. Manuscript and typescript, Eric-Voegelin-Archiv, Geschwister-Scholl-Institut für Politische Wissenschaft der Universität München;

Eric Voegelin Papers, Hoover Institution Archives, Stanford University, Box 51, File 5, p. 2 (roman numeral II in typescript).

13. Eric Voegelin, *Herrschaftslehre*, circa 1930–1932; 146 typed pages; small number of manuscript pages. Eric-Voegelin-Archiv, Geschwister-Scholl-Institut für Politische Wissenschaft der Universität München; Eric Voegelin Papers, Hoover Institution Archives, Stanford University, Box 53, File 5. The first two chapters are incomplete. Chapter One has 22 pages; Chapter Two has 11 pages (numbered 1 to 10a); Chapter Three has 113 pages. Citations from the *Herrschaftslehre* are given in parentheses as *H.*, followed by the chapter number in roman and the page number in arabic numerals: e.g., (*H.*, I. 6). References by Voegelin to St. Augustine's *Confessions* are taken over in the form in which Voegelin cited them; the Latin is replaced with the English translation of William Watts (1631): *St. Augustine's Confessions*, 2 vols., Loeb Classics (Cambridge: Harvard University Press, 1912).

14. *Vom Umsturz der Werte*, 186, 190.

15. *Der Formalismus*, 381–599.

16. *Der Formalismus*, 382.

17. *Der Formalismus*, 395.

18. Voegelin quotes the sentence: "transibo vim meam, qua haereo corpori et vitaliter compagem eius repleo" from X. 7, and adds, after a comma: "gradibus ascendens ad eum, qui fecit me, et venio in campos et lata praetoria memoriae" from X. 8, omitting the beginning of the latter sentence: "transibo ergo et istam naturae meae." This was obviously done to avoid repetition. But, although it does not alter Augustine's meaning, it is not a sentence that Augustine wrote.

19. *Vom Umsturz der Werte*, 187.

20. Compare *Der Formalismus*, 385–93.

21. Eric Voegelin, *Die Politischen Religionen*, 2d ed. (Ausblicke, Stockholm: Berman-Fischer, 1939). My translations follow, with some changes: *Political Religions*, trans. T. J. DiNapoli and E. S. Easterly III, Toronto Studies in Theology 23 (Lewistown, N.Y.: Edwin Mellen Press, 1986). Citations in the text are given in brackets as *PR*, followed by the pages in the English edition: e.g., (*PR.*, 4).

22. Eric Voegelin, "Brief an Alfred Schütz über Edmund Husserl," in *Anamnesis: Zur Theorie der Geschichte und Politik* (Munich: Piper, 1966), 33; this and following quotations are from the English translation, "Letter from Voegelin to Alfred Schütz on Edmund Husserl," in *Faith and Political Philosophy: The Correspondence Between Leo Strauss and Eric Voegelin, 1934–1964*, ed. and trans. Peter Emberley and Barry Cooper (University Park: Pennsylvania State University Press, 1993), 31.

23. "Brief an Alfred Schütz," 35; "Letter from Voegelin to Alfred Schütz," 33.

24. "Brief an Alfred Schütz," 35–36; "Letter from Voegelin to Alfred Schütz," 33–34.

25. "Brief an Alfred Schütz," 36; "Letter from Voegelin to Alfred Schütz," 34.

26. Eric Voegelin Papers, Hoover Institution Archives, Stanford University, Box 72, File 15. The original typescript of the letter, page 20, reads: "Das Dasein Gottes wird also nicht erschlossen, sondern in der Erfahrung der Finitheit des menschlichen Wesens ist das Infinitum gegeben. (Ähnlich in der Problematik,

Schelers Deutung von Sehnsucht und ähnlichen Erlebnissen, in denen ein Negativum positiv gegeben ist). Gott kann nicht im Zweifel sein, denn im Erlebnis des Zweifels und der Imperfektion ist Gott impliziert. In der Grenzerfahrung des Finitseins ist mit dem Diesseits das Jenseits der Grenze mitgegeben." The text I have quoted—without the parenthetical sentence concerning Scheler—is found in *Anamnesis: Zur Theorie der Geschichte und Politik*, 35.

5

Philosophy and Meditation: Notes on Eric Voegelin's View

William M. Thompson

During the 1936–1937 academic year, Eric Voegelin offered a private course at his home in Vienna, which was to introduce students to the theme of philosophical meditation through a study of texts from the Upanishads, Plato, Plotinus, Augustine, Maimonides, Descartes, and others. Philosophical meditation was described as the *"Grundform* of philosophizing." That German term can perhaps be rendered "originary form" in English, indicating that philosophizing not only begins from meditation but that it should be in a continual state of arising from the meditative experience.[1] This "course" indicates that Voegelin wanted to align himself with this tradition of philosophical meditation, and of course he did, as his works amply testify. It also suggests affinities and connections between philosophy as Voegelin understood it and the many religious traditions in which meditative practices are so central. Periodically, in his published writings and correspondence, especially the "latest," he would rather more explicitly and thematically discuss the nature of meditation, and we will make some reference to this as we proceed. But for the most part, he simply practiced the craft, so to speak. His works display what such meditation is. And they evidence something of a spiral effect: each new meditative exercise seems to deepen his proficiency in and view of the craft, and occasionally—for external or personal reasons—he reflects upon the meditative craft itself.

A Meditative Overture

A sustained glance at the preface and introduction found in the first volume of *Order and History* comes first.[2] Together, preface and introduction preside over the entire five volumes of that work and truly serve as an overture to the whole. They are, I think, in some ways an unsurpassed x-ray, taken by Voegelin himself, of what he is about. Interestingly, these pieces, focused on method in a certain sense, are relatively brief. As we know, Voegelin regarded a focus on methodology as a characteristic of positivism: an *angst* over method is a symptom of the breakdown of accepted sources of truth.[3] Appropriately, then, Voegelin wants to keep the focus more on the truth that grounds the method than on the method, which naturally arises from and so is subordinate to the truth. The preface and introduction are modest, then, as befits servants of the truth of the order of history.

The word "meditation" nowhere occurs in either the preface or the introduction.[4] Nonetheless, given what we know of meditation from Voegelin's other writings, this overture to *Order and History* can legitimately be called meditative. As such it is quite disclosive of several key features of a philosophical meditation. Indeed, given the presiding nature of the preface and introduction over Voegelin's major work, if they were not meditative in nature, such would legitimately call into question the view that philosophical meditation is philosophy's *Grundform*.

"Philosophy is the love of being through love of divine Being as the source of its order" (pref., xiv). The word "love" in the context of a philosophical exploration of order indicates that philosophy is rooted in a richer soil than that of a "detached reason." Love has something of an embodied and even conflictual element to it, as all of us can confirm from our own experiences of love in their varied forms. Not surprisingly, then, Voegelin writes of "a struggle for true order" (ix). Philosophy takes place in this real space of the struggle, namely, in history, which accounts for the crucial opening lines of the preface: "The order of history emerges from the history of order" (ix). History, like love, is real, and Voegelin quite deliberately chooses words that underscore this. "Man [sic] . . . is an actor . . . in the drama of being," and the drama is one of "adventure," "decision on the edge of freedom and necessity," with a "disturbing quality" (intro., 1). And because this is history in its reality, there is the fall from truth as well. Philosophy becomes both diagnosis and therapy, "in the modest measure that, in the passionate course of events, is allowed to Philosophy" (pref., xiv).

We are involved in a drama with a "quaternarian structure." A truly realistic view of philosophy strives to be inclusive in its understanding of what constitutes reality. Thus Voegelin writes of the "primordial community of being" whose partners are, on the most general level, "God and man, world and society." Because they form a community, Voegelin will not hesitate to speak of a consubstantiality between the partners, a deeply intimate "experience of participation" within which the partners always find themselves. And this participation is, Voegelin emphasizes, "existence itself"; "no vantage point outside existence" can be had, no "blessed island" of withdrawal (intro., 1).

One might well argue that Voegelin's epistemology is compactly present within this notion of the experience of participation. His is a participationist conception of knowing, which roots knowing immediately in being; there is no splintered subject radically cut off from what is known (though it may try to be so through various postures of alienation). Therefore, although Voegelin had his difficulties with overly objectifying forms of metaphysics, his participationist epistemology made it impossible for him to deny the legitimacy of metaphysics; as there can be no valid separation between knowing and being, so epistemology cannot be divorced from metaphysics, at least in a general sense.[5] His epistemology then is a realism (there is knowledge of being), but one that avoids naivete (since this knowing is known to be situated and participatory); "critical realism" is the typical nomenclature.

What other epistemological features define participatory knowing? It is an experience of "reflective tension" (intro., 2). The phrase is quite significant, for we know that Voegelin's final published work focused on "reflective distance," the basis of that "meditative procedure" appropriate to the true philosopher through which one thematizes the "tensional" elements in existence.[6] "Tension" indicates something of a movement or flow between the partners in the community of being, a mutual tending and attraction. There is no absolute identity between knower and known, but a "space" from within which one can gain a kind of perspective.

Luminosity is a key feature of this reflective tension (intro., 2–5). We are able to identify, or differentiate, partners in the primordial community, and this must mean that there is sufficient "light" to render them apparent and distinct. At the same time, it does not seem to be given to everyone to achieve differentiated understanding of these partners to the same degree. One must practice an "attunement," and such attunement itself ranges along a spectrum from compact (less differentiated) to highly differentiated. This attunement of consciousness is situated *within* the community of being, and so one remains always within a mystery whose outer edges remain obscure, among partners in being who cannot be reduced to mere objects over against subjects. Finally, to complicate matters even more, we tend to fail to attune ourselves adequately; and even when we do attune ourselves appropriately, there remains the mystery of grace. When Voegelin refers to the "greater play of the divine being," he means that we are not fully in control, though this does not mean that we should ignore the call of conscience and its ethical summons of obligation that arises from our partnership in being's community.

The fact that *In Search of Order* introduces the phrase "reflective distance" to thematize meditative procedure strongly indicates the appropriateness of our characterizing the reflective tension of the overture-preface-introduction of *Israel and Revelation* as primordially meditative, at least in Voegelin's lexicon. Also, particularly in *Anamnesis*, meditation in the full sense seems to be a reflective participation within the tensions of existence.[7] If all this be so, then the features noted above would seem to be dimensions of what Voegelin means by philosophical meditation.

In the later *In Search of Order*, Voegelin writes of a "meditative wandering through the paradoxic manifold of tensions," and indeed this describes the very project of *Order and History*.[8] The preface-introduction of volume 1 and the final part of volume 5 in fact form an *inclusio*, framing Voegelin's entire project within a meditative framework. Voegelin's drama of participating with the partners in the community of being is truly a meditative wandering, following former wanderings that broke forth in significant, and especially epochal, experiences of luminosity in human history. (The metaphor of wandering reminds one of the Edwardian Homilies of Anglicanism, which exhort the reader of Holy Writ to "have meditation and contemplation in them; let us ruminate, and, as it were, chew the cud." Going farther back, we are reminded of Anselm's exhortation on the need to meditate on our Redeemer. "Meditate upon [salvation], delight in the contemplation of it. . . . Chew by thinking, suck by understanding, swallow by loving and rejoicing.")[9] Voegelin's meditative wandering interrogates the meditative wandering of humanity in an epic-like way in *Order and History*, and appropriately he returns at its end to a (re)thematization, through a philosopher's "reflective distance," of the meditative method that spontaneously emerged as philosophers and saints attuned themselves to their partnership in being.

Meditation Analogically Understood, and Pseudo-Meditation

It requires only a mild alertness to notice, as one reads through Voegelin's works, that he uses the term "meditation" as a complex symbol for a variety of practices. The various uses share some common meanings, but there are differences among them as well. And one has the sense that Voegelin himself has regularly both discovered new dimensions of the matter and somewhat revised earlier views of the same. He is, in other words, very much an analogical thinker, and so meditation functions as an analogous term. Our treatment above illustrates a rather broad understanding of meditation: meditation as participative knowing, in which, through luminosity and attunement, the partners in the community of being are varyingly differentiated through language symbols. The stress falls upon the reality of participation, itself an enormously crucial symbol in the Voegelinian corpus. One can sense, in moving through *Order and*

History, meditative experience in action—in this broad sense—in all the major sages and saints, as well as in Voegelin's own meditative wandering through the traces left by history.

In this broad sense, meditation is a way of submitting oneself to the challenges posed by sharing in the community of being. It is not spectatorship, but participation, and so engagement, vulnerability, and commitment. The knower who imagines himself or herself to be detached monologues, and so remains unchallenged by partnership. The meditator dialogues, truly submitting himself or herself to the *logia* of humanity's conversation. From this perspective, the borders between meditation and dialogue blur.[10] This may be surprising to some, for I have noticed that certain people quickly think of esoteric introspection and navel-gazing when they hear the word "meditation." This is not partnership but isolation, a flight from the in-between experience of existence, the middle space of Plato's *metaxy*. Interestingly, the very word "meditation" seems related in its Indo-European roots to *me*, which seems to form the root of *medhi*, the word of "between/middle."[11]

The fact that meditation can degenerate into a pseudo-meditative introspection indicates that a certain asceticism or set of practices is required for its proper unfolding. In wandering, some people get lost.[12] The problem becomes one of how to maximize one's chances of not getting lost. There is a "way" that leads somewhere, and then there is a hopeless maze. Not straying from the right way is already implied in the word "attunement." Everyone who attempts to pay attention to nearly anything knows that such exacts its price. A discipline is necessarily involved in attention and attunement, even if the process in its greater aspect is the mystery of being issuing an appeal or even, as the divine ground, drawing us forward in grace. In this regard, Voegelin's brief comment in *The Ecumenic Age* that "precautions of meditative practice" are necessary in order to avoid the dangers of doctrinization seems especially pertinent. The implication of the passage is that such practices keep one inserted "in the experiential Metaxy."[13] Unfortunately the observation is one that needs to be elucidated by all the earlier work in *Order and History* on what immersion in the *metaxy* means.

Voegelin also has his difficulties with methodological obsessions, as we have noted. He refuses to reduce life to a simple list of axioms or techniques. Just as people with "spiritual sensitiveness" who can open their souls to God and submit to the authority of such experiences "do not grow on trees,"[14] so meditators who know by participation do not grow on trees either. And even more emphatically, there are no magic seeds through which we can produce an orchard of meditating seedlings. Thus, there is a set of practices appropriate to meditation, surely; but Voegelin is cautious about identifying meditation too closely with the practices themselves, since even knowledge of meditative practice can degenerate into doctrinization in the negative sense.

Readers of Voegelin will likely bring forth candidates for practices appropriate to meditation, however, and I would suggest that what Voegelin has to say about virtues is especially (though not exclusively) relevant. "Virtues," like "meditation," ought to be treated as an analogous term, as it refers to varied sets of notions in classical philosophy, in Christian theology, and indeed throughout the world's religious traditions. Voegelin, I think, would consider the decisive noetic differentiation of the virtues to be found in the classical Greek and Roman writings. In any case, the virtues, as described within a specific tradition or in a more encompassing way, involve sets of practices that are not mere mindless and soulless techniques. If you will, the virtues are the human "powers" (Latin: *virtus*) of the community of being that enable humans to be members of a community. As those powers are actualized and integrated they become habits of acting and living.[15]

Aristotle's *spoudaios* is perhaps Voegelin's principal representative of the person who is virtuous because of his or her degree of "permeability" for the movement of being."[16] The attractive word "permeability" suggests the manner in which God, world, and society indwell the self on ever deeper levels, enabling the self in turn to indwell God, world, and society. "Indwelling" is another way of speaking of meditative participation, underscoring the aspect of an augmenting, or spiraling, interiorization (which is the development of "habit"). Here, the word "meditative" needs the balance of the term "participation" to bring out the action dimension involved in meditative wandering. There are varied virtues appropriate to this active indwelling, and the master virtues (Voegelin calls them "existential virtues") keep the whole of participation in fruitful tension and balance.[17] The virtues explored by the classical tradition are enriched by those of the Jewish and Christian traditions, the theological virtues of faith, hope, and charity bringing a certain purification and fundamental guidance to the classical life of virtues. Faith and hope, not unknown to Heraclitus, and love, known surely to Plato, for example, are enriched by the *fides caritate formata* of Christianity.[18]

Meditators are people of virtue, then, and through that virtue they avoid derailments into pseudo-meditation. A faithful and hopeful attunement to the community of being nourishes the responsive love already aroused by the loving appeal of being itself. And a life deeply developed in these virtues nourishes the maturity of judgment needed for meditative discernment.

Family Terms

A number of terms with meaningful connections to meditation regularly surface throughout the Voegelinian corpus. It will be useful to examine a few of these. Readers might reasonably wonder what nuance the term "contemplation," which one encounters in Voegelin's studies of Plato and Aristotle, brings to the meditation complex. Contemplation is a dimension of the *paideia*, or educational art, fostered by the *Republic* (518b), a dimension that Voegelin views as "intimately connected" with the *periagoge* (the "turning around" of the soul) and the vision of the Agathon (the Good).[19] Through such *paideia*, one eventually "turns around" and comes to an awareness of the Good. In this context, contemplation seems to mean a gradual ascent toward the Agathon through a discipline of virtuous study of mathematics and dialectics.

Opsis, or the vision of the Agathon, is one of the key results of this experience that "forms the soul through an experience of transcendence."[20] In one study, Voegelin defines the *opsis* as "Plato's technical term for the experiential process in which the order of reality is seen, becomes reflectively known, and finds its appropriate language symbols." In this sense, it is a comprehensive process, a sort of intuition-becoming-differentiated "vision of the Whole of reality."[21] And for our purposes it is significant that he explicitly links vision with meditation. "The philosopher's meditation can operate only within the comprehensive vision and make it self-reflectively luminous for man's existence in tension toward the Beyond."[22] In a wide sense (referring chiefly to *Republic* 507–9, and *Timaeus* 47), vision is equivalent to, or at least very close to, the basic experience of luminous attunement that arises from the process of participation in the quaternarian structure of existence. Vision itself, however, is not precisely meditation; as Voegelin states, the latter occurs within the former.

"Vision" seems to symbolize more emphatically the wholeness of the reality within which we participate, whereas "meditation" seems to emphasize the moments of differentiation or analysis within the visionary whole. If meditation, in its "chewing," wanders so far from the whole that it attempts to split reality into separated objects over against onlooking subjects, then it has severed itself from a proper understanding of its habitat within the more comprehensive reality of the vision. The whole admits of meditative differentiation, but not at the cost of a schism between the partners in being.

Contemplation (*theoria*), thinking now of its meaning in Plato especially,[23] seems so closely associated with vision that it virtually becomes its noetic companion. The contemplative is the visionary, the one attuned to the comprehensive whole of reality. He or she "sees" the whole, even while engaging in an inner exegesis of its dimensions through meditation from time to time. Not surprisingly, then, something of a technical distinction between contemplation and meditation can emerge, although the two terms can be used interchangeably as well. If this somewhat technical

distinction between the two is being employed, one will see contemplation described as more unitary and transanalytic, while meditation is
thought of as more discursive and analytic.[24] In this sense, if you will,
contemplation features attunement to the *community* of being, while
meditation features attunement to the *partners* in the community of
being. In the Christian orbit, the divine Ground is usually especially fea-
tured as the supporting matrix of the other mutual but nonequal partners.
Voegelin is aware of these technical distinctions. Still, I have the impression that he also uses the symbol of meditation in a more comprehensive
way to embrace, at a minimum, the experience of luminosity and attunement in the midst of the community of being by way of vision, contemplation, reason, and the virtuous life.

The Letter to Alfred Schütz on Edmund Husserl

The letter to Alfred Schütz on Edmund Husserl, dating back to 1943,
affords us an opportunity to gain a sense of Voegelin's early view of meditation, and perhaps even of the view somewhat set forth in the 1936–1937
course he offered. It may also amplify or nuance dimensions of the question we have not yet adequately explored. Its original setting in the German edition of *Anamnesis* (1966) indicates that Voegelin regarded its contents as fundamental to his own growing understanding of philosophy.[25]
It is one of the few pieces in which Voegelin lingers, in a thematic way,
over some of the more technical aspects of our theme.

The context is a discussion of Husserl's claim that Descartes's *Meditations* is (in Voegelin's words) "an imperfect form of the phenomenological
reduction, the goal of which is an epoche [bracketing] of the world content in order to reconstitute the world as objective from the egological
sphere."[26] Voegelin agrees with Husserl's view that the goal of Descartes
is to find the epistemological foundation of the world's objectivity; and
he further agrees that Descartes was only partially successful in this effort. He disagrees, however, with Husserl's contention that the Cartesian
Meditations carries only epistemological significance, its religious-theo-
logical dimension carrying no lasting significance.

Voegelin places the Cartesian *Meditations* within the tradition of Christian meditation of the Augustinian type. The late medieval *Cloud of Unknowing* is a further example. On the most basic level, he writes, "[t]he
goal of the meditation is the gradual elimination of the world content,
from the bodily world to the animate, in order to attain the point of
transcendence, in which the soul can, in Augustinian language, turn itself
in the *intentio* toward God." Here it is primarily a biographical experi-

ence, and when it is expressed in verbal form, it "gives rise to the literary form of the meditation." The literary form in Descartes's book is a "literary sediment" of this kind, although only a sediment, for there is a difference. Descartes stands at that point "in the history of the spirit where he *wants* to know the world," and so the traditional Christian theme of the *contemptus mundi* is eliminated. Voegelin interprets the latter as meaning that the Christian meditator, in meditation, "assures himself, if not of the unreality, at least of the irrelevance of the world content." If you want, the reality of the world is not in dispute for the traditional Christian meditator, and so, unlike Descartes, he or she is not in search of a fundamental foundation on the basis of which its reality can be established.[27]

The Christian meditator, Voegelin seems to say, is becoming aware "in a mystical sense of transcendence in the Ground."[28] Earlier in the letter he had interpreted the *contemptus mundi* as meaning that the Christian is not concerned with the world; later he clarifies that the Augustinian *intentio* brings simultaneously a certainty of the self and of God. Conviction about the irrelevance of the world, at least on Voegelin's interpretation of the Augustinian form of meditation, is not aimed at the denial or annihilation of the self (and presumably its world). Nevertheless, in the Augustinian form of meditation as interpreted by Voegelin, it seems to me that the more ample notion of philosophical meditation as a wandering among the partners in the community of being is somewhat restricted in its focus to the transcendent Ground, and perhaps to the self secondarily. On the other hand, Descartes is perhaps too fascinated by the self and the world among the partners in the primordial community.

Voegelin's interest in Augustine directs us to the nonequality among the partners in the community of being. The Ground (God), as ground, is the all-encompassing matrix, it would seem. As he would come to express it in the overture-preface-introduction of *Israel and Revelation*, once the transcendence of the divine partner in the community of being is differentiated, matters change enormously, causing a rethinking of the whole. Augustine is concentrated upon the transcendent divine Ground, seeking to realign his understanding of the other partners in the light of that Ground. This is not easy to do, and again we are back with the theme of a meditative wandering that can get lost, either by an absorption in one/some of the partners in the community of being, or by a lack of attunement to one/some of them. Various people variously estimate Augustine's success in this matter, and Voegelin seems inclined to argue that he insufficiently elaborated the dimensions of world and society.[29] Voegelin was greatly in Augustine's debt, we know, but it seems that he has integrated the saint's thought into a larger and more inclusive view of meditation.[30]

Meditative Forms

Meditations of the Augustinian type suggest the need to introduce distinctions in our study of meditation. The fact that Voegelin speaks of an "Augustinian type" rather than simply of a "Christian type" appears deliberate, for there are any number of types within the Christian tradition. Voegelin's coupling of the Augustinian form with the *Cloud of Unknowing* gives one the impression that he is thinking of a rather more "apophatic" style of meditation. One strives to attend to the transcendent ground, gradually eliminating or "bracketing" finite features of existence in the process. Such would be to enter the "cloud of unknowing," or that which is beyond knowing because it is beyond the finite. Augustine illustrates this when he exclaims that, when he loves his God, such is "[n]ot material beauty or beauty of a temporal order; not the brilliance of earthly light, so welcome to our eyes; not the sweet melody of harmony and song; not the fragrance of flowers, perfumes, and spices; not manna or honey; not limbs such as the body delights to embrace."[31] On the other hand, Christianity could never countenance a pure apophaticism, for it proclaims the incarnation of God in and as a human being. From an "incarnational" perspective, the finite material of this world is not an obstacle to God's presence, except in its sinful distortion. In and through Jesus and Jesus' relation with the world, God's presence is mediated to humanity. Here the finite becomes the medium of the Infinite. "Kataphatic" styles of meditation, then, illustrate this more incarnational aspect of Christianity. When Augustine writes that he "was not humble enough to conceive of the humble Jesus Christ as [his] God," he is indicating that he had been too enchanted by a pure apophaticism. But Christ "[f]rom the clay of which we are made . . . built for himself a lowly house in this world below, so that by this means he might cause those who were to be made subject to him to abandon themselves and come over to his side."[32]

Matters can become rather complex in Christianity, in fact, for even when Christian meditators are drawn toward the more apophatic style, there can never be a bracketing of Jesus Christ, who always remains the incarnate mediator of God's grace. Finite concepts and gestures, for example, may be somewhat bracketed, but somehow, even in the stillness and silence, the Christian believes that the incarnate Savior is present. Teresa of Avila is a fascinating case in point, for at one time she had thought of meditations on the humanity of Jesus as a sort of obstacle to Christian perfection, but in time she came to see that this was contradictory to the Incarnation. Though she still thought it was possible to practice a modified form of apophaticism, she averred that, even in the contemplative silence, "a person walks continually in an admirable way with Christ, our Lord, in whom the divine and the human are joined and who is always that person's companion."³³ Indeed, given God's transcendence, there will always be need for some element of apophaticism in Christianity, but it will be a mixed kind, respectful of the finite as a medium of the Infinite.³⁴

Voegelin does not seem to concern himself with these variations within the Christian orbit to any great extent. Still, his mentioning of the Augustinian type indicates that he is aware of a certain variety.³⁵ I have the impression that he is more concerned with integrating Christian and other religious forms of meditation into his larger project of a philosophy of order. Hence, it is the philosophical form of meditation with which he is most concerned.

It might be useful for us to make some connections at this point with Voegelin's later categories of the "pneumatic" and "noetic" differentiations. Philosophical meditation might appropriately be aligned with the noetic differentiation. *Noesis*, in the classical sense, is a meditative wandering among the poles of human existence, and in fact the noetic differentiation is able to occur when the self achieves a differentiated awareness of itself as the site of the meditative experience. A Jewish, Christian, and Islamic meditation might appropriately be aligned with the pneumatic differentiation. Here the stress falls upon the differentiation of, and attunement to, the transcendent ground and the ground's loving offer in grace. Of course, the Christian strives for attunement to the divine ground become incarnate, and so there would seem to be a certain pressure to keep the focus upon a God who is incarnately united with the other partners in being; and while Jewish and Islamic meditations are similar, I would think they place less stress upon the incarnational dimensions.³⁶ Voegelin's caveat that the noetic and pneumatic differentiations demarcate emphases of focus regarding the effort of attunement within the one community of being, rather than separate types of experience, should be kept in mind, however, lest we overdraw the distinctions.

John Carmody and Denise Lardner Carmody, building upon Voegelin, have suggested that the key religious figure for Judaism, Christianity, and Islam is the prophet. These religious traditions, then, are appropriately understood to be representative of the pneumatic differentiation in various ways, for the prophet is the one who speaks the word of revelation coming from the world-transcendent God. The sage, on the other hand, would be the representative figure for Taoism, Confucianism, and Hinduism in many ways. Professors Carmody choose the sage for the representative figure because here the stress falls upon forms of noesis in search of wisdom, ranging from the very practical noesis of Confucianism to the more esoteric forms encountered in the Upanishads and in Taoism. Again, just as the noetic and pneumatic differentiations are not separate types of experience but overlap, the same is true for the various religions. We may speak of religions of revelation (the prophetic) and religions of wisdom (those of the sage), but in fact each is a mixed genre, although surely the decisive norm is focused upon either revelation or "wisdom" by religious adherents. This form of classification helpfully builds upon *The Ecumenic Age*, which indicates the analogies between Chinese thought and the noetic differentiation of the classical philosophers. Interestingly, the Upanishadic dialogues are characterized as something of an incomplete noetic and pneumatic form, straddling both.[37] If we follow these leads, then, we would need to align pneumatic forms of meditation with the prophetic types of religion, and noetic meditative forms with the religions of wisdom, all the while allowing for overlap.

Finally, the "reflective distance" of the philosopher, with which Voegelin ends his last volume of *Order and History*, might be said to represent the philosophical form of meditation in its most comprehensive sense. To return to our earlier image, reflective distance is a heightened state of awareness—an x-ray—of the features of the process of participation in reality. It is a sort of looking back upon—second level reflection on—the features of such participation. Plato referred to this, somewhat compactly, as *anamnesis*, Voegelin says.[38] It is a meditative experience in an intensified form, for the reflectively distant philosopher attempts to "remember" features of reality, to resist the temptation to "forget" aspects for various reasons, and to become aware of the paradox of the complementary modes of intentionality and luminosity present within participation. Voegelin chooses the word "distance" to highlight the fact that the philosopher cannot attain total knowledge of the process of reality. True philosophical knowledge is always partial, if valid. There is not a simple "identity" (against German identity philosophy) between what one knows and the to-be-known.[39] Participation, in other words, presupposes a certain distance; identity would abolish the flow of participation.

Whether we are speaking of a pneumatic meditation or a noetic, in either case through the philosopher's reflective distance we become aware of ("remember") basic features applicable to both.[40] We remember the reality of the community of being within which we participate. We are aware, as well, both from our own personal experiences and from our study of the history of the search for order, that we can lapse into "imaginative oblivion" of the features of reality. But oblivion also presupposes a certain remembrance. "An imaginative resister may be even more acutely aware of the existential reality he resists than a complacent believer and conformer, as Saint Augustine on occasion observed; he may remember too well what he wants to forget."[41] We are aware, further, of other features involved in our participation in reality, especially our consciousness and language finding expression through both intentionality-concepts and luminosity-symbols. It is a characteristic of this heightened form of awareness—Voegelin calls reflective distance a "third dimension of consciousness," besides intentionality and luminosity—to have a certain critical modesty. It knows that it cannot be exhaustive, and it knows that any insights it reaches will require "supplemental meditations."[42]

Some Examples

Much of Voegelin's work is an extended example of meditative wandering, whether pneumatic or noetic, and/or that of the philosopher in reflective distance. He seeks to participate in the experiences of participation in reality of the saints and sages, for only through such participation can one really share in the luminosity and attunement of such events. To approach the matter nonmeditatively is really not to approach the matter at all. In other words, it is to refuse to submit oneself to the authority of such experiences, a nonsurrender to reality's appeal. It is *anoia*, a sort of deliberate oblivion.[43] At the same time, such participation by Voegelin is a new act of meditative wandering itself. It is not a simple repetition of the past, but a participation in and carrying forward of the past. At the beginning of his major work, he had declared that the "intelligible structure of history [is] . . . a reality to be discerned retrospectively in a flow of events that extends, through the present of the observer, indefinitely into the future."[44] The meditator that is Voegelin is in history's flow, and only through history may he participate. History's flow is not an obstacle to participation but its means. Participation in the community of being is also not simply horizontal, extending "backward" and "forward" into past and future, but vertical, extending to the "beginning" and the "beyond" in a transtemporal sense, since it is a participation in the divine ground. History's flow, grounded in God, connects us with the whole past and opens us to the future, connecting us with all creatures of all times and their Creator. We can sense this interplay of past, present, and future in Voegelin's own studies, which typically analyze the epochal experiences of meditation in history and yet at the same time display his own, somewhat new and somewhat differently differentiated, experience of the matter. The way, for example, in which he more fully differentiates Plato's own profound philosophy of *anamnesis* is a case in point. Meditation, in other words, is an engagement in reality, rather than simply a spectator's look at reality. As such, it is not a pretended stasis in history's flow, but a positive movement of the flow, hoping to contribute however modestly to history's order, and to diminishing its disorder.

In Search of Order is a concentrated illustration of these matters. It is something like the play within the play of *Hamlet*. That play within the

play is an occasion for Shakespeare to display his own artistic self-con-
sciousness, articulating the poetics of drama. Similarly, *In Search of Order*
is a concentrated expression of the poetics of *Order and History*. It is the
drama within the drama of humanity's quest for order, a sustained occasion on which Voegelin self-consciously thematizes his meditative poetics.
The volume opens with a "confession" of his own participation in the
flow of history, and indeed, within the community of being. As he starts
his volume, Voegelin asks himself, "Where does the beginning begin?"
and comes—through a wandering meditation from that interrogative sentence to the paragraph that frames it, and then on to the whole encounter
of reader and text embedded within the dialogue of humanity—to the
conclusion that the beginning is in the middle of reality.[45] And we remember that the middle is the space of meditation, the in-between kind of
thinking. Voegelin's own philosophical meditation is a part of the larger
meditation of humanity, a meditation that always finds expression in
some form of story, whose narrative speaks the language of things and
whose event more comprehensively is the It-reality becoming luminous
for its own meaning.

The many stories told and written by humans can lead to the problems
of relativism or nihilism, Voegelin knows.[46] This is a prescient observation, manifesting an awareness of extreme tendencies now fully broken
out in some forms of postmodernism. Some allege that if there are so
many different stories, there must only be different perspectives, but no
truth; and others allege that, since there is no truth, we should simply
accept a meaningless universe. Voegelin's own meditation keeps him "in
the middle," but we can sense his view that it can be difficult to remain
there, given the climate of opinion. Radical historicists and nihilists seem
to remain on the level of thing-reality, seeing subjects always in relation
to objects, and somehow missing or avoiding the paradoxic fact of the
middle as a site bounded by a beginning and a beyond that cannot be out-
comprehended. The middle is the site where the partners in being become
luminous but never fully transparent, and it presupposes a beginning and
a beyond. We learn that there is a beginning and even a beyond, but they
can be known only from the middle. This is paradoxic, which is to say
that it is humble, in the sense of *humus*, the sort of knowledge that comes
from having feet planted firmly on the ground. Acceptance of this paradox requires a willingness to live with the Mystery.

Apparently the historicist and the nihilist want something less
dense—no "cloud of unknowing" for them. Although that is what they
want, they cannot have it, reality would seem to say. But no matter, they
will not meditatively wander in the midst of reality, hence the subtle
forms of retreat into the "second realities" of a substitute world.[47] Radical
historicism is an ideology legitimating this retreat; nihilism, a drug allow-

ing us to forget it. In either case, the meditation has wandered in such a way that it has become lost. This, of course, makes for great disorder in the community of being, because it mutilates that community in various ways. If the melody of *In Search of Order* is a careful attention to humanity's meditation within the midst of that community, and to Voegelin's participation within that as well, its countermelody is a stubborn attention to the pseudo-meditations of a straying humanity. And Voegelin does not think he is above the possible fall into pseudo-meditation himself.[48]

As we have it, *In Search of Order* is framed between the account in Genesis of the beginning and Plato's own articulation of the mystery of the beyond as it finds expression in the *Timaeus*. Between these, we encounter representative examples of either straying too far from the "in-between" of the beginning and the beyond, or various differentiations, more or less compact, of that middle space. In other words, Voegelin's own meditation is situated within the larger human meditation, participating within it, made possible by it, and prolonging it into a somewhat more differentiated articulation of Plato's *anamnesis* by way of "reflective distance." If you will, Voegelin seeks to remember, rather than to forget, this site of the middle from which he comes along with the rest of humanity. He attends to the symbols through which epochal meditators have imagined and articulated various dimensions of this middle, and, guided and enriched by them, he imaginatively articulates his philosopher's reflective distance.

Voegelin writes, "The authors of Genesis 1 . . . were conscious of beginning an act of participation in the mysterious Beginning of the It," and by pneumatically differentiating the Beginning they "revealed the presence of its consciousness in the compact language of earlier mythospeculations on the Beginning."[49] Voegelin had turned to these authors in an effort to clarify his own beginning of *In Search of Order*. In Genesis we find articulated what Voegelin the meditator has learned repeatedly throughout *Order and History*: meditations are already bounded by a beginning. But "[w]hile in the Biblical story the structure of consciousness remains in the background, it moves into the foreground of exploration in the 'philosopher's' analysis" such as we find it, for example, in Plato.[50] Plato knows of a beginning as well, but he seems to explore more emphatically the questing self, and the site of the questing self, in his movement between a beginning and a beyond. Voegelin finds, especially with Plato's help, that meditations are bounded also by a beyond. He also finds many of the language symbols needed for articulating features of this middle site of consciousness where meditation occurs. The final section of *In Search of Order* (91–107) is, in fact, a complex following—and very meditative in the sense of very "wandering" and very participative—of how Plato, in the *Timaeus*, through a "mutual illumination of symbols," is able to articulate the dimensions of thing-reality and It-reality. Plato, in fact, evidences sufficient reflective distance to be able to thematize, through the symbol of *anamnesis*, the third dimension of consciousness, which Voegelin, through his own participation in Plato's meditation, has differentiated with perhaps somewhat greater clarity.[51] Such is what is meant by meditations within meditations.

Why the New Science of Politics Is New

With a somewhat deliberate irony, Voegelin wrote of the "new science of politics." This was ironical, because what was "new" about it, in contrast to the allegedly new modern science of politics, was that it was old, in the sense that it was a restoration in many ways of the kind of science articulated by Plato and Aristotle, although enriched by revelation. Voegelin was not overly concerned that the restoration would turn into a nostalgic flight into the past of the Classical Age, once one came to understand what the great classical thinkers meant by such science. Typically, modern science claimed to be detached, coolly impersonal, and so rendering objective judgments. It knew that to accomplish this, much would have to be considered unscientific, namely, the entire realms of morality, metaphysics, religion, and theology. Allegedly, these were the realms of the subjective and the personal, and certainly not realms of truly scientific truth. It was not long before what was considered merely subjective collapsed into a mass of conflicting personal opinions, followed by extreme forms of relativism and historicism, on the one hand, and indifference and nihilism on the other.

Voegelin's "new science" did not claim to be impersonal, but instead highly personal and even interpersonal; not detached, but intensively committed; not cool but rather more passionately warm, like the writings of the great sages and saints. There are dangers here, surely. And these dangers are why virtue and such knowledge or science are so closely interconnected—although one might stumble into a bit of information by luck, and we must leave room for the surprising irruptions of grace in history.[52] It would seem that as truly formative knowledge takes hold, it requires the life of the virtues for its unfolding. There is a kind of asceticism demanded in the acquiring of truly personal and interpersonal knowledge. But only through such knowing can the depths of the person, and his or her relations to other persons within a cosmos permeated by the divine Ground, become luminous. Such personal, participatory knowing is a key dimension of what is pointed to by the age-old word "meditation."

It is not by accident that the Jewish and Christian traditions have highly developed forms of meditation, for it was in those traditions that the personally loving dimension of the divine Ground was revealed. A divine Ground that is personal, in a peerless if analogical sense, requires a personal, engaged form of knowing. And such is what meditative forms of knowing claim to be. One might even say that the eventual formulation of the doctrines of the Incarnation and the Trinity were a result of the Christian Church's prolonged meditation on the personal reality of God. Knowing God as not simply remote Ground or source (Creator-Father), but as also personally a Lover (Son Jesus) who is also a Beloved (Spirit) is something of the fruit of meditative prayer. For in prayer we are lifted up *toward* God (the Creator-Father); and yet prayer presupposes that we somehow *know* or are in communication with this God (incarnate Son); and even more, prayer seems to be *within us* (Holy Spirit) as the power moving us in our aspirations (we are beloved because of the Beloved).[53] If you will, because God is a reality of mutual engagement (triune) who engages us, we are called to respond in an "engaged" form of knowing—namely, meditation. Voegelin did not often write of the Trinity, but one of his rather fine observations on it falls within one of his most sustained examples of meditation, an example that includes significant reflections about the nature of meditation.[54]

But under our finite and sinful conditions, such forms of knowing also require discipline and grace if they are to succeed. If love is truly to bring us knowledge and not simply blind passion, it must undergo the purifying fires of the dark night known equivalently by all the saints and mystics, and known analogically by the mystic-philosophers. Further, when we are speaking of the world-transcendent God, even when the Holy One has disclosed the divine self in the world and in the Incarnation, meditation must always take the form of prayer, a sort of "chewing" form of prayer, as the loving attractiveness of the Ground draws us into a sustained attentiveness and exploration. Adoration of the Mystery, thanksgiving for our being invited into knowing, sorrow for our refusals to enter as fully as we might into the relationship, and a growing sense of intercessory concern as we lovingly enter into the divine Mystery's relation to all creation of all times—all of these "existential" theological virtues ought to more and more characterize and surround our meditation.

Voegelin has generalized his studies beyond the Jewish and Christian traditions to a philosophy of order. His work on meditation, then, is integrated into this larger project and needs to be appreciated as such. Those of us who are greatly interested in the religious and theological dimensions thereof need to grapple with its wider, analogical aspects. The philosophical meditation, as Voegelin articulates it, helps the religious and theological scholar to avoid a too narrow fascination for only one or several of the partners in the community of being. On the other hand, the pneumatic form of meditation challenges the philosopher to acknowledge the primacy of the divine Ground.

Notes

1. See "Editors' Introduction," *The Collected Works of Eric Voegelin*, vol. 28, *What Is History? And Other Late Unpublished Writings*, ed. Thomas A. Hollweck and Paul Caringella (Baton Rouge: Louisiana State University Press, 1990), xxvii–xxviii, n19.

2. Eric Voegelin, *Order and History*, vol. 1, *Israel and Revelation* (Baton Rouge: Louisiana State University Press, 1956), ix-xiv, 1–11.

3. See Eric Voegelin, *The New Science of Politics: An Introduction* (Chicago: University of Chicago Press, 1952), 10–11.

4. So far as I can tell, the first and only *explicit* reference to meditation in volume 1 occurs when Voegelin refers to "pieces of a meditative nature" in Isaiah 40–55; see *Israel and Revelation*, 494. In volume 2, Voegelin refers to a meditative prayer of Solon; see *Order and History*, vol. 2, *The World of the Polis* (Baton Rouge: Louisiana State University Press, 1957), 196, 202. In *Order and History*, vol. 3, *Plato and Aristotle* (Baton Rouge: Louisiana State University Press, 1957), the language shifts to that of contemplation. In *Order and History*, vol. 4, *The Ecumenic Age* (Baton Rouge: Louisiana State University Press, 1974), see pages 8 and 56. For *Order and History*, vol. 5, *In Search of Order* (Baton Rouge: Louisiana State University Press, 1987), see the latter part of this essay.

5. See Gerald McCool, *The Neo-Thomists* (Milwaukee: Marquette University Press, 1994), 43ff, for helpful observations on the relation between metaphysics and epistemology.

6. *In Search of Order*, 48ff.

7. See Eric Voegelin, *Anamnesis*, ed. and trans. Gerhart Niemeyer (Notre Dame: University of Notre Dame Press, 1978), 14, 28–29, 32, 36, 96, 152, 175; see also note 33 below.

8. *In Search of Order*, 100.

9. See "The Edwardian Homilies" (1547), in *Creeds of the Churches: A Reader in Christian Doctrine from the Bible to the Present*, 3d ed., ed. John H. Leith (Louisville: John Knox Press, 1982), 239; and St. Anselm, "Meditation on Human Redemption," in *The Prayers and Meditations of Saint Anselm, with the Proslogion*, Penguin Classics edition, trans. Benedicta Ward (New York: Penguin Books, 1973), 230. Meditation in the biblical sense is a form of murmuring (like doves cooing), ruminating (chewing the cud), and so on. See Jos 1:8; Ps 1:2; Lk 2:19. On this, see, for example, Johannes B. Bauer, "Meditation," in *Sacramentum Verbi: An Encyclopedia of Biblical Theology*, vol. 2, ed. idem (New York: Herder and Herder, 1979), 573–74; and *Dictionnaire de spiritualité*, vols. 10 and 2/2, ed. M. Viller (Paris: Beauchesne, 1980 and 1953), s.vv. "Méditation" and "Contemplation." Eugene Webb, *Eric Voegelin: Philosopher of History* (Seattle: University of Washington Press, 1981), chap. 1, is helpful on meditation's influence on Voegelin; see esp. page 30 for Webb's summary of the matter.

10. See *Plato and Aristotle*, 11–12; *The Ecumenic Age*, 186.

11. See James T. Shipley, *The Origins of English Words: A Discursive Dictionary of Indo-European Roots* (Baltimore: Johns Hopkins University Press, 1984), s.vv. *"me IV," "med,"* and *"medhi."*

12. An example I have come across in Voegelin's writings is Comte, whose "meditation" becomes the means by which Comte's "unquestionable" intuition or vision of positivism is achieved; see Eric Voegelin, *From Enlightenment to Revolution*, ed. John H. Hallowell (Durham, N.C.: Duke University Press, 1975), 146–61, esp. 150.

13. *The Ecumenic Age*, 56.

14. *Israel and Revelation*, 195.

15. See *The World of the Polis*, 184–202.

16. *Anamnesis*, 65.

17. See *Anamnesis*, 65ff, where Voegelin refers to justice and *phronesis* as existential virtues. The latter "is the virtue of correct action and, at the same time, the virtue of right speech about action" (65). See also *Plato and Aristotle*, 108ff, 167ff, 297. "Indwelling" is an important notion, with biblical resonances, for Michael Polanyi; see Francis Martin, *The Feminist Question: Feminist Theology in the Light of the Christian Tradition* (Grand Rapids, Mich.: Wm. B. Eerdmans, 1994), 265–68, 289–92.

18. On Heraclitus, see *The World of the Polis*, 228; on love in Plato, see *Plato and Aristotle*, 13ff; on the *fides caritate formata* in this context, see *Plato and Aristotle*, 364.

19. *Plato and Aristotle*, 115–16. Contemplation is also central to the Aristotelian *bios theoretikos* (see *Plato and Aristotle*, 304–14), which Voegelin interprets as "the intellectualized counterpart to the Platonic vision of the Agathon which, in beholding the Idea, transforms the soul and lets it partake of the order of the Idea" (306).

20. *Plato and Aristotle*, 112; see 112–17, esp. 115.

21. "The Beginning and the Beyond: A Meditation on Truth," in *What Is History?*, 229, 232.

22. "The Beginning and the Beyond," 227.

23. See *Republic* 517d, and Voegelin's reference thereto in *Plato and Aristotle*, 116.

24. See, for example, chapter 13 of Teresa of Avila's *Life*.

25. The letter (dated September 17–20, 1943) was not reprinted in the American edition of *Anamnesis*. An English translation appears in *Faith and Political Philosophy: The Correspondence Between Leo Strauss and Eric Voegelin, 1934–1964*, ed. and trans. Peter Emberley and Barry Cooper (University Park: Pennsylvania State University Press, 1993), 19–34.

26. *Faith and Political Philosophy*, 30.

27. *Faith and Political Philosophy*, 31–32. In this letter, Voegelin used terms like "Archimedean point" and Plato's "idealist epistemology" (32), which he would later abandon as inadequate. See *Anamnesis*, 153: "There is no Archimedean point from which participation itself could be seen as an object."

28. *Faith and Political Philosophy*, 33.

29. See *The New Science of Politics*, 109ff.

30. For an interpretation of how Ignatius Loyola attempted to achieve an integration of the partners in the primordial community without abandoning a legitimate sense of the *fuga saeculi*, see Karl Rahner, "The Ignatian Mysticism of Joy in the World," *Theological Investigations*, vol. 3, trans. Karl-H. and Boniface Kruger (Baltimore: Helicon Press, 1967), 277–93.

31. Saint Augustine, *Confessions*, Penguin Classics edition, trans. R. S. Pine-Coffin (Baltimore: Penguin Books, 1961), X:6, 211. A helpful introduction to meditative styles is Peter Toon, *Meditating as a Christian: Waiting Upon God* (London: Collins, 1991).

32. *Confessions*, VII:18, 152. See *In Search of Order*, 79, for a reference by Voegelin to the apophatic and the kataphatic.

33. Teresa of Avila, *The Interior Castle*, Classics of Western Spirituality, trans. Kieran Kavanaugh and Otilio Rodriguez (New York: Paulist Press, 1979), 6:7:9, 147. In the tradition of the French School of Spirituality, there is a form of "adhering to Christ" that is not necessarily discursive, but still real and even profound, for one's union with the incarnate Word is permanent and continual, taking various modes. See my *Christology and Spirituality* (New York: Crossroad, 1991), 201 n39.

34. One might suggest that the crucifixion is also, in some sense, an apophatic phenomenon: the event defeats our concepts (our wisdom) by its very foolishness. It is a sort of intensified apophatic kataphaticism. See 1 Cor 1:21–25.

35. See again *In Search of Order*, 79.

36. See Eric Voegelin, *Science, Politics, and Gnosticism* (Chicago: Henry Regnery Co., 1968), 113–14, for Voegelin's discussion of an Islamic meditation.

37. See John Carmody and Denise Lardner Carmody, *Interpreting the Religious Experience: A Worldview* (Englewood Cliffs, N.J.: Prentice-Hall, 1987), throughout, but esp. 11–12, 49, 105; and *The Ecumenic Age*, 297–98, 321. Voegelin writes very sparingly, and mostly negatively, it seems, about the Buddha's nirvana; the latter is a "shortcut to the divine void behind the world" (*The Ecumenic Age*, 329). Does this mean that Voegelin considers the experiences of nirvana to be more of a pneumatic than a noetic phenomenon? It remains unclear; perhaps appropriately so, Voegelin suggests, since for him, Buddhism, like the Upanishads, reflects an incomplete differentiation of the mysterious process of existence (329). The fact that Buddhism writes of and explores nirvana seems, however, to place the accent upon the "human site" of the experience of transcendence, and in this sense it seems rather more noetic than pneumatic, at least in its originating core. Voegelin likens it, not to gnosticism, but to "the apocalyptic split of consciousness" (328). This is suggestive, for here the split is not as extreme as in the gnostic case; if you will, while trying to transcend the "self," the self still remains.

38. *In Search of Order*, 41.

39. See *In Search of Order*, 41ff, 48ff.

40. "Thus the meditative problem . . . can be accentuated from one side, that is to say, from the human side, as a questing. I would call this the noetic attitude. From the other side, the revelatory side[,] one can accentuate the factor of movement. I would call this the pneumatic attitude. Both are present within the meditative problem" (Eric Voegelin, "The Meditative Origin of the Philosophical

Knowledge of Order," trans. Frederick G. Lawrence, in *The Beginning and the Beyond: Papers from the Gadamer and Voegelin Conferences*, supplementary issue of *Lonergan Workshop, Volume 4,* ed. Fred Lawrence [Chico, Calif.: Scholars Press, 1984], 47).

41. *In Search of Order,* 41.

42. *In Search of Order,* 42, 44. I am presupposing a familiarity with Voegelin's analysis of consciousness as both intentionality and luminosity, and with his categories of thing-reality and It-reality. Through intentionality, conscious subjects "intend" objects, and there is a touch of thinglike objectification involved; consciousness as luminosity is more comprehensive, inasmuch as here "reality is not an object of consciousness but the something in which consciousness occurs as an event of participation between partners in the community of being" (*In Search of Order,* 15; see 14ff). The It-reality is the whole of this partnership in being, within which luminosity occurs. The modes are complementary, each having its appropriate role. Voegelin stresses the tendency of intentionality to derail into dogmatism, but he knows that the pressure of the awareness of our being in the middle of existence (we are "in" the midst of the It-reality) can itself, given certain derailments, issue in "historical relativisms" and even "radical nihilism" (29).

43. *In Search of Order,* 45.

44. *Israel and Revelation,* ix.

45. *In Search of Order,* 13ff, 27.

46. *In Search of Order,* 29.

47. *In Search of Order,* 46–47.

48. See *In Search of Order,* 83.

49. *In Search of Order,* 20, 22.

50. *In Search of Order,* 89–90.

51. For more on how Voegelin understands, and develops, Plato's developing views of *anamnesis,* see his "Consciousness and Order: 'Foreword' to *Anamnesis* (1966)," *Logos* 4 (1983): 17–24; reprinted in Lawrence, ed., *The Beginning and the Beyond,* 35–41.

52. See *Anamnesis,* 63–64.

53. On this see C. S. Lewis, *Mere Christianity* (New York: Macmillan, Collier Books, 1952), 142–43.

54. With reference to the words of Christ in John 16:24 and the counsel of the Spirit that forms their context as treated in Anselm's *Proslogion,* Voegelin writes that "Anselm moves from the first person of the Trinity to the second and third persons, from the Creator to the Christ and the paracletic Spirit, from the mortal imperfection of the creature to its immortal perfection in the beatific vision, from existence in the time of creation to existence in the eternity of the Beyond. For Anselm, thus, the trinitarian Creed is more than the letter of a doctrine to be believed, it has to be lived through as the true symbolization of a reality that moves from creation to salvation; and Anselm can live it through, and can enact the drama of the Trinity in the drama of the Prayer, because the quest of his reason is the proper response to the intelligible movement in the *fides*" ("The Beginning and the Beyond," 195–96).

Part III

Spiritual Sources of
Order and Disorder

6

Brothers under the Skin: Voegelin on the Common Experiential Wellsprings of Spiritual Order and Disorder

Michael Franz

Eric Voegelin's theoretical achievements are so sweeping and varied that scholars from a remarkably wide range of academic fields are now familiar with his name. This familiarity is rather dim in many cases, since Voegelin's writings are notoriously difficult and since he was not given to self-promotion. Such nodding recognition is a mixed blessing. Frequent encounters with a writer's name in footnotes or conversations may prompt serious study, but the more likely results are inaccurate labelings of the author or inappropriate invocations of his authority.[1] Such outcomes are unfortunate but not terribly surprising, at least when they occur at some distance from a thinker's area of academic specialization. However, even in political science, Voegelin's lifelong discipline, misperceptions abound.

American political scientists—especially those who are not well versed in Voegelin's writings—tend overwhelmingly to regard him as a right-wing thinker and a vituperative scourge of the left. This stems partly from a long-standing (and not entirely unjustified) practice among political conservatives to claim Voegelin as one of their own.[2] Also involved is the great likelihood that those who have read only one of Voegelin's fifteen books will have read either *The New Science of Politics* or *Science, Politics, and Gnosticism*.[3] These works are often included in political science reading lists because, in comparison with the remainder of Voegelin's oeuvre, they are relatively accessible and more directly political. They are also unusually sharp in tone, with striking and highly quotable critiques of ideologists like Marx and Hegel as modern "gnostics."

For many readers, this term seemed to suggest an analysis that regarded leftist ideologists as not only mistaken but also wicked, and perhaps even heretical. Readers on the right—especially the Catholic right—were particularly susceptible to this impression, as it offered an opportunity to locate a writer of great erudition and forcefulness within their camp.[4] Here at last, it may have seemed, was a political theorist who could canvass the history of political thought without succumbing to the bland tolerance of the midcentury vogue; Voegelin seemed prepared to rigorously segregate "the sheep from the goats," and to do so in apparently theological language to boot. For his part, Voegelin did little to publicly resist the steady stream of articles portraying him as a political conservative, and since his best-known works seemed to confirm this depiction, it has hardened into a seemingly established fact among American political scientists over the past forty-five years.

Although there are important senses in which Voegelin's thinking corresponds with current understandings of conservatism, depictions of him as a rightist intellectual warrior are biographically problematic and theoretically misleading. The biographical issues are—by comparison to the theoretical ones—more difficult to untangle and less significant for serious appraisals of Voegelin's work, so I shall pursue them only briefly.[5] Of greater importance is the question of whether Voegelin's work may be properly appropriated by those who wish to employ his analyses of "modern gnosticism" in attempts to rigorously segregate ideological thinkers from those deemed more philosophical or theological by type. I shall argue that such appropriations must be regarded as ill-founded when the full sweep of Voegelin's writings is considered, and that his late writings are particularly troublesome for those who would cite his work while seeking to isolate ideological experience and symbolization from modes that are philosophical or theological. Indeed, my reading suggests that a major effect of Voegelin's work on ideological consciousness is a highlighting of the hitherto unappreciated extent to which ideologists, philosophers, and theologians are (at the level of spiritual experience) "brothers under the skin."[6]

Ideology and Its Premodern Antecedents

One of the most distinctive aspects of Voegelin's analyses of ideologies and ideological movements[7] is his lifelong effort to show that their character and origins cannot be contained within modernity. His argument is not entirely at odds with conventional scholarly views of ideology, inasmuch as he locates ideologies as formal systems of thought within modern times, maintaining that such systems were simply unknown prior to the nineteenth century.[8] However, Voegelin held that the consciousness underlying ideological construction and belief is intelligibly linked to a pathological pattern of consciousness that was known to the ancients:

> In fact, the Greek thinkers diagnosed it as a disease of the psyche from the time they had occasion to observe it in the embattled polis. Heraclitus and Aeschylus, and above all Plato, speak of the *nosos* or *nosema* of the psyche; and Thucydides speaks of the expansion of the disease into the disorders of the Peloponnesian War as a *kinesis*, a feverish movement of society. . . . The Stoics, especially Chrysippus, were intrigued by the phenomenon, and Cicero, summarizing the findings of the preceding centuries, deals with the disease at length. . . . He calls it the *morbus animi*, the disease of the mind, and characterizes its nature as an *aspernatio rationis*, as a rejection of reason.[9]

We might say that, for Voegelin, ideologies are modern in their advent and form, but not their content. That is, the time of their appearance, their systematic cast, and their quasiscientific trappings are modern, but the type of consciousness that engenders them is ancient and perhaps even perennial. For this general type of consciousness Voegelin used a variety of designations, including spiritual "disorder," "disease," or "disorientation," as well as "closed" or "pneumapathological" consciousness.

The main theses presented in Voegelin's analysis of ideology and its premodern analogues are not terribly difficult to understand, but access to these theses is rendered extremely difficult by Voegelin's method and peculiarities as a writer. Methodologically, Voegelin's inclinations were empiricist, and his insights are almost always offered up in the course of an exegesis of a specific historical text. Consequently, his analysis of the various types of spiritual disorder are scattered across fifteen books and more than a hundred articles, with no definitive formulation. Moreover, Voegelin never tired of developing new concepts and terms. In addition to the terms for the general pattern of spiritual disorder noted above, he also used a welter of other concepts to designate subtypes of the general pattern, including activist mysticism, egophanic revolt, metastatic faith, demonic mendacity, Prometheanism, parousiasm, political religion, social Satanism, magic pneumatism, and two others that admit of still greater subdivision: gnosticism (intellectual, emotional, or volitional) and immanentization (teleological, axiological, and activist).

Given the confines of this essay, it would obviously take us too far afield to disentangle the complexities of Voegelin's terminology and the various phases through which his analysis was developed over a period of sixty years. Consequently, many of the details and intricacies of Voegelin's diagnosis of disordered consciousness will necessarily be lost in any brief account of his work on spiritual disorder. Nevertheless, I believe it is possible to provide an accurate representation of his view of the parallels that mark the experience and symbolization of the spiritually well-ordered and disordered. This can be accomplished if we tighten our focus, concentrating on the ideological mode of spiritual disorder and emphasizing a single case, that of Marx. An explication of the continuities that characterize the experience and symbolization of exemplars of spiritual order, on the one hand, and ideological figures such as Marx on the other will serve as an illuminating corrective to the image (the caricature, really) of Voegelin as an anti-ideological, anti-leftist warrior. The picture that will emerge will be one that, by contrast, shows him as an appropriately sharp critic who was nevertheless admirably empathetic, balanced, and fair-minded.

Ideology and the History of Spiritual Disorder

Two aspects of Voegelin's analysis of disordered consciousness (and its subtype, ideological consciousness) must be emphasized at the outset. First, diagnostic accounts of disordered or closed consciousness are almost always intertwined with parallel accounts of well-ordered or open consciousness. Purportedly pathological states of the soul are compared with—and theoretically legitimated by—explicit accounts of healthy or well-ordered states. The imbalanced consciousness of a medieval millenarian or an ideological system-builder is not diagnosed in the abstract but by direct comparison to exemplars of balanced consciousness such as Augustine or Plato. The reverse is also true. Voegelin's discussions of what it means to have a philosophic consciousness are articulated in comparative terms by reference to "philodoxers" (lovers of opinion) or "restrictivist" intellectuals or "immanentizing" ideologues. This practice is helpful for understanding what Voegelin means when utilizing controversial terms like "spiritual disease" in a discussion of figures such as Marx or Comte. But there is more at stake than a simple striving for clarity; and we would do well to remember that, for Voegelin, it is the background of an explicitly articulated notion of spiritual health that *justifies* the use of diagnostic terms like spiritual disease.

The second point that must be emphasized is that when Voegelin offers a comparison of thinkers such as, say, Plato and Marx, he is generally undertaking something quite different from a comparison of "true" and "false" propositions about objects in physical reality. Voegelin tries to penetrate the language symbols used in the writings of such men to gain access to the experiences of reality (transcendent and physical), which engendered the symbols in the first place.[10] But again, in moving away from an inquiry regarding the relation of propositions and objects to an inquiry regarding experiences, Voegelin is not merely shifting ground to a comparison of "true" and "false" experiences. Experiences cannot, as such, be false. It would be much better to say that well-ordered consciousness is engendered by experiences that are more inclusive or encompassing.[11] Therefore Voegelin writes (in a discussion of Parmenides):

> The conflict of Truth and Delusion, thus, is not a conflict between true and false propositions. In fact, the Delusion is quite as true as the Truth, if by truth we mean an adequate and consistent articulation of an experience. Truth is the philosophy of the realissimum that we experience if we follow the way of immortalization in the soul; Delusion is the philosophy of the reality that we experience as men who live and die in a world that itself is distended in time with a beginning and an end. The characterization of this philosophy of reality as a Delusion derives its justification from the experience of a superior reality. . . .[12]

Although the differences between well-ordered and disordered consciousness may be traced to the former being based on either a superior reality or a broader horizon on reality, there is yet another possibility. It is a possibility that is often overlooked but that is vitally important for a sophisticated understanding of Voegelin's diagnoses of spiritual imbalance: the experiences of human existence that engender well-ordered and disordered consciousness can be—and often are—essentially equivalent, with the differences arising in the form of varied *reactions* to a common experiential base.

What are the most important experiences that are common to, or shared by, the exemplars of both well-ordered and disordered consciousness? My reading of Voegelin yields four experiences of human existence in reality that are fundamental for the ordering and disordering of consciousness. The first three can be stated succinctly: the human condition is experienced as a condition of uncertainty, contingency, and imperfection. The fourth requires only a slightly more extensive description: it is the experience of mortality in a world in which all things pass away, but beyond which there is a perceived but mysterious lastingness, an eternity beyond the world of things.

The characterization of these experiences as fundamental is intended to suggest several aspects of Voegelin's account. First, they are fundamental in the sense that they are experiences of the foundations of our existence, and therewith of our relation to the ground of being. Second, they are not restricted to particular times or places, but are fundamental for humanity at all times and places. In connection with humanity's contingency, Voegelin writes:

> Man is not a self-created, autonomous being carrying the origin and meaning of his existence within himself. He is not a divine *causa sui*; from the experi-

ence of his life in precarious existence within the limits of birth and death there rather arises the wondering question about the ultimate ground, the *aitia* or *prote arche*, of all reality and specifically his own. . . . [T]his questioning is inherent to man's experience of himself at all times. . . .[13]

Third, these experiences are fundamental in the sense that all persons partake of them. I hasten to add the caveat that the experiences of different individuals will, nevertheless, be marked by varying degrees of frequency, intensity, clarity, and transformative impact. But that said, it is important to emphasize that one need be only a normally self-conscious person and not a philosophical genius to partake of the experiences:

> For we find ourselves referred back to nothing more formidable than the experiences of finiteness and creatureliness in our existence, of being creatures of a day as the poets call man, of being born and bound to die, of dissatisfaction with a state experienced as imperfect, of apprehension of a perfection that is not of this world but is the privilege of the gods, of possible fulfillment in a state beyond this world, the Platonic *epekeina* [Beyond], and so forth.[14]

Thus, the fundamental experiences that are common to the well-ordered and the disordered soul are also common to all of humanity, though it remains true that the great majority of individuals will not be motivated to absorb themselves in contemplating or symbolizing the experiences. Rather, for the majority of humans who lack the spiritual sensitivity and reflectiveness that characterizes those such as Plato or Hegel, the experiences will be relatively fleeting, usually occasioned by personal turbulence or tragedy (perhaps the death of a beloved or the apprehension of one's own death) and followed by an absorption not in the experience but in the more comfortable routines of everyday life that are disturbed by the experience. Importantly, what sets figures like Plato, Aquinas, Hegel, or Marx apart from the majority of humanity is precisely that which unites them with one another as a human type. In cases such as theirs, the fundamental experiences are not banished to the periphery of life and consciousness but, rather, become the motivating center of life and consciousness.

To be sure, one such as Marx is motivated toward a very different sort of project than is Plato. Yet there are important continuities that run through the experiences that result in such different reactions, and it will be helpful to give them specific consideration by way of Marx's example. Plato seeks to attune himself to the divine measure, and to symbolize his experiences of participation in the divine in writings that will assist those driven by a parallel desire. Marx, by contrast, seeks to make humanity the measure, and to symbolize his revolutionary consciousness in writings that will help humanity achieve independence by means of communist productive relations, which will banish scarcity and the attendant need for religious opiates. Yet Marx's quest for human emancipation is motivated just as surely as Plato's search for attunement by the basic experiences of uncertainty, contingency, and imperfection. As the young Marx writes (in a passage to which Voegelin accorded great significance):

> A being only counts itself as independent when it stands on its feet and it stands on its own feet as long as it owes its existence to itself. A man who lives by the grace of another considers himself a dependent being. But I live completely by the grace of another when I owe him not only the maintenance of my life but when he has also created my life, when he is the source of my life. And my life necessarily has such a ground outside itself if it is not my own creation. The idea of creation is thus one that it is very difficult to drive out of the minds of people. They find it impossible to conceive of nature and man existing through themselves since it contradicts all the evidences of practical life.[15]

This passage suggests that, whatever else one may think of Marx, he was not a spiritually obtuse man. He had partaken of the experiences underlying Aristotle's meditations on the *prote arche*. What sets him off from an Aristotle is not a different foundation in experience, but a different pattern of response to an essentially equivalent experience.

What Voegelin calls existential or ideological closure is not a condition with which one is born, or an insidious process that befalls a passive or unwitting victim. It is an active "existence-in-revolt" against a condition experienced as intolerably flawed and incomplete. The case of Marx helps to illustrate this crucial point. He tacitly acknowledges that his own existence must have a ground beyond itself, and thus we might ask why this observation did not prompt him to inquire into the nature of that ground, or to explore the extent to which he could know or participate in its order. But the answer is already before us. Marx's philosophical training informs him in advance that the very presence of such a ground will place him—and the rest of humanity—in a condition of contingency. Moreover, since the ground of being is not of the physical world but beyond it, such a ground cannot be fully known, and thus its very presence will leave Marx and the rest of humanity in a condition of permanent uncertainty. Additionally, if humanity and the world do not originate from out of themselves, but require a source outside of their existence if they are to come into being, then the apprehension of a ground of being entails an awareness that the human condition is one of structural incompleteness that can never attain the perfection that may lie beyond the world of things. Finally, if humanity and the world came into being rather than existing eternally out of themselves, they must have been preceded by a ground of being that exists out of itself and is eternal; therefore, since it is readily apparent that everything in physical existence passes out of existence, mortality will bring each of us to physical destruction regardless of our apprehension of a reality that is immortal.

Since these conclusions are the upshot of Marx's fundamental experiences of the human condition within reality, and since Marx finds this condition intolerably flawed and incomplete, he must revolt against the experiences and, to the greatest degree possible, close himself off from them and their implications. This is exactly what he tries to do. Although he is privy to the experience of contingency, he rebelliously asserts that "for socialist man what is called world history is nothing but the creation of man by human labour. . . ."[16] However implausible the notion of humanity having created itself may be, this is Marx's only option if he insists on declaring human independence from metaphysical contingency. Of course, the notion will seem less implausible (or the implausibility may be less bothersome) if Marx can surround himself with followers who share his militant immanentism. But in 1844, Marx has not yet been able to attract his followers, his "socialist men," since he is just beginning his advocacy of scientific socialism. This helps to explain the anxious tone of this section of the "Paris Manuscripts," particularly the ominous sentence in which Marx reflects that "the idea of creation is one that it is very difficult to drive out of the minds of people." Why should Marx care whether the idea of creation occurs to people? Is it because he knows that his theory, in which humanity creates itself through productive activity, begs rather than answers Aristotle's question of the *arche*? If he believes that his theory can pass scrutiny when measured against "all the evidences of practical life," would he have any reason to wish that the idea of creation might be driven from people's minds? And by what means might the driving out be accomplished? Not by education in the principles of scientific socialism, it would seem, since Marx's radically immanentist theory is structurally such that it can only sidestep and not answer the question. And thus Marx's final response to an imaginary critic (who pursues Aristotle's argument for a *prote arche*) is, "Give up your abstraction and you will give up your question. . . . [D]o not think, do not ask me questions."[17]

Orders and Disorders of the Soul

The foregoing section suggests that Voegelin may be correct in according significance to the experiences of contingency, uncertainty, imperfection, and mortality to Marx's case of spiritual revolt. Yet several important questions remain: How does Marx's disordered pattern of response compare to patterns that Voegelin would consider well-ordered? And how representative is Marx's case in relation to the many writers to whom Voegelin referred as ideologists?

To compare Marx's response with one that Voegelin cites with approval, we may turn to Aristotle.[18] Whereas Marx responds to a ground he can experience but not fathom with a curious mixture of escapism and aggressiveness, Aristotle describes the philosopher's response with the symbols of wondering (*thaumazein*), seeking or searching (*zetein*), search (*zetesis*), and questioning (*aporein, diaporein*).[19] The philosopher feels himself moved (*kinein*) by some unknown force to ask the question of which the search consists; he feels himself drawn (*helkein*) into the search. This is the experience recounted in the cave allegory of Plato's *Republic*, in which the prisoner is forced by an unknown entity to turn around (*periagoge*) and begin his ascent to the light.[20]

Though Aristotle's account emphasizes the philosopher's perception of his own ignorance rather than the unknown entity that moves him, he presents that perception of ignorance less as a first piece of information than as a restless stirring within the soul: a person "could not know that he does not know, unless he experienced an existential unrest to escape from his ignorance (*pheugein ten agnoian*) and to search for knowledge (*episteme*)."[21] In Voegelin's reading, Aristotle, no less than Plato, finds the origins of the loving openness to the *sophon* outside the seeker: "The mind (*nous*) is moved (*kineitai*) by the object (*noeton*)."[22] For Voegelin, this object that moves the mind of the philosopher is not an object in the external world of things but the transcendent ground of those things and of the philosopher's own existence. And the ignorance that the lover of wisdom perceives, and to which he or she responds with wondering and searching, is the very ignorance of the ground of being that prompts Marx's rebellion:

> The search from the human side, it appears, presupposes the movement from the divine side: Without the *kinesis*, the attraction from the ground, there is no desire to know; without the desire to know, no questioning in confusion; without the questioning in confusion, no knowledge of ignorance. There would be no anxiety in the state of ignorance, unless anxiety were alive with man's knowledge of his existence from a ground that he is not himself.[23]

Plato and Aristotle conceive of the ground of being as an entity beyond being, as God, and it is interesting to note that Marx also formulates the experience of contingency in terms of "living by the grace of another." We cannot make too much of this parallel without running a risk of overburdening the text, but it seems reasonably safe to suggest that Marx, Plato, and Aristotle all understand the experience and its logical implications in strikingly comparable terms. The great parting of the ways is a matter not of experience or even interpretation, but of response. Plato and Aristotle respond with wonder, a searching questioning, and with love, hope, and trust. Marx responds with a resentful closure that issues into an activist intellectual's project of imaginatively transfiguring the human condition, as well as a revolutionary's project of populating the newly imagined world through ideological persuasiveness and public agitation.

The parallels that can be spun out of this passage from Marx are surely impressive, but how might Voegelin respond if pressed to show that Marx's case is representative of a more general ideological consciousness that can be found in other movements? I believe he would respond with several points. First, he might suggest that few ideologists will possess sufficient philosophical acumen to symbolize their experiences in a manner that will dovetail so neatly with the symbolizations of authentic philosophers. Second, one cannot expect that ideologists will often muster the candor to offer written accounts of disturbing spiritual experiences or of their personal reactions to them. Third, Voegelin might explain that many ideologists revolt not against primary experiences of contingency, uncertainty, incompleteness, and mortality, but rather against the doctrines, creeds, treatises, and traditions that are the symbolic repositories where modern thinkers encounter ancient responses to our fundamental experiences. Thus, while we cannot compile a list of passages from other ideological system-builders that will serve to bolster Voegelin's argument as nicely as our passage from Marx,[24] we could certainly compile volumes of passages in which they rail against theological and philosophical doctrines that spring from the fundamental experiences.

Despite the considerable variation that characterizes the many movements Voegelin identified as ideologies (see note 7), hostility toward Christianity and classical Greek philosophy is a recurrent theme across the set of ideologies. One would be hard-pressed to identify a major ideologist who was simply indifferent to these traditions. Why is this the case? Voegelin's perspective suggests that even an indirect or secondary exposure to the fundamental experiences of the human condition will prove unsettling, and that reactive longings for independence, certainty, perfection, and immortality will be expressed against the doctrines and institutions in which the experiences survive—however faintly or opaquely. Ideology must, by its very nature, be hostile to authentic religion and philosophy, for both are enduringly frustrating to the ideologist's project. Philosophy and theology call for faith, hope, trust, love, humility, and reverence for an eternal, transcendent ground that cannot be known with certainty or made to do the bidding of humans. Whether one is a gifted and self-conscious ideologist (like Marx or Hegel) who knows that the call comes from the fundamentals of human experience, or a relatively unpenetrating thinker (like Helvétius or Vauvenargues) who merely revolts against the opaque symbols of an incompletely fathomed tradition, the call will be rejected for the same reasons.[25]

One who wishes to be independent, certain, and perfect can never have his or her way as long as a realm experienced as transcendent is present to consciousness, and thus the reformulated world of an ideological system must be a truncated, intramundane construct. The personal closure of the ideologist will be expressed in a stubborn theoretical immanentism. The divine will be eclipsed by the worldly, and the ground of being will be relocated to some immanent aspect of worldly existence such as productive relations, racial composition, scientific rationality, historical progress, libidinous drives, and so forth. Once the transcendent ground has been immanentized, it becomes conceivable that one might not only understand reality completely but also manipulate it to one's liking. The drive for certainty and the will to power that we found in the initial reaction to the fundamental experiences will both get their way, simultaneously, through the act Voegelin calls "the decapitation of being" or the "murder of God."[26]

The speculative murder of God can be accomplished in a more or less subtle manner, but it must be accomplished in some way if humanity is to emerge as the measure of all things. Hegel, Feuerbach, Marx, and Nietzsche are fairly explicit about their intentions, whereas others perform the feat indirectly. Thinkers such as Bacon and Descartes do not mount a frontal assault but push the transcendent ground out the back door by isolating nature as a self-contained object of inquiry. When nature is declared to be nothing more than matter-in-motion, devoid of design and purpose, God can be reduced to the status of a hypothesis and relegated to theologians so that scientists and philosophers can get on with the "real" business of enhancing human power and longevity.[27] Hobbes abolished the tension between love of self and love of God in an equally efficient way. By stating that "there is no such *Finis ultimus*, (utmost ayme,) nor *Summum Bonum*, (greatest Good,) as is spoken of in the Books of the old Morall Philosophers," Hobbes makes the passions the center of the person.[28] Voltaire simply exchanges the transcendental *pneuma* of Christ for an intramundane *esprit humain* as the object of general history, and the change of heart is replaced by progress toward ever more enlightened opinions.[29] Helvétius discards the traditional understanding of the growth of the soul as an internal process that is nourished by communication with transcendent reality in favor of the formation of conduct through external manipulation by an enlightened legislator.[30] Turgot, Saint-Simon, and Comte relegate spiritual experience to a bygone phase of human immaturity, with the obvious implication

that those who still order their existences by reference to such experiences
are unfit for the new age of positivistic rationality.[31] Finally (or at least
most recently), in what Voegelin called the ideologies of biologism and
psychologism, the direction in which the *realissimum* of existence is to
be sought is inverted from the transcendent realm to genetic coding or
psychological conditioning.[32] Voegelin characterized this sequence of de-
formations as a

> movement of intramundane religious sentiments, pressing the interpretation
> of history and politics downward from the spirit to the animal basis of exis-
> tence. Neither the "model" of the secular "sacred history," nor the dogmatic
> symbols on the level of the "thesis of generality" remain constant; they
> change continuously in accordance with the stratum of human nature that
> commands the attention of the time and becomes the object of the process of
> deification. The rapid descent from reason, through technical and planning
> intellect, to the economic, psychological and biological levels of human na-
> ture, as the dominants in the image of man, is a strong contrast to the impos-
> ing stability of the Christian anthropology through eighteen centuries. Once
> the transcendental anchorage is surrendered, the descent from the rational to
> the animal nature, so it seems, is inevitable.[33]

In each of the cases discussed above, the thinker has, according to Voegelin, defined nature or humanity in such a way that the transcendent
ground of spiritual experience is eclipsed. As we have seen, for Voegelin
this equivalence on the level of results arose from a deeper equivalence at
the level of motivating experiences. Each of these projects was engendered
by an inordinate drive for certainty and power, and thus Voegelin could
argue for an intelligible unity among these efforts, despite their pheno-
typical differences.

This inordinate drive for certainty and power is, for Voegelin, the crucial thread of continuity that runs through the various ideologies. To be
sure, relations among ideologies have generally been as bitter as those
that marked the relations of religious sects in earlier eras, but far from
disconfirming Voegelin's analysis, this fact helps to corroborate it. The
ideological "dogmatomachy," as Voegelin described it, is intelligible because each of the ideologies arises from dissatisfaction with the degree of
independence and certainty afforded by the reality depicted in classical
philosophy and Judeo-Christian theology. Since the various ideologies
are, in Voegelin's view, efforts to construct a "Second Reality" in which
humans achieve greater power and certainty, and since certainty is diminished by the presence of rival "Second Realities," internecine warfare is
to be expected in the ideological camp.

Thus, the inordinate drive for certainty and power that divides ideologies in practice nevertheless serves to bind them to one another in Voege-

lin's analysis. It is a thread of continuity that runs horizontally, we may say, through modernity, but also backward through time, binding ideologies to premodern manifestations of spiritual revolt against contingency, uncertainty, imperfection, and mortality. Voegelin found an equivalence—at the level of experience and symbolization—between modern ideology and the "antidivine self-assertiveness" diagnosed by Jeremiah and the prophets,[34] the *ate* or blindness of passion diagnosed by Homer,[35] the *hybris* (hubris) and *pleonexia* (unjust will to power) diagnosed by Aeschylus, Plato, and other Greek thinkers, the *morbus animi* (disease of the mind) and *aspernatio rationis* (rejection of reason) diagnosed by Cicero and the Stoics, and the apocalyptic and millenarian excesses diagnosed by the fathers of the early church and detailed by historians such as Norman Cohn.[36]

The Precarious Balance of Consciousness

As we have seen, Voegelin argued that well-ordered and disordered consciousness arise as distinct patterns of response to a single complex of fundamental experiences. The complex of experiences arises, in turn, from the essentially timeless and universal tendency of human beings to inquire into the ground of their existence. The questions of "where-from" and "what-for" arise from the human condition itself, and Voegelin, following Aristotle, regards the human as the *zoon noetikon* who is defined in relation to other animals by its search for understanding. When the search pursues questions of an ultimate nature—questions concerning the ground of being and nature of reality—the search will carry a plurality of motivations: the seeker desires a true understanding of the ontological structure of reality, but also a release from the pressure of anxious uncertainty and the prospect of meaninglessness. These motivations will have been present, according to Voegelin, regardless of whether the search produces formative or deformative results in the soul, and regardless of whether the results are subsequently expressed mythologically, philosophically, theologically, or even ideologically.

Both truth and certainty are sought. But what happens if the truth turns out to be that the order of being is essentially mysterious? What if the seeker is not rewarded with a comforting certainty but rather a demanding call to faith, hope, and trust? What if the search results not in possession of facts but instead in a call to the love of wisdom? When anxious desires for truth and certainty motivate a search, but the outcome is a truth that is mysterious rather than certain, the original anxiety may be deepened rather than alleviated in the course of the search. A truth that requires faith for its confirmation will leave many a seeker unsatisfied.

Those who do not have—or cannot maintain—the capacity for gracefully accepting a truth that does not slake the natural human thirst for certainty will have ample motivation to strike out again in search of something more tangible and less trying. The imaginative construction of a human condition that would prove more tangible and less trying is a common element Voegelin finds in all the various forms of spiritual disorder, from the most otherworldly forms of apocalypticism or millenarianism to the most stubbornly immanentist, scientistic forms of ideology.

Once one begins to follow Voegelin in recognizing the commonalities that bind the various forms of spiritual disorder, as well as in recognizing the contrasting pattern of response that marks a consciousness that is open and balanced, there is a strong temptation to regard symbolic ex-pressions of well-ordered consciousness (such as Christianity or Platonic philosophy) as *alternatives* to—or even *cures* for—disordered conscious-ness. This may be the temptation that made Voegelin so attractive to anti-ideological Christian conservatives: he seems to offer such clear lines of distinction between Christian faith and ideological activism that one might be tempted to regard a renewed ascendancy of Christianity as the solution to the convulsions of ideological modernity. But those who were reading closely could have seen (as early as *The New Science of Politics* in 1952) that Voegelin's analysis shows that Christianity (and the open consciousness that it demands of the faithful) resembles something like a *cause* of spiritual revolt more closely than a viable "cure":

> [W]hen the world is de-divinized [i.e., the intracosmic gods replaced by the world-transcendent God of Judaism and Christianity], communication with the world-transcendent God is reduced to the tenuous bond of faith, in the sense of Heb. 11:1, as the substance of things hoped for and the proof of things unseen. Ontologically, the substance of things hoped for is nowhere to be found but in faith itself; and, epistemologically, there is no proof for things unseen but again this very faith. The bond is tenuous, indeed, and it may snap easily. The life of the soul in openness toward God, the waiting, the periods of aridity and dulness, guilt and despondency, contrition and repentance, forsakenness and hope against hope, the silent stirrings of love and grace, trembling on the verge of a certainty which if gained is loss—the very lightness of this fabric may prove too heavy a burden for men who lust for massively possessive experience.[37]

This passage shows that Voegelin did not regard authentic Christianity as a refuge for the seeker of certainty. However, I must stress that my use of the language of "causes" and "cures" in relating Christianity and pneumapathology is heuristic only. Christianity is not a "cause" of disor-dered consciousness, but rather a highly differentiated expression of the tension toward the ground of being, which tension is *itself* the agitating factor underlying spiritual revolt. However, in the broader sense of Christianity's social impact in history, Voegelin does indeed come close to speaking of it as a cause of ancient "heresy," medieval millenarianism, and modern ideology. In the sentences that follow immediately from the passage just quoted, Voegelin writes:

> The danger of a breakdown of faith to a socially relevant degree, now, will increase in the measure in which Christianity is a worldly success, that is, it will grow when Christianity penetrates a civilizational area thoroughly, supported by institutional pressure, and when, at the same time, it undergoes an internal process of spiritualization, of a more complete realization of its essence. The more people are drawn or pressured into the Christian orbit, the greater will be the number among them who do not have the spiritual stamina for the heroic adventure of the soul that is Christianity.[38]

Although this passage is certainly remarkable, it is not an aberration but rather an expression of a view held consistently by Voegelin from at least the late 1940s onward.[39] Voegelin regarded Christianity not as an assuaging but as an aggravating factor in the advent of spiritual disorder and ideology, and he held this view comprehensively in the sense of regarding the appearance of Christ, the worldly activity of the Church, and the spiritual impact of Christian doctrine in this same way.

With the publication of *The Ecumenic Age* in 1974, Christian readers came to understand that Voegelin was up to something much more complicated than what they thought they had seen in *The New Science of Politics*. He was not erecting a wall between spiritual order and disorder, and then placing Christianity on one side and gnosticism on the other. Rather, he was treating the two as historically and spiritually intertwined: "Considering the history of Gnosticism, with the great bulk of its manifestations belonging to, or deriving from, the Christian orbit, I am inclined to recognize in the epiphany of Christ the great catalyst that made eschatological consciousness an historical force, both in forming and deforming humanity."[40] Again and again in *The Ecumenic Age*, Voegelin stresses the structural equivalence that characterizes the experiences and efforts at symbolization of ideologists and the exemplars of spiritual order:

> The search of the ground, thus, remains recognizable as the reality experienced even in the modes of deformation. However much the symbolisms of deformation may express existence in untruth, they are equivalent to the symbolisms of myth, philosophy, and revelation.[41]

> Egophanic deformation notwithstanding, the Hegelian speculative revelation is an equivalent to the Pauline vision. Both symbolisms express experiences of the movement in reality beyond its structure. The experience of transfig-

uration, thus, emerges from the confrontation between Hegel and Paul as one of the great constants in history, spanning the period from the Ecumenic Age to Western modernity.[42]

[T]he modern revolt is so intimately a development of the "Christianity" against which it is in revolt that it would be unintelligible if it could not be understood as the deformation of the theophanic events in which the dynamics of transfiguration was revealed to Jesus and the Apostles. Moreover, there is no doubt about the origin of the constant in the Pauline myth of the struggle among the cosmic forces from which the Son of God emerges victorious. The variations on the theme of transfiguration still move in the differentiated form of the eschatological myth that Paul has created. This is an insight of considerable importance, because it permits one to classify the ideological "philosophies of history" as variations of the Pauline myth in the mode of deformation.[43]

Lest the intention behind the selection of these passages be misunderstood, I must emphasize that I am not suggesting that Voegelin came to view figures such as Marx, Hegel, Comte, and Nietzsche as the moral or theoretical "equals" of Plato, Aristotle, or Paul. The point, rather, is that there is a common complex of experiences underlying the thought and activity of all these men, and that they must be understood by reference to the deepest sources of their motivation.

Voegelin's work offers no support to those who would equate Marx and Paul. But neither does it support those who would equate Marx and Stalin. Though both Stalin and Marx are surely reprehensible characters, Voegelin's work shows them to be utterly different, as will be seen when one tries to conjure an image of Stalin, pacing the floors inside the Kremlin, speculating on how he might circumvent Aristotle's conclusions regarding the *prote arche*. Voegelin was a careful and fair-minded thinker. He criticizes Marx in appropriately harsh terms, calling him an intellectual swindler and a connoisseur of his own dream world. Yet he knows that Marx is not a fool or a thug but a man who, for all of his (historically catastrophic) failings, wrestles with the great questions and problems of human existence. Marx was also a man of high intelligence, and Voegelin did not begrudge his accomplishments. In a passage (written in the 1940s but published in 1975) that must have caused great consternation for Voegelin's admirers on the political right, Voegelin applauds Marx's insight as an economist while also criticizing the conservative orthodoxy that prevails among economists:

Marx has laid his finger on the sore spot of modern industrial society, on the cause of serious trouble (even if the trouble should not take the form of a general communist revolution), that is the growth of economic institutions into a power of such overwhelming influence on the life of every single man, that in the face of such power all talk about human freedom becomes futile. . . . That no economic theorist after Marx was sufficiently interested in the philosophical foundations of his science to explore this problem further, that no modern school of economic theory exists that would understand and develop the very important beginnings of Marx, casts a significant light on this whole branch of science.[44]

Voegelin was a scholar of remarkable independence and intellectual honesty. He felt no impulsion to curry favor with those of any particular belief or political stripe, and all those who hope to find his writings useful in bolstering some doctrinal "position" will, if they read long enough, be sorely disappointed. Engaged in the open exploration of reality, Voegelin followed the insights acquired from his investigations wherever they led, offering praise for men like Marx and Hegel where he felt it was deserved, and criticism of figures such as Isaiah, Aristotle, Paul, and Aquinas when necessary. When his investigations pointed up problems in his own programs and pronouncements, he was equally unflinching. In such cases he was no less willing to use his legendary critical sharpness on himself than he had been with others. Explaining why he abandoned a four-thousand-page manuscript on the history of political ideas, Voegelin said "it dawned on me that the conception of a history of ideas was an ideological deformation of reality."[45] And after he had reworked these investigations into the highly acclaimed first three volumes of *Order and History*, he broke with this new project as well, finding in his sequential history of types of order the very flaw (termed "historiogenesis") that characterized the ideological philosophies of history he sought to surpass.[46]

Everyone who has read one of Voegelin's books knows that there is plenty of criticism to go around. But those who have read only *The New Science of Politics* or *Science, Politics, and Gnosticsm* may not be aware that there is plenty of understanding and even empathy to go around as well. It is true that Voegelin's account accuses Marx of losing the "balance of consciousness," of closing himself off from the transcendent ground of being, and of seeking to draw the ground into the intramundane realm of existence. But this account also shows that Marx's thought springs from experiences that are common to a host of philosophers, prophets, and saints, many of whom had their own difficulties maintaining balance in the *metaxy*, the tensional realm of human existence in-between the worldly and the divine.

Well-ordered consciousness, or what Voegelin called the "balance of consciousness," is not the "normal" condition of the person on the street but an accomplishment of considerable difficulty and rarity that is—even when attained—easily lost in the tensions of the *metaxy*. With regard to the immanent pole of experience, it involves a balance between virtuous action in the world and upholding one's responsibilities in private and public life, and the acknowledgment of the limitations and imperfections of worldly existence. With regard to the transcendent pole of experience, it involves a balance between a relentlessly searching and questioning existence that seeks to fathom the divine, eternal source of order, and sober recognition that this order can neither be fully comprehended nor enlisted in worldly struggles. The balance of consciousness is enduringly precarious: the *periagoge*, the turning toward the divine and eternal, always threatens to take on the character of a turning away from the world, resulting in escapism, quietism, or attempts to make the order of transcendence operative in the world. This last form of imbalance, which Voegelin called "metastatic faith" in his analysis of Isaiah, has its analogue in those who, like Marx, perceive a transcendent source of order but know that humans cannot attain certainty and perfection unless it is imaginatively dragged into the world. Voegelin's theory of spiritual disorder helps us to understand the nature of Isaiah's or Marx's fall from the balance of consciousness, but also the formidability of the spiritual challenges to which they succumbed. And since these challenges stem not from their historical circumstances or personal idiosyncrasies but from the fundamental conditions of human experience, we do well to remember that Isaiah and Marx are brothers under the skin not only to one another but also to each of us.

Notes

1. Voegelin not only anticipated this problem, but also experienced it well before his death: "On my religious 'position', I have been classified as a Protestant, a Catholic, as anti-semitic and as a typical Jew; politically, as a Liberal, a Fascist, a National Socialist and a Conservative; and on my theoretical position, as a Platonist, a Neo-Augustinian, a Thomist, a disciple of Hegel, an existentialist, a historical relativist and an empirical sceptic; in recent years the suspicion has frequently been voiced that I am a Christian. All these classifications have been made by university professors and people with academic degrees. They give ample food for thought regarding the state of our universities" (Eric Voegelin, "On Readiness to Rational Discussion," in *Freedom and Serfdom*, ed. Albert Hunold [Dordrecht: D. Reidel, 1961], 280).

2. See, for example, M. E. Bradford, "A Generation of the Intellectual Right: At the Head of the Column," *Modern Age* 26 (1982): 292–96; Ian Crowther, "Conservative Thinkers: Eric Voegelin, A Philosopher in Search of Order," *Salisbury Review* 1 (1985): 18–22; John P. East, "Eric Voegelin and American Conservative Thought," *Modern Age* 22 (1978): 114–32; Paul Gottfried, "On the European Roots of Modern American Conservatism," *Thought* 35 (1980): 196–206; Russell Kirk, "Eric Voegelin's Normative Labour," in *Enemies of the Permanent Things*, ed. Russell Kirk (New Rochelle, N.Y.: Arlington House, 1969), 253–81;

Ted V. McAllister, *Revolt against Modernity: Leo Strauss, Eric Voegelin, and the Search for a Postliberal Order* (Lawrence: University Press of Kansas, 1996); Gerhart Niemeyer, "Conservatism and the New Political Theory," *Modern Age* 23 (1979): 115–22; David W. Noble, "Conservatism in the USA," *Journal of Contemporary History* 13 (1978): 635–52; and James Patrick, "Modernity as Gnosis," *Modern Age* 31 (1987): 222–33.

3. Eric Voegelin, *The New Science of Politics: An Introduction* (Chicago: University of Chicago Press, 1952); *Science, Politics, and Gnosticism* (Chicago: Henry Regnery, 1968).

4. James M. Rhodes argues that "[w]hen Eric Voegelin published *The New Science of Politics* and *Order and History: I–III* in the 1950s, Christian political theorists acclaimed him their champion. . . . It is clear that Christians followed Voegelin without carefully scrutinizing his premises" (James M. Rhodes, "Voegelin and Christian Faith," *Center Journal* 2 (Summer 1983): 55, 60).

5. Clearly Voegelin was, at the very least, not uncomfortable traveling in conservative circles. He wrote several articles for *Modern Age* and *The Intercollegiate Review*, periodicals that are not just conservative in tone but avowedly enlisted in a conservatism conceived as both an intellectual and political movement. He engaged in correspondence and maintained friendships in which political conservatives are conspicuously prominent, and concluded his career in a position at the conservative Hoover Institution named after (and presumably endowed by) Henry Salvatori, a prominent benefactor of conservative enterprises. However, it is one thing to say that Voegelin was comfortable with conservatives and quite another to say that he conceived of himself as a conservative. Voegelin's unwillingness to be enlisted in the conservative movement is set forth in unambiguous fashion in a letter to Gerhart Niemeyer dated October 8, 1964 (Eric Voegelin Papers, Hoover Institution Archives, Stanford University, Box 27), the body of which I reproduce here in its entirety: "At the Chicago meeting of the American Political Science Association, I have been told, there was a breakfast meeting conducted by you. According to my informations, the subject matter apparently was my work in political science, given a strong slant toward conservative politics. Among those present apparently there were a number of persons who would hardly qualify as political scientists, but rather looked like adherents of some radical rightist group. I do not want to inquire further into these happenings, as I have other things to do. Still, they are somewhat disquieting. Hence, you would oblige me to take note of the following cautionary statement: Any move undertaken by whomsoever, apt to associate my work as a scholar with any political party, group, or movement whatsoever, but especially with Goldwater, conservatism, or rightist groups, is made, not only without my permission or tacit consent, but against my declared intention. I consider any such attempt at association as an attack on the intellectual integrity of my work." Years later, in a retrospective article considering Voegelin's relation to conservatism, Niemeyer himself reflected that Voegelin ". . . had no message to proclaim. Nor did he conduct a conservative polemic against liberals and socialists. On the contrary, he inclined to regard conservatives as ideologists whose thinking began with 'a position' and aimed at 'positions,' which to Voegelin was the very opposite of the philosopher's

'open soul' and open mind" (Gerhard Niemeyer, "Eric Voegelin, 1952," *Modern Age* 26 (1982): 262–66, at 263). Also illuminating is a passage in a letter dated March 20, 1957 (Eric Voegelin Papers, Hoover Institution Archives, Stanford University, Box 20) in which Voegelin responds to a request for an evaluation of Wilmoore Kendall from Kendall's department chair: "On the debit side must be set, at least as far as I am concerned, his publicistic activities for the cause of ideological conservatism. One could, of course, make a case for it by saying that in the economy of public opinion one foolishness should be balanced by another one, so that neither one will run to extremes. And under that aspect, one might esteem this activity a public service—certainly Kendall sees his activity in this light—though he would not consider every ideology, regardless of content, a foolishness, as I do."

6. Voegelin used this arresting phrase to link Isaiah with modern ideologists at the very outset of *Israel and Revelation*, the first volume of *Order and History*. James M. Rhodes, recollecting the reaction of Christian readers who had been attracted to Voegelin by *The New Science of Politics*, suggests that Christians were not overly alarmed because "Voegelin seemed to have contained this trouble within the Old Testament. It appeared that he would finish his work by illuminating the Christian foundations of right order and by clearing the spiritual rubble of modernity off the site of a new Christian culture" (Rhodes, "Voegelin and Christian Faith," 59). Rhodes goes on to suggest that Christians should have been more aware of the theoretical grounds dividing them from Voegelin, who was not taken to task for his understanding of Isaiah for nearly twenty years. See Eric Voegelin, *Order and History*, vol. 1, *Israel and Revelation* (Baton Rouge: Louisiana State University Press, 1956), xiii, 452–58.

7. Voegelin refers, at various points in his writings, to each of the following intellectual movements as ideologies: anarchism, behavioralism, biologism, constitutionalism, existentialism, fascism, Hegelianism, liberalism, Marxism, positivism, progressivism, psychologism, scientism, and utilitarianism. For specific citations for each of these see Michael Franz, *Eric Voegelin and the Politics of Spiritual Revolt: The Roots of Modern Ideology* (Baton Rouge: Louisiana State University Press, 1992), 8.

8. Eric Voegelin, *Conversations with Eric Voegelin*, ed. R. Eric O'Connor (Montreal: Thomas More Institute, 1980), 13–18, 147.

9. Eric Voegelin, "Wisdom and the Magic of the Extreme: A Meditation," in *The Collected Works of Eric Voegelin*, vol. 12, *Published Essays, 1966–1985*, ed. Ellis Sandoz (Baton Rouge: Louisiana State University Press, 1990), 322.

10. An adequate account of what is generally called Voegelin's "theory of experience and symbolization" cannot be offered here. For an exceptionally clear explication, see "Experience and Language," chapter 2 in Eugene Webb's *Eric Voegelin: Philosopher of History* (Seattle: University of Washington Press, 1981), 52–88.

11. On the issue of the inclusiveness of experiential horizons, see "Remembrance of Things Past," a 1977 foreword to the English edition of Voegelin's *Anamnesis*, ed. and trans. Gerhart Niemeyer (Notre Dame: University of Notre Dame Press, 1978), 3–13; reprinted in *Published Essays, 1966–1985*, 304–14.

12. Eric Voegelin, *Order and History*, vol. 2, *The World of the Polis* (Baton Rouge: Louisiana State University Press, 1957), 216.

13. Eric Voegelin, "Reason: The Classic Experience," in *Published Essays, 1966–1985*, 268–69.

14. Eric Voegelin, "On Debate and Existence," in *Published Essays, 1966–1985*, 41–42.

15. Karl Marx, "Economic and Philosophical Manuscripts of 1844," in *Karl Marx: Selected Writings*, ed. David McLellan (Oxford: Oxford University Press, 1977), 94. For Voegelin's analysis of this passage and Marx's ensuing remarks, see *Science, Politics, and Gnosticism*, 23–28, and Eric Voegelin, *From Enlightenment to Revolution*, ed. John H. Hallowell (Durham, N.C.: Duke University Press, 1975), 289–91.

16. Marx, "Economic and Philosophical Manuscripts of 1844," in McLellan, 95.

17. Marx, "Economic and Philosophical Manuscripts of 1844," in McLellan, 95.

18. Since Voegelin argued that the engendering experiences of prophets, philosophers, and saints are structurally equivalent (in the sense that what is experienced is the same participatory tension toward the one ground of being), it would be equally legitimate to concentrate on the experiences of, say, Moses or Paul as on those of Aristotle and Plato. However, as Voegelin maintained that "the adequate articulation and symbolization of the questioning consciousness as the constituent of humanity is . . . the epochal feat of the philosophers," we will concentrate here on philosophical symbols of health, openness, and balance. See "Reason: The Classic Experience," 269.

19. "Reason: The Classic Experience," 269.

20. As an example of the parallels running through the experiences and symbols of spiritual order and disorder, we might note that the imagery of the "cave allegory" would prove entirely suitable for a text from the ancient Gnostic traditions. The description of ignorance as a condition of darkness and imprisonment within the world and society that can be overcome only by an ascent to true knowledge in an upper realm could easily pass for a gnostic one; all that would be required would be a hypostasis of these symbols of an internal process of the soul into the literal depiction of an escape from a malevolent cosmos. See also Plato's *Theaetetus*, 176a–b.

21. Eric Voegelin, *Order and History*, vol. 4, *The Ecumenic Age* (Baton Rouge: Louisiana State University Press, 1974), 190.

22. Voegelin's translation of Aristotle, *Metaphysics*, 1072a30, in *The Ecumenic Age*, 190.

23. Voegelin, *The Ecumenic Age*, 190. The movement from the divine side mentioned in this passage—the pull *from* the ground that induces a search *for* the ground—is the philosophical equivalent of the "call" answered by the prophet and the saint. Voegelin repeatedly inveighs against the medieval distinction between natural reason and supernatural revelation, arguing that it was based upon a misunderstanding of the mystical character of Platonic-Aristotelian noesis, which carries a revelatory component. See Eric Voegelin, "Toynbee's History as a Search

for Truth," in *The Intent of Toynbee's History*, ed. Edward T. Gargan (Chicago: Loyola University Press, 1961), 196–98; "The Gospel and Culture," in *Published Essays, 1966–1985*, 187–88; *Conversations with Eric Voegelin*, 104; *The Ecumenic Age*, 48; "Wisdom and the Magic of the Extreme," 337; and Eric Voegelin, *Order and History*, vol. 5, *In Search of Order* (Baton Rouge: Louisiana State University Press, 1987), 43.

24. Voegelin seems to have been content with a few model cases as evidence for his general reflections on ideological consciousness. He identifies Marx as a model case in "Wisdom and the Magic of the Extreme," 319, and also speaks of Hegel as a "prototypical case." See *The Ecumenic Age*, 21; *Science, Politics, and Gnosticism*, 40; and "Response to Professor Altizer's 'A New History and a New but Ancient God?' " in *Published Essays, 1966–1985*, 295–96.

25. See Eric Voegelin, "On Classical Studies," in *Published Essays, 1966–1985*, 259–60; *From Enlightenment to Revolution*, 36–42, 59; and *In Search of Order*, 48, 53, 61–62.

26. *Science, Politics, and Gnosticism*, 54.

27. See Francis Bacon, *The Great Instauration* (Arlington Heights, Ill.: Harlan Davidson, 1980), 15–17; René Descartes, "Discourse on the Method of Rightly Conducting the Reason and Seeking Truth in the Field of Science," in Descartes, *Discourse on Method and Meditations*, trans. Lawrence J. Lafleur (Indianapolis: Bobbs-Merrill, 1960), 44–47.

28. Thomas Hobbes, *Leviathan* (Harmondsworth: Penguin, 1968), Book I, ch. 11, 160. Compare with Augustine's analysis of this tension in his commentary on Psalm 64 in *St. Augustine on the Psalms*, trans. Scholastica Hebgin and Felicitas Corrigan (Westminster, Md: Neuman Press, 1960), which Voegelin calls "philosophically perfect." See "Configurations of History," in *Published Essays, 1966–1985*, 105.

29. See *From Enlightenment to Revolution*, 10.

30. *From Enlightenment to Revolution*, 70.

31. On Turgot see Eric Voegelin, "Philosophies of History: An Interview with Eric Voegelin," *New Orleans Review* 2 (1973): 135–36, and *From Enlightenment to Revolution*, 88–123; on Saint-Simon and Comte, see *From Enlightenment to Revolution*, 136–94.

32. *From Enlightenment to Revolution*, 69. Voegelin did not deny that these are important factors in explaining human nature or behavior; biology and psychology become biologism and psychologism only when these factors are said to be all there is to human nature. See "Reason: The Classic Experience," 289–91.

33. *From Enlightenment to Revolution*, 13.

34. *Israel and Revelation*, 433.

35. *The World of the Polis*, 80, 87, 107–8. On the relation between the diagnosis of the prophets and the Homeric *ate*, see Franz, *Eric Voegelin and the Politics of Spiritual Revolt*, 39–41.

36. This has become a broad and active field of scholarship, but the most essential reference point is still Norman Cohn, *The Pursuit of the Millennium* (New York: Oxford University Press, revised edition, 1970).

37. *The New Science of Politics*, 122.

38. *The New Science of Politics*, 122–23.

39. See the section on Bossuet, Voltaire, and the turn toward secularized conceptions of history, originally written for Voegelin's abandoned history of political ideas, in *From Enlightenment to Revolution*, 18–23. Voegelin's analysis places primary responsibility on the medieval church for the Reformation, the militancy of secularism, the abandonment of its own spiritual leadership of society, and the "respiritualization of the public sphere from other sources, in the forms of nationalism, humanitarianism, economism both liberal and socialist, biologism, and psychologism" (20).

40. *The Ecumenic Age*, 20.

41. *The Ecumenic Age*, 192.

42. *The Ecumenic Age*, 266.

43. *The Ecumenic Age*, 269.

44. *From Enlightenment to Revolution*, 299–300. This is not an isolated case of praise for the critical accomplishments of ideologists; see also Eric Voegelin, "History and Gnosis," in *The Old Testament and Christian Faith*, ed. Bernhard Anderson (New York: Herder and Herder, 1969), 65, 82–83; "On Hegel: A Study in Sorcery," in *Published Essays, 1966–1985*, 222–24; and "The Eclipse of Reality," in *The Collected Works of Eric Voegelin*, vol. 28, *What Is History? And Other Late Unpublished Writings*, ed. Thomas A. Hollweck and Paul Caringella (Baton Rouge: Louisiana State University Press, 1990), 114–16.

45. Eric Voegelin, *Autobiographical Reflections*, ed. Ellis Sandoz (Baton Rouge: Louisiana State University Press, 1989), 63.

46. See *The Ecumenic Age*, 1–11, 57–113.

7

Balanced and Imbalanced Consciousness

Glenn Hughes

One of the most useful of the diagnostic concepts developed by Eric Voegelin for analyzing order and disorder in history is his notion of "the balance of consciousness." The concept is most fully presented and explained in chapter 4 ("Conquest and Exodus") of the fourth volume of *Order and History, The Ecumenic Age*, where the context is an analysis of certain dangers accompanying the discovery of divine transcendence.[1]

A major problem introduced by the discovery, Voegelin explains, is that the conceptual separation of the cosmos into the two distinct realms of finite world and transcendent reality not only fails to "solve" the mystery of existence—the questions regarding the where-from and the where-to of existence, its meaning and value, and its obligations—but rather makes the human situation even more perplexing and demanding. The human search for purposeful living is now revealed to have the character of a "tension" (as Voegelin describes it) between finite world and transcendent truth; and human consciousness is revealed to be that place in reality where finite being recognizes its orientation and obligation toward a transcendent—and therefore inescapably mysterious—origin and meaning. The burdens of these insights weigh heavily. So there ensues a constant temptation, Voegelin writes, to try to reduce or escape the "tension of existence" by identifying one of the disclosed realms—either immanence (the finite world) or transcendence—with true reality and demoting the other realm to the status of meaninglessness or untruth. To succumb to this temptation, however, is to lose the "balance of consciousness," where the "balance" consists precisely in appreciating and accepting both the given finite world and transcendent reality as facts; in acknowledging the implications of these facts; and in embracing one's own, and all of human, existence as a life of tension between the "poles" of immanence and transcendence.[2]

Although the phrase "the balance of consciousness" doesn't appear in Voegelin's work until quite late in his career, the notion itself and the diagnoses related to it are a central concern throughout his mature work.[3] His studies often trace a distorted perspective on reality, or a dangerously misguided assumption, to its source in a "loss of balance" in this sense. As a result, the full sweep of his writings provides an extensive survey of modes and consequences of "imbalanced" consciousness.[4]

Regarding different types of imbalance, as already mentioned, the fundamental distinction pertains to which realm of reality, immanence or transcendence, is rejected or ignored—though it is also possible to turn away from both at once, for example in denying that transcendent reality exists while at the same time refusing to accept the world as given. Still, the basic distinction between rejecting immanence or transcendence is helpful, and we will use it to organize a survey of interpretations of reality that reflect imbalanced consciousness. It should be stated right away, however, that this survey of interpretations is most emphatically not offered as science, but only as a suggestive catalogue, a provisional patterning of imbalanced attitudes.

Before beginning the survey, I will discuss more completely the notion of the balance of consciousness itself, and also consider some of Voegelin's remarks on requirements for maintaining the balance. After the survey, a few remarks will be offered on causes of the loss of balance and on the significance of Voegelin's analysis.

The Balance of Consciousness

It is the discovery of transcendence, the discovery that the divine ground of reality is somehow "beyond" the world of space and time, that creates the conditions in which the balance of consciousness becomes a requirement for a realistic appraisal of the human condition. The balance needing to be kept is an existential equilibrium in the face of two sorts of experience: on the one hand, experiences of worldly things, of their truth and reality and lastingness; on the other hand, experiences of human consciousness reaching toward and discovering a divine "beyond" as the ultimate source of worldly things. The difficulty of keeping this equilibrium is, as already indicated, the difficulty of not letting the discovery of divine transcendence frustrate or frighten one to the point that one either (1) distorts one's appreciation of or response to finite reality, or (2) denies or distorts the truth of transcendence.

This problem of equilibrium cannot arise in human living until the explicit identification of transcendent reality dissociates the cosmos into the two realms of finite world and divine beyond. In cosmological societies, there can be no problem of the balance of consciousness in this sense. Since in cosmological consciousness experiences of the divine ground and of worldly things are still interwoven, still unified in compactness—since divine substance and thingly substance remain to some degree fused in the imagination—the balance is not endangered. One can neither devalue the universe in favor of a beyond, nor deny the existence of a beyond, before an explicit conception of a beyond has arisen. Cosmological myth, then, as the symbolic habitat of peoples preceding the discovery of transcendence, may understandably evoke a certain nostalgia in latter-day students of ancient cultures since through it the elementary human experiences of divine reality and worldly life remain satisfyingly bound to each other. As Voegelin explains, the "cosmogonic" myths—cosmological myths of ultimate origins—"adequately express a balanced manifold of experiences" and thus promote and preserve "balanced order in the soul of the believers."[5]

With the discovery of transcendence, this protection of balance provided by cosmological myth is shattered. In the West, the discovery—flowing from experiential wellsprings in Israel and Hellas into first their own and then into surrounding cultures—gradually establishes the authority of language reflecting the dissociation of the cosmos into a realm of worldly things and a transcendent divine ground. This "differentiation of transcendence," as Voegelin calls it, turns out to be a decidedly mixed blessing. To be sure, the human search for truth has been rewarded with a transformative leap, a qualitative change in humanity's apprehension both of the structure of reality and of its own existence. The conceptual dissociation of divine powers from worldly phenomena opens finite being to its study as a network of intelligible structures, causes, and laws; and the sciences of nature are complemented by the recognition and study of the structure of consciousness itself by Greek philosophers. The human soul discovers itself, mapping out its own meaning as the invisible center of the personal and social struggle for truth and dignity, as the passionate and intelligent questioner who inhabits and explores the world while also finding, in its own infinite depths, the transcendent source of all order. The soul recognizes and describes its unique function and status as a participant in both worldly process and divine creativity, as the creative "in-between" of human-divine encounter. But also it discovers its daunting responsibility as the being who may or may not succeed in bringing the order of soul and society into adequate harmony with the truths and values of transcendent being. So the blessing of the discovery of transcendence is also a burden, making it more difficult to appreciate and accept the human situation, and introducing new temptations by which to be drawn away from successful and sanctified living, now measured by the heightened standards of the philosophers and prophets. By considering a few of these difficulties and temptations in more detail, Voegelin's notion of the balance of consciousness may be further clarified.

First, there are what might be called the intellectual difficulties ushered in by the discovery of transcendence. It is not straightforwardly obvious to just anyone with common sense what symbols of transcendence, whether of Greek, Hebrew, Christian, or other origin, refer to. The most problematic aspect of affirming transcendent reality lies in grasping its radical otherness from finite existence, its nonexistence in spatiotemporal terms. The general human tendency to rely on mental pictures in determining what is real frequently leads people to confuse divine transcendence with some kind of thing or location. This tendency to "hypostatize" (Voegelin's usual word) the transcendent ground of reality leads into a dead-end spiral of misunderstood assertions and misdirected counterassertions, a progression succinctly described by Voegelin in *The Ecumenic Age*:

> For whatever the [transcendent] ground is, it must be something; but as soon as the term *something* is introduced it suggests a "thing" of the type of existent things; but as the ground is not an existent thing, it can only be "nothing"; but as "nothing" is really nothing in terms of existent things, the question of the ground is illusionary; and so forth, until the pole of nonexistence [i.e., transcendent reality] in the experienced tension of reality has dissolved in hypostatic negations of its reality.[6]

And then, even when the profoundly "other" character of transcendent reality is recognized and granted, there are the problems of adequately understanding the relation of divine reality to immanent reality in light of the differentiating insights. Understanding this relation calls for the most subtle discernments. If the discovery of transcendence dissociates the divine ground and the finite universe into conceptually distinct realms of reality, still the structure of worldly things and human existence isn't affected by this discovery in any substantial way. It doesn't alter the practical conditions of living in the cosmos; and especially, the discovery does nothing to invalidate the apprehension of divine reality as experienced in the creation and order of the cosmos itself. How, then, is one to understand a divine reality that is present through the presence of immanent things and is also simultaneously a "beyond" of all immanent things? From this and related questions there arises the long history of speculative efforts to explain and symbolize a structure of reality so complex and, to the human mind, so full of logical insults and impasses, that the best responses to the questions have received only a minimal recognition.

Closely linked with the intellectual difficulties introduced by the discovery of transcendence are what one might call existential difficulties.

As the differentiation of transcendence separates divine perfection from the world, it causes the shadow of imperfection to fall over the whole of finite reality. The world of human life and struggle is revealed to be a partial reality, incomplete. It becomes a land of sojourn, where one's thirst for communion with the truly real, the divine source of truth and goodness, can never be fully satisfied. And the burdensome experiences of pain and suffering, misery and evil, are made even more disturbing as it becomes clear that they have no lasting solution in the world of time— that disorder in worldly existence, for all the order that may be achieved, is permanent and inescapable. To consciously endure and embrace one's own existence as a tension between immanence and transcendence, to accept that under the conditions of earthly existence the highest human aspirations remain unattainable, requires certain virtues of courage and confidence—indeed, as we shall see, of faith, hope, and love—that not everyone is able to muster.

Then there are the difficulties involving the problem of history. The discovery of transcendence impresses itself on the discoverers as a radical, decisive advance in the human knowledge of reality and in human self-understanding. The experience of a radical, transformative leap in the search for truth prompts the question of history: why is there such an advance? Why is there historical development? If the meaning of human existence includes the transformations that human consciousness achieves as it unfolds through time, what is the point or the goal of this historical process?

The question cannot be answered definitively, for not only does history remain open-ended toward the future, but its origin and ultimate meaning rest in a divine source of meaning beyond time. Nevertheless, the fundamental clue regarding the direction of historical development is given with the decisive, transformative leap from cosmological consciousness to differentiated consciousness, to consciousness explicitly aware of its participation in transcendent meaning. History in general is the process in which divine presence meets human response. The differentiating responses constitute a qualitative leap in human knowledge of and attunement with divine transcendence. With the decisive event in historical advance being this emergence within finite consciousness of an explicit grasp and affirming embrace of its own participation in and obligation toward transcendent divine reality, the movement of history would appear to be above all a movement in which the finite world, through the medium of human consciousness, advances toward fuller, more emphatic participation in the timeless divine ground. History is a process of "transfiguration," to use Voegelin's term, in which finite and perishable being is drawn into more complete, more eminent, participation in the imperishable divine ground. And finally, with the recognition of this as the struc-

ture of historical advance, there comes the suggestive image of a completion to the movement: of arrival at some final, transfigurative participation
of finite in transcendent being. This is a promise that has no consummation so long as the world and human history continue to exist. But ever
since the discovery of transcendence, it is a promise that has haunted the
human imagination with dreams of a transfigured and glorified existence,
of a new heaven and a new earth, of a redemptive conclusion to the long,
bloody, perplexing story of human effort and achievement. Thus the
awareness of history, and especially of its permanently unresolved relation to transcendence, complicates the challenge of sustaining a realistic
and balanced view of the human situation.

What I have identified here as intellectual, existential, and historical
difficulties are quite obviously not discrete but overlapping concerns; and
their scope has merely been adumbrated. But enough has been stated to
indicate the formidable challenge of orientation in existence posed by the
discovery of transcendence. Voegelin's summary way of referring to this
challenge, in his later writings, is to describe it as the task of ordering
one's life as "existence in the tension of the *metaxy*," with the Greek
word *metaxy*, "in-between," referring primarily to the in-between of immanence and transcendence.[7] Every dimension of human concern unfolds
in the tension of the *metaxy*. The search for individual happiness and
dignity, for political order and the social good, for redemptive historical
achievement—all unfold in the tension between the imperfections of life
in time and the apprehension of timeless perfection. Existence in cosmological society, it should be stressed, was already if not consciously this
tension. It is the very nature of human consciousness to be structured as
the in-between of immanence and transcendence, whether or not that nature is identified and known as such. But the postcosmological awareness
of one's own consciousness as precisely such an in-between *heightens* the
tension of existence, by making explicit that one's consciousness participates in the mystery of transcendence. To consciously acknowledge one's
own life as existence in the tension of the *metaxy* and to order it accordingly, therefore, requires embracing the mysteriousness of transcendence.
And herein lies the principal obstacle to maintaining the balance of consciousness.

The mystery of reality is hard to bear. The discovery of transcendence
reveals an unavoidable "blind spot at the center of all human knowledge
about man," an "ignorance with regard to the decisive core of existence"
that frustrates our desire for answers to our deepest questions about our
origins, purposes, and destinies.[8] We long for certainty: for absolute
knowledge about what we are and where we came from, for assurance
that our lives have some permanent meaning in the scheme of things, for
immortality. The revelation of transcendence makes it certain merely that

we *cannot* humanly know the ultimate truths about human origins and destiny; that our yearnings for truth, righteousness, and goodness are uncertain of consummation; and that though we do participate as long as existence lasts in the permanence of transcendent meaning, we know nothing of our future or ultimate relation to imperishable being. The *metaxy*, the human-divine in-between, is also the in-between of ignorance and knowledge, of imperfection and perfection, and of contingency and permanence. Nothing is more true of existence in the *metaxy* than that it has no resolution, no solution, in worldly time. All human accomplishment is an unfinished search within a horizon of divine mystery. This is a most disturbing fact to admit, one that understandably gives rise to anxiety. But to face this anxiety and respect the truth of the *metaxy* is precisely what is involved in maintaining the balance of consciousness.

The balance of consciousness, then, is psychological and existential equilibrium in full openness to the mystery of reality, honoring the truth of transcendence, while remaining committed to the search for truth and goodness in worldly existence. Slipping away from the balance is easy. The *mysterium fascinans et tremendum* of transcendence may lead one to the conviction that it is transcendent reality alone that counts, that the transfigurative process in history revealed through the differentiating insights is as good as completed, that concern with existence in the world is misplaced in light of the differentiating "theophanies" that have revealed the truth of the transcendent beyond. Conversely, love of the world and commitment to the struggle for human dignity and well-being can lead one to reject transcendence as a danger to that very commitment, to regard it as a misplacement of the divine in a false beyond, a conceptual error undermining a sense of responsibility to the world, an illusion created by haters of their own lives. Either of these false resolutions to the tension of existence in the *metaxy* makes the human situation easier to understand and to live with: the mystery of reality is reduced; a responsible course of action is more readily discerned; and enemies—the promulgators of untruth—are more easily identified. But either alternative is a betrayal of the more difficult truth of the actual human situation. The balance of consciousness requires one to reject both alternatives as distortions of reality, and thus to preserve, in Voegelin's words, "the balance between the experienced lastingness [of the cosmos] and the theophanic events" in such a way that neither discredits the other.[9] The balance is finally, then, a matter of accepting one's human role *as a mediator between immanence and transcendence*, loving the world while acknowledging it to be oriented toward a transcendent meaning and fulfillment.

Loving the world, while loving divine transcendence: this is a primary requirement for keeping the balance of consciousness. It was the loving search for, and loving responsiveness to, the divine source of reality that led to the discovery of transcendence in the West by Greek philosophers and Hebrew prophets, as Voegelin points out. And it is only loving openness toward the whole of reality that can at the same time sustain fidelity to the presence of divine transcendence as apprehended in consciousness and also to divine presence revealed through cosmic order.[10] Such openness acknowledges that the goodness and fulfillment we most long for are not to be granted in the time of existence, that our expectation of them must rest on hope; and so hope, too, plays its part in keeping the balance. And finally faith—basic trust in reality and confidence in its ultimate meaningfulness—is needed to remain open to the mystery of reality. So Voegelin argues that faith, hope, and love, the familiar triad from St. Paul's first letter to the Corinthians, are elementary requirements for suffering openness to reality in its fullness, and thus deserve to be called "the virtues of existential tension": habits of orientation without which the anxieties and uncertainties of meaning belonging to existence in the tension of the *metaxy* would be unbearable.[11]

Many do lose their equilibrium. Frustration and anxiety in the face of mystery; desire for absolute certainty and control; intolerance of ambiguity; moral passion that cannot bear waiting for the envisioned, possibly unattainable good; a longing to escape the burden of human responsibility; all of these can contribute to a flight from the tension of the *metaxy* and a loss of the balance of consciousness. It must not be thought, either, that intellectual talent, or purity of moral intention, is a safeguard against that loss. In fact, as Voegelin's portrayals of such figures as the prophet Isaiah, Hegel, and Nietzsche indicate, it is sometimes the moral fervor witnessing to a supreme sensitivity to human distress, or an intellectual sophistication that penetrates the mystery of reality so deeply that it imagines it to have solved it, which inspires devotion to a distorted interpretation of reality. As the following survey will show, the modes of imbalanced outlook are many and derive from many motives. As to the two major orientations of these modes, in general it may be said that imbalanced outlooks from the ancient world tend toward devaluation of the world in favor of transcendence, while among moderns the tendency is toward the reverse, favoring the denial or misconstrual of transcendence. The descriptions and examples in the following brief survey will indicate these trends (and the extent of exceptions to them), and also in passing testify to human ingenuity, so successful in devising interpretations of reality that assuage the unease of differentiated consciousness.

Attitudes toward Reality Reflecting Imbalanced Consciousness

The most basic distinction for identifying imbalanced attitudes reflects the two directions in which escape is sought from the tension of balanced consciousness. One may, through fascination with transcendence, turn away from the challenge of living in the world and so adopt an attitude that devalues worldly reality; or one may attempt to eclipse the troublesome truth of transcendence. The following survey includes five examples of each of these modes of escape. Each example given, it should be stressed, is merely an *attitude*, perhaps functioning as merely an assumption or habit of perception, though an attitude capable of expansion into a sophisticated argument or worldview. Further, these attitudes, as shall be noted, are frequently complementary. It is possible, for example, to view the immanent realm as both irrelevant and ultimately illusory— while it is also possible to hold only one of these attitudes and not the other. Also, the two basic modes of imbalance, rejection of transcendence and rejection of immanence, are not always mutually exclusive. A person may be closed toward transcendence and also reject the truth of worldly order—an example being Karl Marx, who both dismisses transcendence as an illusion and rejects the given structure of the world in favor of an unrealizable ideal. A final, eleventh example in the survey will in fact be an attitude that combines both forms of imbalance in the extreme position of what I call "absurdism," constituting, I suspect, a certain limit to the suppression of awareness of the *metaxy*.[12]

Attitudes That Devalue Worldly Reality

The discovery of a divine beyond, by imaginatively splitting the cosmos into finite and transcendent realms, can create the impression that the divine is no longer present in the world. In this way the discovery of transcendence—which led, inevitably, to the waning of belief in the gods of cosmological myth—is allowed, quite unjustifiably, to radically dedivinize the finite universe altogether. "By a non sequitur," as Voegelin puts it, "immanence may become perverted from a world empty of the gods of polytheism to a world empty of divinity."[13]

Common to these viewpoints is a gap in perception: to some degree, the experience of divine reality *as present through the presence of finite things* is lost or obscured. Thus they evidence a lack of respect for the world, and for the conditions of human existence.

1. *Immanence as irrelevant.* Once a distinction is made between immanent world and divine transcendence, the finite world's incompleteness, imperfection, and perishability stand out in sharp contrast to the perfect and imperishable divine ground. The conviction may then grow that only the transcendent source of the world is truly meaningful, and that the imperfect and perishing world does not deserve our deep concern—that worldly existence is a mere waiting period in an inconsequential abode, while our transcendent homeland alone deserves our real attention. "Lay

up for yourselves treasures in heaven" (Matthew 6:20) can be taken to mean that existence under worldly conditions is not to be granted real importance, that poverty, injustice, inequality, and other worldly evils should not too much distract us as we stay focused on our transcendent destiny; likewise the world of nature should not be considered too significant or unduly fussed over.

Here the loss of balance involves, among other oversights, forgetting that the transcendent ground is only discovered through consciousness searching for the ground of the world it experiences—that the divine ground *is the ground of the world*, which therefore, for all its imperfections, enjoys the sanction of divine perfection.[14] An otherworldly focus leading to indifference toward such evils as poverty, disease, oppressive social conditions, and exploitation and destruction of the natural environment, betrays a desire to reduce the tension of existence by rendering the immanent pole of experience irrelevant. Balanced consciousness, on the contrary, accepts the responsibility of being a mediator between transcendent and immanent reality, and so also the duty to "shepherd" the world into as close an attunement as possible with transcendent values and ideals.

2. *Immanence as evil.* Once the divine ground recedes to a beyond, the shadow of imperfection that falls on the world can be misconstrued as the shadow of evil. Goodness then becomes identified with transcendence, while existence in the world, with its dangers, accidents, pain and sickness, poverty, hunger, war, and death, is perceived as imprisonment in evil. In this view, what is good in ourselves is "spirit" or whatever in us that is not "of" the world; while whatever binds us to the finite universe—our bodies, sense-based desires, worldly concerns—is a demonic burden. Existing only as a hell to be escaped from, the given world is regarded as darkness, delusion, and evil, the antithesis of divine light, truth, and goodness.

An example of this attitude, and in Voegelin's view a particularly telling symptom of imbalanced consciousness, is the viewpoint of ancient Gnosticism. In the ancient Gnostic writings, the physical universe is portrayed as the creation of an evil divinity and as a prison into which our spirits, "sparks" of transcendence, have "fallen," and from which they must find their way back to their proper abode beyond this universe through action based on the right knowledge (gnosis). Human spirits are sparks of goodness, deriving from a supratranscendent divinity, while the order and history of the existing world are alien to goodness.

Voegelin treats in some detail the existential motives underlying the ancient Gnostic images of reality and the enduring appeal of various types of gnostic vision, ancient and modern. At times he presents them as understandable responses to profound anxiety in the face of the miseries and mysteries of existence.[15] Still, a severe loss of balance is indicated in the Gnostic rejection of the significance and goodness of participating in world and history. The rejection—which again depends on a misleading reification of transcendent meaning—is a betrayal of the fact that existence in the world is the very condition of human concern for the good. Any *questioning* about purpose, goodness, and the where-to and where-from of human existence belongs to the structure of the human psyche as it emerges within the hierarchy of being that includes finite being. Consequently any "beyond" discovered as an *answer* to such questioning cannot reasonably be considered alien to the cosmic process in which the questioning has emerged. The Gnostic rejection of the world is an attempt to escape the tension of existence and its uncertainties by irresponsibly aligning the self with transcendence in an aggressive posture against immanence and declaring solved the mystery of existence in the *metaxy*.

3. *Immanence as illusory.* This response to existence is similar to the preceding attitude, only in this case the accent falls on truth and illusion rather than on good and evil. Again a strict dichotomy is imposed: only the transcendent dimension and insights regarding it are accorded the status of "truth," while the immanent realm and knowledge pertaining to it are reduced to the rank of "illusion." Meaning that does not perish must be transcendent, so transcendence is alone accorded the status of *true* reality, while the world known through the senses is dismissed as a flux of appearance, a shifting mirage mistaken by the ignorant for true reality. The essential struggle of existence is that of escaping from this ignorance, and most fail in the task: all humans begin life subject to the illusion that the world of the senses is something solid and enduring, and this illusion is reinforced by sensory pleasures and attractions that typically keep people from discovering or acknowledging that true reality is the imperishable oneness beyond the world of multiplicity and perishability.

This attitude is sometimes associated with Hindu culture, where the Vedantic tradition identifies truth with *Brahman*, the one transcendent reality, and subsumes all of physical reality and individuality under the heading of *maya*, or cosmic illusion. The Vedantic reduction of immanence to the rank of illusion is certainly more benign than the Gnostic condemnation of it as evil; it allows room, after all, for a loving and respectful posture toward the world. But it, too, is based on a misleading hypostatization of immanence and transcendence. Transcendence, as Voegelin might say, is not elsewhere; its truth is not that of another world.[16] Transcendent truth is the real completeness of meaning attested to by the finite universe, whose incomplete meaning awakens consciousness to the divine self-sufficiency that grounds both universe and consciousness. As completeness of meaning, it is neither "here" nor "there";

it is the ineffable fullness of divine presence suggested by divine presence as experienced. Indeed, the significance of the world is guaranteed, rather than made spurious, by the truth of transcendence. The designation of immanence as *maya* leans away unjustifiably from balance in the *metaxy* toward escape into transcendence, and by doing so devalues the very real, if difficult, problems of worldly and historical responsibility.[17]

4. *Immanence as an abandoned mechanism.* In the early modern period, with the rise of natural sciences based on or inspired by mathematical analysis, it became possible to conceive of the physical universe as a vast machine whose workings could in time be exhaustively known through application of the proper scientific method. The resulting mechanical model of the universe was especially attractive to philosophical materialists, for whom reality can on principle be fully explained in terms of matter and motion. But a machinelike universe may also be understood to imply by necessity a machine-maker, a divine inventor. Granting both machine and divine maker, then, how ought one to understand the relation between the two? If the disclosure of causal relations and predictive laws through scientific investigation is accepted as promising, in time, a complete explanation of all finite phenomena, what role is left in an explanation of reality for transcendent divinity? Nothing more, it may seem, than that of one-time manufacturer of this fabulously intricate machine, who, after having set it into motion, remains apart from and uninvolved in its functioning. By the seventeenth and eighteenth centuries, such a view of world (immanence) and God (transcendence) had entered Western popular imagination.

The view is misleading in numerous ways. A general problem is that it tends toward reductionist interpretations of psychological, intellectual, and spiritual phenomena, interpretations that claim to explain all of reality strictly in terms of the "building blocks" of physical elements, chemical compounds, and/or biological structures and functions. With respect specifically to its devaluation of the immanent realm, though, the point is this: if the mechanical analogy is taken to mean that finite reality is a closed system, in relation to which divine transcendence is no more than an absentee First Cause, then it distorts the relation between immanent and transcendent reality by obscuring the human experiences of divine presence as costructuring consciousness and as informing cosmic order. Again a reified transcendent ground and reified world are divorced from each other, falsely positioning the divine in a spatial "elsewhere" and eclipsing the human-divine *metaxy* of consciousness through the imaginal incorporation of conscious existence into an immanent mechanical scheme. Any affirmation of divine transcendence that also affirms the universe to be an autonomous mechanism reflects an imbalancing dullness of sensitivity to the divine presence in world and consciousness.

5. *Metastatic faith.* A final and dramatic example of human attitudes that devalue worldly reality is *metastatic faith.* Voegelin coins the phrase in *Israel and Revelation* to describe the prophet Isaiah's conviction that God will reward a faithful Israel by intervening in worldly affairs on its behalf, an intervention that would in fact entail a transfiguration of the conditions of worldly existence to bring them into conformity with divine will and perfection. This faith in an impending alteration, or *metastasis*, in the constitution of finite being through divine grace reflects Isaiah's impatience with the conditions of the actual world, an impatience magnified by his trust in Yahweh into the certainty that his own desire for a new world coincides with the divine plan. Out of this mix of passion and presumption comes Isaiah's "vision of a world that will change its nature without ceasing to be the world in which we live concretely."[18]

For Voegelin, such a faith is unfounded, involving as it does a denial of the experienced truth and lastingness of the order of mundane existence, as well as a confusion about the implications of transcendence. But it should be noted that Voegelin's critique of Isaiah on this issue is more complex than some commentators have assumed. He emphasizes that the existential roots of metastatic faith lie in the sublime realizations of the prophets about the true nature of personal harmony with divine reality and in their painful sensitivity to the disparity between the order realized in their own souls and any actual—or actualizable—social order. Transfiguration, Voegelin reminds us, has actually occurred in the souls of the prophets; the prophetic insights into the nature of true existence under God were "essentially metastatic."[19] The problems arise when the metastatic *experience* erupts into faith in a *concrete metastasis of worldly order.* The balance of consciousness is lost when the value of living in the world is ignored in impatient anticipation of its miraculous transfiguration.

The problem of metastatic faith, writes Voegelin, "is of importance for the understanding not only of Israelite and Jewish order but of the history of Western Civilization to this day." For not only have symbols of world-transformation and organized activity deriving from metastatic experience been a constant in Western religious life—the Christian elaboration of metastatic insights animated heresies throughout the Middle Ages, and has continued to give birth to millennialist and chiliastic expectations among religious groups of the most diverse and colorful persuasions—but they have also become in recent centuries a crucial force in secular culture and politics. Voegelin mentions "progressivist metastatic faith," and also the heralded "communist metastasis," as recent examples of the expectation of a miraculous perfection of world or society.[20] In these secular instances, faith in world transfiguration has become divorced from acknowledgment of divine transcendence, but the perspective is structurally identical insofar as the world's order as given is rejected in favor of its miraculous metastasis.[21]

Attitudes That Eclipse Transcendent Reality

In secular forms of metastatic faith, the given world is rejected, but not in favor of transcendence—transcendence is ignored or dismissed as an illusion. The eclipsing of transcendence is a second major means of obscuring reality and fleeing the tension of the *metaxy*. Though, as we see, it can be combined with devaluing the truth of the world, usually the rejection of transcendence is linked to a willful embrace of the immanent realm as acceptable, good, and even sacred.

Resistance to the fact of transcendence may be quite innocent, merely a result of its elusiveness. As stated earlier, it is not immediately clear to just anyone what language about transcendence signifies. Unless a person has undergone experiences in some degree parallel to those of the original discoverers of transcendence, the language symbols arising from those discoveries may well seem unpersuasive, if not fantastical.[22] On the other hand, the rejection of transcendence is not always so benign. It may be the reaction of a consciousness frustrated, or enraged, by its awareness of a transcendent truth that causes the world's and its own imperfection, dependence, incompleteness, and perishability to stand glaringly forth. Imbalanced attitudes that eclipse transcendence, then, arise from existential origins ranging from gross ignorance to conscious revolt against divine power and authority.

6. *Transcendence as irrelevant.* Divine transcendence is by definition a reality beyond the reach of direct, or substantive, human understanding. Through the discovery of transcendence, the divine ground takes on "the ambiguity of an unknown that becomes known as the unknown," an ambiguity that can easily be misconstrued.[23] For example, knowing of the divine's essential unknowability may lead to the conclusion that, whatever the divine is, it is not worth thinking about at all. Or there is the more reasoned error of the agnostic, the "nonknower," who mistakes human ignorance about the *what* of the divine ground for lack of evidence as to *whether* there is a divine ground, and so declares that our search for the divine is and must remain inconclusive. In both cases, the "no-thing" of transcendence is reduced to a mere blank, something irrelevant to our search for direction in life.

Dismissed as irrelevant, the transcendent ground sinks below the horizon of acknowledgment. But all the time concern with ultimate meaning persists. The consequence is a collapse of human yearning for ultimacy into a concern with finite objects and considerations, and a consequent distortion of values and goals reflecting the assumption that only the worldly is significant.

7. *Transcendence as evil (Prometheanism)*. In Greek tradition, Prometheus was a divinity who rebelled against the community of gods by stealing the divine fire and giving it to humans, a transgression for which Zeus, leader of the gods, imposed a terrifying punishment. Aeschylus, in *Prometheus Bound*, portrays a chained Prometheus staunch in his defiance: "In one word, I hate all the gods who received good from me and wrongfully returned evil."[24] One may with a little license, then, define as a "Promethean attitude" one in which divine power and authority are seen as an encroachment on human freedom and dignity, justifying the rejection of the divine for the good of human self-determination.

Prometheanism as just described is an attitude made possible through the differentiation of immanent and transcendent being, since a human revolt against divine will can only be based on the apprehension of independent human powers of reason, judgment, and decision—that is, on the clear distinction of human will and divine will achieved through the conceptual separation of immanent nature and divine transcendence.

Since the Promethean stance only makes sense on the presumption that divinity is real, its rejection of divine transcendence is essentially an act of defiance: a refusal to give allegiance to a divine reality perceived to be a threat to human dignity. It is imbalanced consciousness in the purest posture of revolt against transcendence.

8. *Transcendence as illusory*. Again, one may become convinced that transcendence is a hoax, that there can be no reality beyond the reality intrinsically conditioned by space and time. To the hardheaded materialist, a term such as *transcendence*, or *God*, or *nirvana* is just the symbol of an illusion, born of human gullibility or mendacity. In the early nineteenth century, Ludwig Feuerbach explained that transcendent divinity is only a projection of human desires and capacities onto a fictional "beyond" of the world. Karl Marx further developed Feuerbach's thesis by identifying the origins of religious projection in the oppressive social and economic conditions that create the need for soothing illusions of an omnipotent divinity and a just afterlife. As atheists, Feuerbach and Marx argue that all conceptions of divinity originate in human creativity, aspiration, and community; as materialists, they view the immanent realm—the physical universe including human consciousness—as the whole of reality.

It is possible to regard transcendence as an illusion and not be an atheist: as we shall see in the cases of our next two categories, there are those for whom denying transcendence is part of a religious response to the world and an effort to reawaken awareness of divine presence in nature. But in modern culture the most familiar denunciations of transcendence as an illusion belong to the atheist intellectual current that flows from late Enlightenment materialism, through Feuerbach, Marx, Nietzsche, and

Freud, into the popular materialisms and vague scientisms of our contemporaries who find notions of divine reality both incredible and quaint.

Voegelin's response to atheist materialism, or to any portrayal of reality as "wholly immanent," rests on the critical realization that *immanence* and *transcendence* are not separable descriptive terms, but in fact a single, linked notion, the notion of *immanence-transcendence*, originating in meditative experiences in which the one complex of reality experienced in the tension of consciousness becomes conceptually differentiated into a world of things and their incommensurate ground. The experience of a ground of things is always an element in the human awareness of reality: consciousness is always conscious of there being a ground of its own and worldly being. *Transcendence* is merely the designation of this ground following the insight into its incommensurability with finite and limited being, which in contrast with the ground becomes *immanence*. *Immanence* and *transcendence* are linked exegetical concepts that only together explain an experience of reality. Neither term means anything in isolation.

But the image of a "wholly immanent" world, however nonsensical, maintains its appeal, since human consciousness prefers to think in concrete images, and so creates for itself a "world" of immanence and a second "world" of transcendence of which one may quite justifiably become suspicious.

9. *Pantheism.* Pantheism asserts that the totality of things is identical with God or divinity. From Voegelin's standpoint, such a view may be charged with an indiscriminate fusing of immanence and transcendence, arising from either an unwillingness or an inability to acknowledge the real incommensurability of the divine ground and finite things.

The viewpoint of pantheism is only attainable once the divine has dissociated from specific entities and powers in the natural world—that is, once the compact cosmos of cosmological consciousness has differentiated into nature and transcendence. Only then is nature free to have divinity dispersed throughout it in a general fashion rather than identified with particular forces, object, and locales; and again only then is divinity vague and impalpable enough in its characteristics to be able to be thought of as being present everywhere. Pantheism, therefore, employs the differentiated categories of nature and transcendent ground only to mismanage them by refusing their distinction, insisting on an identity between the nature that attests to divine presence and the ultimate and ineffable divine ground of being. It eclipses transcendence by identifying it with immanence.

10. *Neopaganism.* We may describe as *neopagan* a religious attitude guided by the attempt to re-evoke experiences of, and to reestablish practices of worship relating to, intracosmic divinities. The neopagan attitude views the historical displacement of the cosmological gods and goddesses

by the world-transcendent God of Judaism, Christianity, and Islam as an error and a curse, a replacement of natural religion opening the way to a debased, mechanistic view of nature and to an arrogant indifference to environmental values that shows itself in greedy exploitation of the natural world. A remedy is seen in the recovery of outlooks and beliefs characteristic of the cosmological religions of ancient, Native American, and to some extent Eastern cultures. The recovery of cosmological-mythic experiences in resistance to doctrines and institutions that teach divine transcendence is a goal common to numerous contemporary grassroots and "new age" spiritual movements.

The goal is unattainable. The discovery of transcendence, whatever its consequences for good and ill, was not a mistake; the disappearance of the cosmological gods and goddesses cannot be reversed, however intense the nostalgic devotion to their original truth as experiences of divine presence; and one cannot in full sincerity ignore the cultural and linguistic heritage of the differentiating insights and "play existence in cosmic-divine order" as if they had never occurred.[25] The eclipse of transcendence in the neopagan outlook involves a willful denial of the *metaxy* that can only maintain itself by ignoring the omnipresent symbols and vastly complex articulations of differentiated spiritual truths in the major Western and Eastern religious traditions.

An Attitude That Both Devalues Worldly Reality and Eclipses Transcendent Reality

11. *Absurdism.* Finally, it is possible to hold both that transcendence is an illusion and that there is nothing either sacred or even intrinsically meaningful about worldly reality—that nothing at all in reality bears witness to enduring value or purpose. Neither a world-transcendent truth nor the world of nature is understood to provide a measure or standard for determining what constitutes meaningful direction in life. The human situation then appears absurd: not absurd in the noble sense of Kierkegaard or Camus, each of whom had faith in some kind of enduring meaning, but absurd in the sense of pointless or meaningless: a situation without aim beyond the obvious psychological urges toward pleasure and power.

In this final attitude of absurdism, a certain limit would appear to be reached in the dulling of sensitivity to the tension of living in the *metaxy* and thus to the value of achieving a "balance of consciousness" in Voegelin's sense. Intransigent denial of both transcendent reality and the world's value, total closure to enduring meaning, would appear to constitute the antithesis to the existential openness that values the world's truth while acknowledging and loving the transcendent source of its order.

Conclusion

There is no need, after this survey of attitudes, to argue Voegelin's point that the balance of consciousness is a rare achievement. The appeal and widespread acceptance of imbalanced viewpoints is obvious. And scarcely less obvious is the principal cause of the loss of balance. Every one of the attitudes sketched above simplifies reality and reduces existential uncertainty at some cost to the truth about the human situation. Each attitude attempts to lessen the mystery of existence—by turning away from the truth of transcendence, by diminishing the importance of the given world, or by doing both at once—and so induce a sense of greater human control over our situation and destiny. The balance of consciousness requires above all a high tolerance for uncertainty about the outcome and ultimate meaning of personal existence and historical transformation.

Two concluding points may be made about Voegelin's analysis of the balance of consciousness. First, he stresses that, although the achievement of the balance is relatively rare, since the time of classic philosophy it has successfully provided a normative critical perspective from which to recognize as deformed those attitudes or philosophies that either devalue the world or deny transcendence, and in so doing "has determined the life of reason in Western civilization up to our own time."[26] Second, Voegelin's own study of the balance of consciousness, an essential component of his analysis of human existence in the *metaxy*, constitutes a unique theoretical clarification of that critical perspective and is thus—as this essay has tried to indicate—a particularly useful instrument in the contemporary effort to diagnose disorder and unreason.

Notes

1. Eric Voegelin, *Order and History*, vol. 4, *The Ecumenic Age* (Baton Rouge: Louisiana State University Press, 1974), chap. 4, § 3, "The Balance of Consciousness," 227–38.

2. For one of Voegelin's most concentrated and sustained accounts of human life as a "tension of existence" between "poles" of immanence and transcendence, see his essay "Eternal Being in Time," in Eric Voegelin, *Anamnesis*, ed. and trans. Gerhart Niemeyer (Notre Dame: University of Notre Dame Press, 1978), esp. 124–36.

3. As far as I can tell, the phrase proper first appears in *The Ecumenic Age* and "Reason: The Classic Experience," both published in 1974. See Eric Voegelin, "Reason: The Classic Experience," in *The Collected Works of Eric Voegelin*, vol. 12, *Published Essays, 1966–1985*, ed. Ellis Sandoz (Baton Rouge: Louisiana State University Press, 1990), 266. Related notions of psychological, or existential, balance appear in earlier works. For example, in *Plato and Aristotle* (1957), Voegelin describes the "balance of openness and separateness" that must be achieved if

myth—as the expression of openness to the cosmic ground of being—is to help one endure the separateness of finite existence; and in "What Is Political Reality?" (1966), Voegelin writes of the mystic's "balance of tolerance . . . between the areas of silence and of symbolic expressions" that preserves awareness of the ineffability of the divine ground of reality while acknowledging or using symbols to evoke it. See Eric Voegelin, *Order and History*, vol. 3, *Plato and Aristotle* (Baton Rouge: Louisiana State University Press, 1957), 188; and "What Is Political Reality?", in *Anamnesis*, 197–98. In the works that follow *The Ecumenic Age*, the notion of "the balance of consciousness" is again made thematic in "Wisdom and the Magic of the Extreme: A Meditation" (1977). The treatment here, which introduces some refinements to the notion while linking it more immediately to Voegelin's account of the structure of consciousness, is an integral part of Voegelin's meditation on the topic. See Eric Voegelin, "Wisdom and the Magic of the Extreme: A Meditation," in *Published Essays, 1966–1985*, 326–28.

4. I have chosen to write of "imbalanced" rather than "unbalanced" consciousness for a number of reasons. First, I want to avoid the connotations popularly associated with the notion that someone's mind or consciousness is "unbalanced" in a psychological sense. Second, "imbalanced" more readily suggests degrees of "lack of balance," while "unbalanced" might suggest simply "not balanced." And third, there is the precedent of Voegelin's use of the term as both noun and adjective (for example: "the Gnostic imbalance of consciousness," *The Ecumenic Age*, 234; "imbalanced and distorted images of reality," "Wisdom and the Magic of the Extreme," 327).

5. Eric Voegelin, *Order and History*, vol. 1, *Israel and Revelation* (Baton Rouge: Louisiana State University Press, 1956), 84.

6. *The Ecumenic Age*, 74.

7. Voegelin takes the term *metaxy* from Plato, who, he claims, used it (principally in *Symposium*) to designate the distinctive ontological realm of human consciousness, where the search for meaning, happiness, and divinity takes place. See "Reason: The Classic Experience," 279–82. For Voegelin's most concentrated description of human existence as having the structure of an "in-between" or *metaxy* , see "Equivalences of Experience and Symbolization in History," in *Published Essays, 1966–1985*, 119–20.

8. *Israel and Revelation*, 2.

9. *The Ecumenic Age*, 228.

10. On love as an element in the philosophical discovery of transcendence, see Eric Voegelin, "Science, Politics, and Gnosticism," trans. William J. Fitzpatrick, in Eric Voegelin, *Science, Politics, and Gnosticism* (Chicago: Henry Regnery Co., 1968), 18: "In the experiences of love for the world-transcendent origin of being, in *philia* toward the *sophon* (the wise), in *eros* toward the *agathon* (the good) and the *kalon* (the beautiful), man became philosopher. From these experiences arose the image of the order of being. At the opening of the soul . . . the order of being becomes visible even to its ground and origin in the beyond, in the Platonic *epekeina*, in which the soul participates as it suffers and achieves its opening." See also "Reason: The Classic Experience," 273–74.

11. "Equivalences of Experience and Symbolization in History," 122. Earlier

in the same essay (119) he refers to the triad as "virtues of openness toward the ground of being."

12. Michael Franz in his study of Voegelin has also provided categories for mapping out types of imbalanced consciousness. He arranges them under four headings, with each of the two basic orientations, "eclipse of worldly reality" and "closure against transcendent experience," divided into two chronological segments, the Christian epiphany constituting a dividing line. Eclipse of worldly reality is given the headings of "metastatic faith" (B.C.) and "parousiasm" (A.D.); closure against transcendent experience the headings of "promethean revolt" (B.C.) and "ideological consciousness" (A.D.). See Michael Franz, *Eric Voegelin and the Politics of Spiritual Revolt: The Roots of Modern Ideology* (Baton Rouge: Louisiana State University Press, 1992), 3–20. Franz describes his categories as merely "heuristic suggestions," and reminds the reader that the "two characteristic patterns of 'imbalanced' consciousness—closure against transcendent experience and eclipse of worldly reality—are often observable in a single writer" (10). Franz's work has been helpful in developing my own survey of imbalanced attitudes, though the results of our respective organizing efforts reflect somewhat different questions and criteria.

13. Eric Voegelin, "Anxiety and Reason," in *The Collected Works of Eric Voegelin*, vol. 28, *What Is History? And Other Late Unpublished Writings*, ed. Thomas A. Hollweck and Paul Caringella (Baton Rouge: Louisiana State University Press, 1990), 78.

14. As Voegelin puts the matter in *The Ecumenic Age* (324), "[T]he discovery of the [transcendent] ground does not condemn the field of existent things to irrelevance but, on the contrary, establishes it as the reality that derives the meaning of its existence from the ground; and inversely, the [search for ultimate reality], as it ascends over the hierarchy of being, leads toward the ground because the ground is the origin of the hierarchy."

15. See especially the introduction (3–12) to "Science, Politics, and Gnosticism"; also *The Ecumenic Age*, 17–29.

16. "Such terms as *immanent* and *transcendent* . . . do not denote objects or their properties but are the language indices arising from the Metaxy in the event of its becoming luminous for the comprehensive reality, its structure and dynamics. The terms are exegetic, not descriptive. They indicate the movements of the soul when, in the Metaxy of consciousness, it explores the experience of divine reality and tries to find the language that will articulate its exegetic movements" ("The Beginning and the Beyond: A Meditation on Truth," in *What Is History?*, 185).

17. The Vedantic attitude may be interestingly contrasted with the poem of the pre-Socratic philosopher Parmenides, as analyzed by Voegelin. The Parmenidean distinction between Truth (*aletheia*) and Delusion (*doxa*) recalls the *Brahman-maya* distinction, but according to Voegelin, Parmenides (as far as the text permits conjecture) shows less tendency toward misleading hypostatization of the two "realities" described in his poem. See Eric Voegelin, *Order and History*, vol. 2, *The World of the Polis* (Baton Rouge: Louisiana State University Press, 1957), 203–19.

18. *Israel and Revelation*, 452. On metastatic faith, see especially 447–58 and 481–91.

19. *Israel and Revelation*, 484. "The metastatic experience of Isaiah, which hitherto has been considered under the aspect of a sterile withdrawal from the realities of Israel's order, will appear in a new light if it is considered as an experience of the gulf between true order and the order realized concretely by any society, even Israel. And Jeremiah's experience of the tension between the two orders . . . is even articulate enough to make it certain that the prophet had at least a glimpse of the terrible truth: that the existence of a concrete society in a definite form will not resolve the problem of order in history . . ." (491).

20. *Israel and Revelation*, 481–82 n13, 484.

21. It may be said that the secular forms of metastatic faith that reject the given world in favor of an imagined perfected world have in fact not truly abandoned transcendence, but rather allowed imagination to confuse the perfections of transcendence, conceived specifically as the goal of historical transfiguration, with the conditions of immanence; they have, in Voegelin's phrase, "immanentized the eschaton." See Eric Voegelin, *The New Science of Politics: An Introduction* (Chicago: The University of Chicago Press, 1952), 117–21.

22. "[W]hen the experience engendering the symbols ceases to be a presence located in the man who has it, the reality from which the symbols derive their meaning has disappeared. The symbols in the sense of a spoken or written word, it is true, are left as traces in the world of sense perception, but their meaning can be understood only if they evoke, and through evocation reconstitute, the engendering reality in the listener or reader" ("Immortality: Experience and Symbol," in *Published Essays, 1966–1985*, 52–53). "[T]heory as an explication of certain experiences is intelligible only to those in whom the explication will stir up parallel experiences as the empirical basis for testing the truth of theory. Unless a theoretical exposition activates the corresponding experiences at least to a degree, it will create the impression of empty talk or will perhaps be rejected as an irrelevant expression of subjective opinions" (*The New Science of Politics*, 64–65).

23. "The Beginning and the Beyond," 217.

24. Lines 975–76, quoted in *The World of the Polis*, 259–60. For Voegelin's discussion of Aeschylus's *Prometheus Bound*, see *The World of the Polis*, 253–64. Karl Marx famously quoted the line, "In one word, I hate all the gods," in the preface to his doctoral thesis, adopting Prometheus as a symbol of his own atheistic position. See Franz, *Eric Voegelin and the Politics of Spiritual Revolt*, 13–14.

25. *Israel and Revelation*, 465.

26. *The Ecumenic Age*, 228.

8

Voegelin's Challenge to Modernity's Claim to Be Scientific and Secular: The Ancient Theology and the Dream of Innerworldly Fulfillment

Stephen A. McKnight

From *Die Politischen Religionen* of 1938 to the final volume of *Order and History* published in 1987, religion remained a primary focus of Eric Voegelin's work. Moreover, for better or worse, Voegelin is best known for his claim that modernity is not secular and scientific but derives instead from Gnosticism, an ancient esoteric rival to Christianity. In this chapter I intend to relate recent research on the Renaissance revival of Hermeticism and other forms of esoteric religion to Voegelin's critique of modernity. My purpose is to demonstrate that this recent scholarship confirms Voegelin's basic insights, while it broadens and deepens the range of esoteric religious influences affecting modernity.

Many readers of this volume will be familiar with Voegelin's work, but may not be acquainted with recent research on the Renaissance revival of the *prisca theologia* tradition. I have, therefore, decided to proceed in the following manner. First, I want to begin on familiar ground by briefly reviewing the basic characteristics Voegelin identified with modernity, and then explain how and why he juxtaposed science to gnosis and secularization to a pseudomorphosis of ancient religion. I will then have a background against which I can discuss the Renaissance *prisca theologia* tradition, especially Hermeticism, and explain its connections to science and utopianism. I will then compare this "optimistic" immanentist *prisca theologia* tradition to "pessimistic," dualistic Gnosticism. This comparison will make the relevance and significance of the *prisca theologia* to Voegelin's critique of modernity clear. In order to underscore its impor-

185

tance, however, I will offer a brief case study relating Voegelin's concept of "Puritan Gnosticism" to recent work on Francis Bacon's Hermetic and millenarian dream of a great instauration.

Before taking up these tasks, however, I want my intent and purpose to be clear. My intent is to show that recent scholarship verifies that Voegelin's basic insights into the character of modernity are correct. At the same time, this scholarship diminishes the status of ancient Gnosticism as the primary source of modern epistemological and political disorder. In pointing to a broadening and deepening of the sources of esoteric religion and pseudoscience, I am not attempting to correct or disparage Voegelin's work. On the contrary, I think I am working very much in the Voegelinian mode. Voegelin was always open to the implications of new research and always willing to revise his theoretical and methodological position in light of new findings. Moreover, as will become clear in the course of this essay, Voegelin was already acknowledging problems with a unilinear emphasis on Gnosticism and encouraging the exploration of other esoteric traditions like magic, alchemy, and Renaissance neoplatonism. Were he still living, I think he would be very interested and deeply immersed in the work of Renaissance scholars and historians of science on the revival of the *prisca theologia* and its close ties to science and the utopian dreams of innerworldly fulfillment.

Gnosticism and Modernity

Three aspects of Voegelin's analysis of Gnosticism and modernity are going to be the focus of my discussion. The foremost is modernity's claim of an epochal break with the past. The second is the claim that the source of this epochal break is an extraordinary epistemological advance that equips humanity with both the knowledge and the ability to perfect society. The third element of this modern configuration is the conviction that this epistemological breakthrough allows humanity to alter the conditions of existence and, for the first time in human history, render it able to shape its own destiny. Modernists from the seventeenth century to the present have linked this epistemological leap and this confidence in humanity's capacity for self-determination with science and secularization. Voegelin makes these claims the focus of his critical analysis and develops the counterposition that the epistemological foundations of modernity are gnostic in nature.[1]

The gnostic believes that he has a direct grasp of the ultimate issues concerning human nature, human purpose, human meaning, and human destiny. With the possession of this knowledge, he is convinced that he is able to recognize accurately the sources of alienation and to escape from the prison of the world. Voegelin found this characteristic gnostic element in the epistemological and soteriological operations of modern political revolutionaries from the Puritan gnostics of the seventeenth century to Comte and Marx in the nineteenth century. The knowledge that modern revolutionaries put their faith in is purportedly modeled after science, but Voegelin demonstrates that these "social science" projects took natural science far beyond the boundaries proper to it. Whereas Galileo and Newton readily acknowledged the limits of the field to which the new methodologies could be applied, the seventeenth-century Baconians, the eighteenth-century *philosophes*, and nineteenth-century "social scientists" disregarded those limitations and used the method in the way that the ancient Gnostics used esoteric knowledge, that is, as a means to escape alienation and transform existence.

Voegelin's analysis of the transformation of science into the equivalent of an esoteric religion by radical social and political reformers not only undermines the powerful link that social science attempts to establish with natural science but also undercuts another basic tenet of modernity—that it is secular. Secularization, another fundamental modernist theme, developed in the eighteenth century and has expanded in our own time to the point that Hans Blumenberg can claim that the terms *modernity* and *secularization* are virtually identical.[2] Voegelin's analysis shows, however, that modernity is not overwhelmingly secular. The root concept of knowledge and the basic views of society and history are religious in origin and function.

The juxtaposition of science to *gnosis* was a central feature of Voegelin's analysis of modernity in the 1940s, 1950s, and 1960s. Beginning in the 1970s, however, Voegelin acknowledged that other esoteric traditions also played a major role in shaping the character of the modern age. This realization came from the study of new historical data and from new theoretical insights that convinced him that the configuration of ideas that he was analyzing was far more complex than he had originally realized. He subsequently published essays on magic and sorcery in the writings of Hegel and others,[3] and we know from his lectures and from his research notes that he had a strong interest in work on the Renaissance recovery of Hermeticism and related esoteric traditions.[4]

The Renaissance Recovery of Ancient Wisdom

The work most directly relevant to Voegelin's analysis of modernity focuses on what is called the *prisca theologia* or ancient theology tradition. This *prisca theologia* is a compendium of a wide array of esoteric religious and pseudoscientific traditions, including Orphism, Zoroastrianism, Hermeticism, Cabala, alchemy, and magic. The term *prisca theologia*, which was used by Marsilio Ficino (1433–99) and other theologians and philosophers of the Renaissance, reflects their opinion that these materials contained the pristine theological and philosophical revelations to the great wise men, the magi, of the ancient Near East and Mediterranean.

One of these ancient wisdom traditions, the Hermetic, was of particular interest. A clear indication of the high regard for Hermes Trismegistus is the fact that Ficino, the head of the Platonic Academy, set aside his work on recently acquired Platonic dialogues to analyze newly found Hermetic materials. The reasons for giving primacy to Hermes Trismegistus was that he was believed to be the first in a series of ancient wise men who received revelations regarding the true nature of the world and of humanity's place in it.[5] Scholarship on the *Corpus Hermeticum* has long recognized that it is a compendium of a wide range of materials, some radically dualistic, others intensely immanentistic. It has only fairly recently been recognized, however, that Ficino and other influential early modern thinkers concentrated on the highly optimistic, immanentist elements of the Hermetic tradition that portrayed humanity as a terrestrial god able to master nature and perfect society.[6] I intend to examine the optimistic, immanentist strands and show their similarities and differences with ancient Gnosticism. I wish to make two key points through this comparison: (1) the Hermetic materials are gnostic in the generic sense, that is, they have a doctrine of saving knowledge, but (2) the worldview of the Hermetic materials is profoundly different from the Gnostic pessimistic view. To demonstrate that this is the case, I will develop the themes in the Hermetic creation story and compare it to Gnostic views presented in the classic text, "The Hymn of the Pearl."

Hermetic Views of Human Nature: Man as a Terrestrial God

The Hermetic text that Ficino was responsible for translating and introducing into the mainstreams of modern thought was the *Pimander*, which contains a creation myth often referred to as the "Egyptian Genesis." This compact but comprehensive myth is revealed when Hermes is called into the presence of Pimander, "the mind of sovereignty," who asks him: "What do you want to hear and see; what do you want to learn and know from your understanding?" Hermes replies: "I wish to learn about the things that are, to understand their nature, and to know god."[7]

Pimander tells him that God created the Demiurge, who created the seven celestial Governors who encompass the world and whose rule is known as Fate. He is then told of man's creation, and the first important feature to note is that the Supreme God and not the Demiurge is man's creator. "Mind, the father of all, who is life and light, gave birth to a man like himself whom he loved as his own child. The man was most fair: he had the father's image; and god, who was really in love with his own form, bestowed on him all his craftworks."⁸ When man sees the creation of the Demiurge, he wants to participate in creation, and God the Father orders the celestial powers to teach man how the cosmos is governed. After receiving knowledge and creative power from the cosmic sources, man enters into the world of Nature and Matter.

> Having all authority over the cosmos of mortals and unreasoning animals, the man broke through the vault and stooped to look through the cosmic framework, thus displaying to lower nature the fair form of god. Nature smiled for love when she saw him whose fairness brings no surfeit [and] who holds in himself all the energy of the governors and the form of god, for in the water she saw the shape of the man's fairest form and upon the earth its shadow. When the man saw in the water the form like himself as it was in nature, he loved it and wished to inhabit it; wish and action came in the same moment, and he inhabited the unreasoning form. Nature took hold of her beloved, hugged him all about and embraced him, for they were lovers.

The narrator then explains the implications of this union for man's nature. "Because of this, unlike any other living thing on earth, mankind is twofold—in the body mortal but immortal in the essential man. Even though he is immortal and has authority over all things, mankind is affected by mortality because he is subject to fate. . . ."⁹

Later on, Pimander asks if Hermes understands how death (loss of immortality) can be avoided and Hermes replies that man must turn toward the light (knowledge/*nous*) because it is the essence of God and the essence of man. But Hermes is still somewhat troubled. Don't all men possess God-given minds; are not all men capable of salvation? Pimander answers, "I myself, the mind, am present to the blessed and good and pure and merciful—to the reverent—and my presence becomes a help. . . . But from these I remain distant—the thoughtless and evil and wicked and envious and greedy and violent and irreverent—giving way to the avenging demon. . . ." Hermes then asks about the stages of the ascent to God and is told of the seven stages and of the final union with God: "This is the final good for those who have received knowledge: to be made god."¹⁰ Pimander then commands Hermes to use what he has learned to save other men from damnation.

Several important features emerge from this compact myth. First of all, the cosmogony makes the creation a work of beauty and harmony that is divinely inspired and maintained by celestial influences. The material world is not intrinsically evil or an inherent threat to humanity. On the contrary, Primal Man and Nature love each other. Nevertheless, there are aspects of the world that are turned away from the divine influence and retain the properties of the *prima materia*—the tendency to dissolve or to revert to their original state as part of moist-humid Nature. Despite this inclination, the world is a work of beauty and a suitable home for humans, especially when they become actively involved in it. The explanation of humanity's loss of immortality makes it clear that the world is not inherently evil. For one whose life is oriented toward the light (knowledge and God), the world is not a temptation or an obstruction. Only if a person has turned from the light is he or she susceptible to the attraction of the flesh and inclined toward darkness (a material existence). This pursuit of material pleasure is a willful choice; it is not the result of original sin or of inherent evil in the world. The myth, therefore, stands in dramatic contrast to dualistic views of the tension between the flesh and the spirit, the secular and the sacred.

Another feature to note is the emphasis the myth places on humanity's capacity for godlike knowledge and on knowledge as the means of salvation. At the creation God provides man with the knowledge needed to exercise his role as a divine co-creator, and the myth contains repeated references to parallels between the divine *Nous* and man's *nous* and to the role of the *Logos* as the link between man, the creation, and the Supreme God.[11] Man becomes damned to a material existence only if he willfully ignores or denies the noetic dimension of his soul.

The *Asclepius*, which Ficino regarded as the second divine book of Hermes Trismegistus, contains a section worthy of brief note because of its explanation of the problem of evil in the world. In the texts we have already examined, evil is not inherent in the world, and humanity is not flawed with original sin. Yet, the *Asclepius* warns that it is possible for humanity to become so disoriented that chaos and despair will consume the world. Egypt, the holy land that Hermes has served as priest-king, will be overrun by barbarians who will destroy the true religion and the gods will leave the earth and go back to heaven leaving only evil angels who will goad people to commit every conceivable crime. "Then neither will the earth stand firm nor the sea be sailable; stars will not cross heaven nor will the course of the stars stand firm in heaven. . . . The fruits of the earth will rot; the soil will no more be fertile; and the very air will droop in gloomy lethargy."[12] The lament does not explain the origin of this time of troubles, except to say that it will occur when barbarians, who do not understand the true religion, overrun Egypt. Instead, the purpose of this passage is to provide a reassurance that the condition is only temporary and that God will intervene to renew the world and humankind.

> Such will be the old age of the world: irreverence, disorder, disregard for everything good. When all this comes to pass, Asclepius, then the master

and father, the god whose power is primary, governor of the first god, will look on this conduct and these willful crimes, and in an act of will—which is god's benevolence—he will take his stand against the vices and the perversion in everything, righting wrongs, washing away malice in a flood or consuming it in fire or ending it by spreading pestilential disease everywhere. Then he will restore the world to its beauty of old so that the world itself will again seem deserving of worship and wonder, and with constant benedictions and proclamations of praise the people of that time will honor the god who makes and restores so great a work. And this will be the geniture of the world: a reformation of all good things and a restitution, most holy and most reverent, of nature itself, reordered in the course of time [but through an act of will,] which is and was everlasting and without beginning.[13]

Here again, then, we have repetition of a theme noted earlier. Evil and disorder are not the permanent state of the world. They are temporary conditions that will be alleviated by divine redemption that will turn the world again into paradise and restore humanity to its proper state.

Ficino regarded the Hermetic writings as a prefiguring of the Christian revelation. His commentary on book 1 of the *Pimander*, "the Egyptian Genesis," draws several parallels to the Mosaic Genesis. Moses describes a darkness over the abyss and the spirit of God brooding over the waters: Hermes sees a darkness and the Word of God warming the Moist Nature. Moses describes creation by the word of God: Hermes identifies the word with the Logos or Son of God. Both describe humanity being made in the image of God, both contain a command to the species to be fruitful and multiply, and both explain how humanity may regain its immortality.[14]

There are, however, significant differences between the two myths. The most striking contrast is in the emphasis on knowledge. In two of the stories of Genesis 1–11, man is punished for his effort to obtain knowledge that would make him like God. The first occurs in the third chapter when mankind is tempted to eat from the Tree of Knowledge (and of the Tree of Life). For this sin, man is driven from Eden and punished not only with physical suffering but also by a profound rupture in his union with God. This theme of divine knowledge being forbidden to man is also a central element in the story of the Tower of Babel. In this myth, man decides to build a tower that will permit him to storm the heavens and occupy the place of God. To confound man's attempt to overstep his boundaries in such a defiant way, God disrupts his ability to communicate. By contrast, the Hermetic myths underscore man's divinity and describe man as possessing both godlike knowledge and the creative capacity to use that knowledge to emulate God's creation. Rather than denying or forbidding man to possess knowledge that would make him truly like

God, the Hermetic myths portray this as man's basic nature and the most precious gift of his Father.

Several other important comparisons also need to be made. First of all, man precedes creation and has a cosmogonic role to play. He is not made by God out of the dust of the earth; he is an emanation of God and is of the same substance (*nous*). Second, man is given the magus's dominion over the macrocosm and not just the earth. Third, godlike knowledge is the source of man's salvation; it is not the source of sin. Moreover, the Hermetic ascent up the seven stages toward union with God seems analogous to the effort to build a Tower of Babel. The Hermetic theme of salvation through spiritual knowledge suggests a parallel with Gnosticism. It is, therefore, appropriate to provide a brief comparison and contrast of the Hermetic views described above with the basic understanding of creation and man's place in the world expressed in the ancient Gnostic materials.

Gnostic and Hermetic Knowledge of Salvation

One of the classic Gnostic texts is known as "the Hymn of the Pearl." This text opens as follows:

> When I was a little child and dwelt in the kingdom of my Father's house and delighted in the wealth and splendor of those who raised me, my parents sent me forth from the East, our homeland, with provisions for the journey. From the riches of our treasure-house they tied me a burden: great it was, yet light, so that I might carry it alone. . . . They took off from me the robe of glory which in their love they had made for me, and my purple mantle that was woven to conform exactly to my figure, and made a covenant with me, and wrote it in my heart that I might not forget it: "When thou goest down into Egypt and bringest the One Pearl which lies in the middle of the sea which is encircled by the snorting serpent, thou shalt put on again thy robe of glory and thy mantle over it and with thy brother our next in rank be heir in our kingdom."[15]

The narrator then gives an account of his journey into Egypt. While in Egypt he meets "one of my race" who warns against the Egyptians and "contact with the unclean ones." Despite his precaution, the Egyptians "ingratiated themselves with me, and mixed me [drink] with their cunning, and gave me to taste of their meat; and I forgot that I was a king's son and served their king. I forgot the Pearl for which my parents had sent me. Through the heaviness of their nourishment I sank into deep slumber."[16]

This "ingratiation" is a trap deliberately sprung on the royal visitor by the Egyptians. The son's predicament causes great anxiety in his father's kingdom, and it is decided that all of the royal governors and officers of the land will prepare a letter and send it to the son.

> From thy father the King of Kings, and from thy mother, mistress of the East, and from thy brother, our next in rank, unto thee, our son in Egypt, greeting. Awake and rise up out of thy sleep, and perceive the words of our letter. Remember that thou art a king's son: behold whom thou hast served in bondage. Be mindful of the Pearl, for whose sake thou hast departed into Egypt. Remember thy robe of glory, recall thy splendid mantle, that thou mayest put them on and deck thyself with them and thy name be read in the book of the heroes and thou become with thy brother, our deputy, heir in our kingdom.

The message is given over to an eagle who is capable of avoiding "the children of Babel and the rebellious demons of Sarbûg." Upon receipt of the message, the son remembers his royal origin and awakens from the slumber that he had fallen into. Immediately he sets out "to enchant the terrible and snorting serpent" to recover the pearl and return home to his father's kingdom. "Their filthy and impure garment I put off, and left it behind in their land, and directed my way that I might come to the light of our homeland, the East." Upon return, his mission accomplished, there is much joy that the pearl is returned and that the son is safely home.[17]

Even if one is unfamiliar with the specific Gnostic meaning of certain symbols, the thrust of this myth is clear and its contrast to the Hermetic myths evident. The king of kings is the supreme God, and the son who is sent is the son of God comparable to Primal Man in the Hermetic myth. In attempting to recover the pearl, he becomes trapped in matter and forgets his divine origin and mission. The pessimistic, dualistic view of the physical is expressed in references to food and drink being the source of trickery, the garments put on to be like the Egyptians as filthy, and the consequences of the treachery as slumber and sleepwalking. The eagle is a universal symbol of a divine messenger. The meaning of the symbol, the pearl, is not so readily apparent, though myths of a great treasure lost in the dross of the world are a frequent component of dualistic religions and most often refer to the soul that becomes imprisoned in matter and has to be rescued by divine action. This is the meaning here. Without explaining how the divine soul becomes entrapped, the myth, nevertheless, expresses this as the fundamental condition. The effects of the material world are so strong that even God's son forgets his true nature and his real home.

This text stands in stark contrast to the Hermetic materials. In the Gnostic myth, salvation, or regaining one's divine station, depends on escaping from the world. In the Hermetic myth, by contrast, the world is necessary for humanity to exercise its divine creativity, and it is in the world that humanity creates the social microcosm that completes creation. In the Hermetic myth, the threat posed by the material world is not due to its inherent evil, but is the result of human ignorance of the proper relation of the material and the divine. The two esoteric traditions also have very different understandings of the benefits of knowledge. In the Gnostic myth, knowledge frees humanity from an ignorant effort to find meaning and purpose in the world. In the Hermetic material, knowledge enables humanity to master nature and perfect society, that is, to create a utopian existence.

Even though these fundamental differences exist, a sharp contrast between Gnosticism and Hermeticism has not always been made. Festugière, who is one of the most important early scholars of the *Corpus Hermeticum*, referred to it as Gnostic.[18] The reason for doing so was because of the Hermetic emphasis on knowledge as the means of salvation. But, as we have now seen, the Hermetic materials contain a very different understanding of what is meant by salvation from the disorder of the world. Moreover, to use such a broad definition of "Gnostic" would mean that many esoteric traditions, such as Orphism, Pythagorianism, Zoroastrianism, and Cabala, would have to be placed under this elastic term. To do so, however, obscures the characteristic differences that distinguish them.

Festugière attempted to deal with the differences between the Gnostic dread of the world and the Hermetic immanentism we have examined by distinguishing between optimistic and pessimistic forms of Hermetic Gnosticism. But this attempt, which was subsequently adopted by Walker and Yates and introduced into Renaissance Hermetic studies, only causes unnecessary confusion.[19] There is a wide variety of esoteric traditions that have a doctrine of saving knowledge. Moreover, it is the optimistic strands of the Hermetic and other ancient wisdom traditions (*prisca theologia*) that influenced Ficino and other Renaissance thinkers interested in mastering nature and perfecting society and "overcoming fate." Therefore, the themes that enter modern thought through Renaissance neoplatonism have a thrust profoundly different from those associated with ancient and modern gnostic nihilism.[20] In pushing for recognition of the Hermetic pattern in modern thought, I do not mean to discount the influence of pessimistic Gnosticism as examined, for example, by Hans Jonas, who draws parallels to modern nihilism and existentialism. Rather, my purpose is to argue that another mode of esoteric saving knowledge gains attention in the Renaissance and becomes part of a different pattern in modernity—one that emphasizes human dominance over nature and stresses the transformation of the natural and social order into paradise. These features are usually linked with science and secularization and not with esoteric religion. It is necessary, therefore, to look carefully at the transmission of this set of ideas from the Hermetic materials into the mainstream of modern thought and then relate them to Voegelin's critique of modernity.

Puritan Gnosticism and Bacon's Great Instauration

In order to show the relevance of this material, I intend to take as a case study Voegelin's concept of "Puritan Gnosticism" in *The New Science of Politics* and recent scholarship on Francis Bacon's vision of a Great Instauration. The phrase "Great Instauration" is taken from the title of one of Bacon's best-known works. In it he presents his program for the transformation of England into a utopian society through the reform of religion and the use of science to master nature and bring relief to man's estate. In developing this analysis of Bacon's vision, I not only want to show the presence of Hermetic or ancient wisdom themes, but also to relate my discussion to Voegelin's analysis of Puritan Gnosticism in *The New Science of Politics.*

Before turning to Bacon, I need to mention that Voegelin makes no reference to Bacon in his discussion of Puritan Gnosticism. I am prepared to argue, however, that Bacon's work, developed in the Puritan revolutionary framework, offers a clear, concise articulation of the features Voegelin identifies as characteristic of Puritan Gnosticism. Moreover, I intend to indicate that an analysis of Bacon makes a fundamental connection with Voegelin's analysis of the transformation of science into scientism, another central theme in *The New Science of Politics.*

Francis Bacon is usually presented as a great hero of science and progress during the seventeenth century Battle of the Ancients and Moderns.[21] Recently, however, this placement of Bacon and other leading figures of the seventeenth century into the modern camp of science and technology, which stands at odds with the ancient camp of religion and philosophy, has come under critical scrutiny. There is, for example, Charles Webster's important book, *The Great Instauration: Science, Medicine and Reform,* which documents the complex interplay of religious yearnings, political ideologies, and the rise of science between 1626 and 1660. Webster gives particular emphasis to the distinctive variety of Puritan eschatology and millenarianism that linked scientific progress to the reversal of the intellectual decline that had plagued humanity since the Fall of Adam, and saw in the advances in learning the prospects of restoring humanity's dominion over nature and its paradisical existence prior to Original Sin.

Francis Bacon lived and wrote prior to the period Webster focuses on. His significance for the period is attested to, however, by Webster's title,

The Great Instauration, which is borrowed from Bacon. According to Webster, Bacon's term and the project it describes are emblematic of the Puritan millenarian expectation. That is, it presents the advancement of learning as a necessary means to usher in the religious millennium of peace, harmony, and prosperity.

Recently, Charles Whitney has added substantial insight into the meaning of Bacon's root symbol of instauration by establishing its primary Renaissance and classical uses. The primary meaning in Bacon's time derives from the Vulgate edition of the Bible, where the term occurs in more than two dozen passages alluding to the apocalyptic restoration of Jerusalem and the golden age of the Davidic-Solomonic Kingship. This theme is particularly significant in Bacon's time because James I was heralded as the new Solomon who would restore Jerusalem.[22] The term is also used in a broader apocalyptic meaning in several Vulgate passages referring to Christ's redemption and restoration of humanity to its prelapsarian condition prior to Original Sin.[23] Like Webster and Whitney, I am interested in the sources of Bacon's central concept of "instauration." My focus, however, is not on orthodox Judeo-Christian sources, which have now been well documented. Rather, I am interested in the possible influence of the *prisca theologia* or ancient wisdom tradition of esoteric religion and occult science, which was revived by Ficino and the Platonic Academy as part of the Renaissance recovery of ancient learning.

The ancient wisdom tradition augments or complements the Judeo-Christian apocalyptic and millenarian themes at two points that help us to understand Bacon's concept of *instauration*. First, the Hermetic and alchemical traditions purported to contain the wisdom necessary to restore humanity to its primordial state. In this aboriginal condition, man lived in harmony with God, had dominion over nature, and lived in a utopian world free from want. Second, these traditions parallel the traditional Judeo-Christian apocalyptic or millenarian pattern in their description of an ideal, primordial condition that was lost through human ignorance and error, but will be restored at a time appointed by God.

A text of Bacon's dedicated to James I and linking the ancient, pure esoteric knowledge of nature and of government is "A Brief Discourse Touching the Happy Union of the Kingdoms of England and Scotland" (1603). The private dedication states that

> the education and erudition of the kings of Persia was in a science which was termed by a name then of great reverence, but now degenerate and taken in ill part: for the Persian magic, which was the secret literature of their kings, was an observation of the contemplations of nature and an application thereof to a sense politic; taking the fundamental laws of nature, with the branches and passages of them, as an original and first model, whence to take and describe a copy and imitation for government.[24]

Another reference to the original, pure form of Persian magic occurs in a later work, *De . . . augmentis scientiarum* (1623), the expanded Latin version of the *Advancement of Learning* (1605). Here it occurs in the context of a discussion of the accuracy and adequacy of various forms of natural philosophy. Bacon distinguishes what he calls "popular and degenerate" natural magic from the ancient magic of the Persians, which he asserts should "be again restored to its ancient and honourable meaning." For among Persians "magic was taken for a sublime wisdom, and the knowledge of the universal consent of things; and so the three kings who came from the east to worship Christ were called by the name of Magi."[25]

These two allusions to a pure natural magic that has been lost or corrupted helps us to set the stage for an analysis of Bacon's reference to the recovery and advancement of the original pure state of knowledge that has been lost through the passage of time. The principal source for developing this theme is *De sapientia veterum* (*Wisdom of the Ancients*, 1609). Only one of the fables can be discussed here: that of Orpheus. For Bacon, the fable of Orpheus is the story of the decline of philosophy as it descends from the natural philosophy of the ancient wise men to moral and civil philosophy and finally to a state of almost total disintegration.[26] In its pristine state, "natural philosophy proposes to itself as its noblest work of all, nothing less than the restitution and renovation [*instauratio*] of things corruptible, and (what is indeed the same thing in a lower degree) the conservation of bodies in the state in which they are, and the retardation of dissolution and putrefaction."[27] The effort at retardation, however, means arduous labor, and failure leads to frustration and to the adoption of the easier task—the management of human affairs through moral and civil philosophy. This stage of philosophy remains stable for a time, but then men return to "the depraved conditions of their nature" and these perturbations put moral and civil laws to silence. "And if such troubles last, it is not for long before letters also and philosophy are so torn in pieces that no traces of them can be found but a few fragments, scattered here and there. . . ." When philosophy and civilization reach this low point, barbarism sets in and disorder prevails "until, according to the appointed vicissitude of things, they break out and issue forth again, perhaps among other nations, and not in the places where they were before."[28]

With this brief analysis in mind, I want to turn to Bacon's own fable of instauration, the *New Atlantis*. Bacon's tale has European voyagers discovering the utopia of the title, called Bensalem by its inhabitants, when a storm throws them off course, and they learn what makes this land so different through a series of interviews with the Governor of the House of Strangers and an elder of Solomon's House. I will discuss the substance of two of these conversations: the founding of Solomon's House, and Bensalem's miraculous conversion to Christianity.

In the *New Atlantis*, Bacon presents Bensalem as the one civilization that stands as the exception to the general pattern of civilizational disintegration and decay. According to the Governor of the Stranger's House, the source of Bensalem's success is Solomon's House founded 1,900 years ago by King Solamona. Solomon's House, or the College of the Six Days' Works, as it is also called, was created for "the finding out of the true nature of all things (whereby God mought have the more glory in the workmanship of them, and men the more fruit in the use of them)."[29] The Governor further explains that the name Solomon's House was inspired by the biblical Solomon's reputation for wisdom, which is known in Europe, but also because Bensalem had possession of Solomon's *Natural History*, a text that had been lost to the Europeans. This text held special knowledge of the working of nature that Solomon's House used as the guide for its own remarkable work.

In a subsequent interview with an elder of Solomon's House, the Europeans are told: "The end of our Foundation is the knowledge of causes, and secret motions of things; and the enlarging of the bounds of Human Empire, to the effecting of all things possible." A detailed description of the investigation of the natural world then follows: from caves to mountain observatories to marine investigations. These investigations produce a breadth and depth of knowledge beyond anything imagined in Europe. Experiments in the Lower Region, for example, produced new artificial metals that are used for curing diseases and prolonging life. There is also a "great variety of composts, and soils, for the making of the earth fruitful," and blended mineral waters, including one called Water of Paradise that was created by the brethren "for health, and prolongation of life." The Elder further indicates that "[w]e have also large and various orchards, and gardens . . . [and] make them also by art greater much than their nature; and their fruit greater and sweeter. . . . And many of them we so order as they become of medicinal use."[30] Many scholars have linked this description of the activities of Solomon's House to the advancement of learning that Bacon hoped James I would have the Solomonic wisdom to support. But one can see that it also mirrors the descriptions discussed earlier of the ancient forms of learning and of the civilizational accomplishments of the Persians, Egyptians, and Greeks. More specifically, it parallels the descriptions of an ancient learning that was able to retard age and prolong life and to restore corruptible things to their original, pure state.

The final segment of Bensalem's history that requires attention is the account of its conversion to Christianity. The governor explains that the conversion occurred as the result of a miraculous event that happened about twenty years after the Resurrection and Ascension of Christ. One night a great column of light appeared about a mile out on the ocean and some of the braver souls of the nearest city boarded boats and sailed out toward it. One of the boats had a member of Solomon's House on board, and he begged God to reveal the meaning of this miraculous event. The pillar of light was then transformed, leaving an ark (small chest) floating in the water. As he approached it, the chest opened to reveal a book and a letter. The letter was from the apostle Bartholemew, who stated that he had received a vision in which God appeared and told him to "commit this ark to the floods of the sea." When the ark reached its appointed destination, the people of that land would receive a special benediction: on the day the ark reaches them there will "come unto them salvation and peace and goodwill from the Father, and from the Lord Jesus." The book found in the ark contained the canonical books familiar to the Europeans and other "books of the New Testament, which were not at that time written. . . ."[31] This last phrase is peculiar, but makes it evident that the Bensalemites received sacred texts in addition to those that make up the European canon.

What is most noteworthy in this account is the fact that Bensalem's conversion occurs as the result of direct intervention by God, who has chosen the island for a special benediction. The evidence of this special election is found in the two symbols of the hierophany: the Pillar of Light and the ark. A Pillar of Light guided the Hebrews out of bondage in Egypt, and through the desert to Mt. Sinai, where God made his covenant with them. The ark is the prime symbol of God's selection of the Hebrews as his chosen people. Following the revelations on Mt. Sinai, Moses placed the law in the Ark of the Covenant, which also served as the throne of God's presence among his chosen people. This ark subsequently played a ritual role in the crossing of the Jordan into the Promised Land, and it is linked directly to the establishment of the Davidic-Solomonic kingships and the consecration of Jerusalem as the center of religious and political order. The use of the ark and the account of the miracle of Bensalem's conversion make it evident that the Bensalemites have been specially selected as God's new chosen people and the kingdom as the New Jerusalem.

At several places in his writings, Bacon argues that the damage done by Original Sin could be overcome in humanity and in nature, that is, humankind could, allegorically speaking, return to Eden. In the *Advancement of Learning*, for example, Bacon speaks of the purpose of learning as "a restitution and reinvesting (in great part) of man to sovereignty and power . . . which he had in the first state of creation."[32] A similar statement occurs in the *Novum Organum*: "For man by the Fall fell at the same time from his state of innocency and from his dominion over nature.

Both of these losses, however, can even in this life be in some part repaired; the former by religion and faith, the latter by the arts and sciences."[33] The notion that a restoration is possible through right knowledge also occurs in the "Proemium" to the *Instauratio Magna*. According to Bacon, "all trial should be made, whether that commerce between the mind of man and the nature of things . . . might by any means be restored to its perfect and original condition, [or at least] reduced to a better condition than that in which it now is."[34]

If we place these several references to the instauration of humanity to its prelapsarian condition in the context of the *New Atlantis*, we see that Bensalem has the benefit of both of the means for repairing the ruptured union with God caused by Original Sin. For its religious instauration, Bensalem has the benefit of a pure, apostolic form of Christianity and has both canonical and noncanonical books to guide it and keep it pure. For the instauration of the arts and sciences, Bensalem has the ancient wisdom contained in the Solomonic *Natural History* to guide its ongoing research. This ancient wisdom closely parallels the knowledge of the Persian magus that Bacon refers to in the passages read earlier. Quite clearly, both elements are necessary for instauration to occur.

Much more could be said about the ties between the *prisca theologia* tradition and Bacon's writings. Further analysis of the activities of Solomon's House can show parallels between them and alchemical practices, and Solomon's *Natural History* can be linked to the Cabala and other forms of ancient wisdom.[35] Likewise, Bacon's account of Adam's prelapsarian condition can be shown to have strong affinities with the Hermetic creation myth discussed earlier. Unfortunately, space does not permit further elaboration; instead, I must simply reiterate the main points being made, and then relate them to Voegelin's analysis of "Puritan Gnosticism."

I have tried to make two points regarding the relation of Bacon's program for the advancement of learning and the myths and symbols of the ancient wisdom tradition. First, Bacon's advancement of learning is also an instauration of ancient learning that had been lost or corrupted in the course of time. Second, this ancient wisdom tradition parallels and augments the Puritan apocalyptic and millenarian traditions that link science and the advancement of learning to a prelapsarian state where humanity has dominion over matter and lives in an ideal world in complete harmony with God.

If we now review the characteristic features of Voegelin's concept of Puritan Gnosticism, we can see that the basic pattern parallels Bacon's call for a Great Instauration. Voegelin identifies four characteristic features of modern gnosticism in the Puritan case: (1) It entailed "the successful invasion of Western [religious and political] institutions by Gnostic move-

ments" aiming at the creation of a world-immanent apocalyptic or eschatological fulfillment of history. (2) It included the systematic formulation
of a new doctrine in scriptural terms, which sanctified and legitimated
the gnostic call for transformation of the existing political order and the
intellectual and institutional foundations on which it rested. (3) It constituted an attack on "classic philosophy and scholastic theology; and, since
under the two heads came the major and certainly the decisive part of
Western intellectual culture," an attack in which this culture received a
destructive blow from which it has been unable to recover. (4) And finally, the Puritan revolution had "for its purpose a change in the nature
of man and the establishment of a transfigured society."[36]

In Bacon's age, England becomes persuaded that it has an apocalyptic
role to play in salvation history. The fulfillment of this destiny is possible
because of an advancement in knowledge, this knowledge becoming the
basis for human action as the agent for the fulfillment of history. Moreover, in Bacon we see not only the transformation and appropriation of
apocalyptic symbols, we see these symbols conjoined with the esoteric
view of humankind as a terrestrial god able to transform society through
science.

This brief case study of Voegelin's account of Puritan Gnosticism and
Bacon's Great Instauration demonstrates, I believe, the significance of the
prisca theologia materials for Voegelin's analysis of modernity and sup-
plies a response to a major criticism of Voegelin's analysis of parallels
between ancient Gnosticism and modernity. Voegelin's critics rightly note
that ancient Gnosticism had no interest in transforming the world as
modern reformers yearn to do. Ancient Gnosticism portrayed the world
as a prison to be escaped because it is irredeemable. In fact, Gnostics
believed that the primary symptom of profound ignorance (*agnoia*) was
expressed in the belief that the world could be made into a suitable home
for humanity. Critics, therefore, claim that Voegelin inappropriately
transforms a radically dualistic loathing of the world into a messianic
yearning for innerworldly perfection. Such a transformation, they maintain, so alters the nature of traditional Gnosticism that it ceases to be what
it originally was—a radical yearning for release from the prison of the
world through saving knowledge.

The *prisca theologia* materials, on the other hand, contain a concept of
saving knowledge that is directed at transforming this world into a perfect
home for humanity. These materials, therefore, confirm Voegelin's basic
insight. Voegelin's primary point was to demonstrate that modern dreams
of innerworldly perfection are not grounded in science but are modern
versions of esoteric religion and pseudoscience. The current work by Renaissance specialists and historians of science supply the theoretical and
historical data to confirm this key insight but locate the origins in the

prisca theologia. It is important to note, however, that this recent work does show that Voegelin and his contemporaries were using the term "Gnosticism" in a far too elastic manner. It is not the specific ancient religion Gnosticism that is the root of modern dreams of innerworldly perfection. It is rather a broad stream of esoteric religion and pseudoscience that entered the modern age through the Renaissance reverence for the tradition as a *prisca theologia.*

Conclusion

We can summarize the importance of these recent developments by noting that they demonstrate the presence of a broad-based ancient theology tradition that can be shown to have direct formal and historical connections with those features of the modern age that Voegelin identified with Gnosticism. The significance of these materials for the analysis of the origins of modern thought and experience has been obscured in part because early work on the Hermetic materials by Festugière and others referred to them as Gnostic. This was because the *prisca theologia* shares the Gnostic emphasis on saving knowledge. But emphasis on this general trait eclipses fundamental distinctions. The Hermetic materials, as already noted, contend that humanity can find innerworldly fulfillment; the gnostic regards the search for innerworldly fulfillment as a sign of ignorance (*agnoia*), not *gnosis.* It would, therefore, be formally and historically more accurate to differentiate between the elements of modernity that parallel ancient Gnosticism, such as nihilism and existentialism, and those that parallel the *prisca theologia* tradition, such as modern utopian movements. This differentiation would be especially useful to Voegelinians and others who want to explore the esoteric origins of scientism and utopianism. Another consequence of this research is that it moves toward a fundamental reevaluation of the core concept of science itself, a reevaluation that supports Voegelin's juxtaposition of modern science with religious, esoteric-knowledge systems that inform modern programs of social reformation.[37]

Notes

1. See Eric Voegelin, *The New Science of Politics: An Introduction* (Chicago: University of Chicago Press, 1952); *Science, Politics, and Gnosticism* (Chicago: Henry Regnery, 1968); and *From Enlightenment to Revolution*, ed. John H. Hallowell (Durham, N.C.: Duke University Press, 1975).

2. See Hans Blumenberg, *The Legitimacy of the Modern Age*, trans. R. M. Wallace (Cambridge, Mass.: MIT Press, 1983), a translation of the second revised edition of the German original, *Die Legitimität der Neuzeit.*

3. Eric Voegelin, "On Hegel: A Study in Sorcery," in *The Collected Works of Eric Voegelin*, vol. 12, *Published Essays, 1966–1985*, ed. Ellis Sandoz (Baton Rouge: Louisiana State University Press, 1990), 213–55, and "Wisdom and the Magic of the Extreme: A Meditation," in *Published Essays, 1966–1985*, 315–75.

4. Voegelin made Renaissance neoplatonism the subject of his 1971 Notre Dame lecture, which celebrated the twentieth anniversary of *The New Science of Politics*, and he stated the need to qualify the use of the term "Gnosticism" and to investigate other sources of modernity in his plenary lecture at Vanderbilt in 1978.

5. For a discussion of the terms *prisca theologia* and *prisci theologi* and the genealogies of the Ancient Wisdom developed by Ficino, see D. P. Walker, *Spiritual and Demonic Magic: From Ficino to Campanella* (London: Warburg Institute, 1958), and *The Ancient Theology* (Ithaca, N.Y.: Cornell University Press, 1972).

6. I provide a more detailed discussion of the Renaissance recovery of the *prisca theologia* and of Ficino's use of it in "Eric Voegelin, The Renaissance *Prisca Theologia* Tradition, and Changing Perspectives on the Gnostic Features of Modernity," in *International and Interdisciplinary Perspectives on Eric Voegelin*, ed. Stephen A. McKnight and Geoffrey L. Price (Columbia: University of Missouri Press, 1997).

7. The English quotations are from Brian P. Copenhaver, *Hermetica* (Cambridge: Cambridge University Press, 1992). This passage is found on page 1. The standard edition of the *Corpus Hermeticum* is by Festugière and Nock, 4 vols. (Paris: J. Gabalda, 1954–1960); see vol. 4, 26ff. Ficino's Latin translation and commentary are found in Marsilio Ficino, *Opera Omnia*, reprint (Turin: Bottega d'Erasmo, 1959), vol. 4, 1837ff.

8. *Hermetica*, 3.

9. *Hermetica*, 3.

10. *Hermetica*, 5–6.

11. The myth, like classical philosophy's concept of the cosmos, emphasizes the link between *Logos* as the source of order and *logos* as humanity's understanding of the ordering principles of creation.

12. *Hermetica*, 83.

13. *Hermetica*, 82–83.

14. Ficino, *Opera Omnia*, vol. 4, 1850.

15. The translation is found in Hans Jonas, *The Gnostic Religion: The Message of the Alien God and the Beginnings of Christianity*, 2d ed. (Boston: Beacon Press, 1963), 113. Jonas uses this myth as characteristic of ancient Gnosticism and draws parallels to modern nihilism and existentialism.

16. Jonas, *The Gnostic Religion*, 113–14 (brackets in original).

17. Jonas, *The Gnostic Religion*, 114–15.

18. A.-J. Festugière, *La Révélation d'Hermès Trismégiste*, 4 vols. (Paris: J. Gabalda, 1949–54).

19. See Walker's *Spiritual and Demonic Magic* and *The Ancient Theology*. Of Frances A. Yates's several books, the most influential has been *Giordano Bruno and the Hermetic Tradition* (London: Routledge, 1964).

20. I briefly discuss the difference between optimistic Hermeticism and pessi-

mistic Gnosticism in "Eric Voegelin and the Changing Perspective on the Gnostic Features of Modernity," in *The Allure of Gnosticism*, ed. Robert A. Segal (Chicago: Open Court, 1995), 136–46.

21. See, for example, Richard F. Jones, *Ancients and Moderns: A Study of the Rise of the Scientific Movement in Seventeenth-Century England*, 2d ed. (St. Louis: Washington University Press, 1961).

22. Charles Whitney, *Francis Bacon and Modernity* (New Haven: Yale University Press, 1986), and "Bacon's *Instauratio*," *Journal of the History of Ideas* 50 (1989): 371–90.

23. More than two dozen references to the instauration of Solomon's Temple appear in the Vulgate. The Vulgate also uses the verb to describe God's renewal of the world and the apocalyptic Christ's renewal of the world and the fulfillment of time. For example, in Ps. 104 *instaurabis faciem terrae* is translated by Bacon as "the Earth . . . Doth now return to the former state" (Francis Bacon, *Works*, 14 vols, ed. James Spedding, R. L. Ellis, and D. D. Heath, reprint of 1857–1874 edition [Stuttgart: Friedrich Fromann, 1963], vol. 7, 283). According to Whitney, "the Vulgate in effect creates a typology or symbolism of *instauration* by lexically connecting the architectural instauration of Solomon's Temple both to a prophetic 'rebuilding' of Israel and to a Christian instauration of all things in the apocalypse." This typological connection is the creation of the Vulgate. It does not exist in the Hebrew and Greek originals; see Whitney, "Bacon's *Instauratio*," 271.

24. Francis Bacon, "A Brief Discourse Touching Upon the Happy Union of the Kingdoms of England and Scotland," in *Works*, vol. 10, 90.

25. Francis Bacon, *De . . . augmentis scientiarum*, in *Philosophical Works of Francis Bacon*, ed. J. M. Robertson, reprint of 1905 edition (Freeport, N.Y.: Books for Libraries Press, 1970), 474.

26. It is important to note that the source for the myths that Bacon reinterprets, Natale Conti's *Mythologiae* (1551?), does not use the term *instauro* in the Orpheus myth or in the related myth of Deucalion. Orpheus represents the natural philosopher, and Eurydice, nature. To lead Eurydice from Hades with music is "the noblest work of natural philosophy," "the restitution and renovation [*restitutio et instauratio*]" of things corruptible. Deucalion and Pyrrha, sole survivors of the world deluge, pray "that they might know by what means to repair mankind" (*instaurandi generis humani*). Bacon's interpretation of the myth presents it as a "magical" instauration of nature (*verum renovationes sive instaurationes*)—that is, the technological transformation of nature that can lead to the instauration of humanity. See Whitney, "Bacon's *Instauratio*," 277.

27. Francis Bacon, *De sapientia veterum*, in *Philosophical Works*, 835–36.

28. Bacon, *De sapientia veterum*, 836.

29. Francis Bacon, *New Atlantis*, in *Philosophical Works*, 58.

30. Bacon, *New Atlantis*, 71.

31. Bacon, *New Atlantis*, 79.

32. Francis Bacon, *Advancement of Learning*, in *Works*, vol. 3, 222.

33. Francis Bacon, *Novum Organum*, in *Works*, vol. 4, 247–48.

34. Francis Bacon, *Instauratio Magna*, in *Works*, vol. 4, 7.

35. The Paraclesian text *Liber de Renovationis et Restaurationes* refers to the

extraction of pure chemical substances from compounds as the restoration or "instauration" of their original forms. These forms, the first entities, primal essences, or radical moistures of things, enable bodies to be renewed, refreshed, or brought back to youth and health (Whitney, "Bacon's *Instauratio*," 277). This clearly seems to be the thrust of the work of Solomon's House, and this parallels Bacon's references to the restoration and prolongation of life in *De sapientia veterum* and in *Historia Vitae et Mortis* where he also refers to "the instruments and dispensers of God's power and mercy in prolonging and renewing [*instaurandu*] the life of man" (Bacon, *Works*, vol. 2, 103; English transl. vol. 5, 215). In his *Oration on the Dignity of Man*, Pico associates the instauration of the Second Temple with the transmission of the Kabbalah. Frank E. Manuel, in *Utopian Thought in the Western World* (Cambridge, Mass.: Harvard University Press, 1979), 258, notes that "The Thirty-Six Elders of Solomon's House" bears overtures of the Judaic belief in thirty-six just men who sustain the world.

36. *The New Science of Politics*, 134, 140–41, 152; see 133–52.

37. For further indication of how these materials can be related to this theme, see the essays by David Walsh and Klaus Vondung in *Science, Pseudo-Science, and Utopianism*, ed. Stephen A. McKnight (Columbia: University of Missouri Press, 1992).

Bibliography

This bibliography is divided into three parts. The first part is an alphabetical listing of the published works by Eric Voegelin used in this study, along with other significant published writings, predominantly from the later years of his career. The second part contains a selection of English language studies by others on Voegelin that either address the topic of religion or religious experience or treat this basic area of his thought in a broadly helpful way. The third part is a list of other important works consulted by the contributors in the writing of their essays.

A complete international reference bibliography on Voegelin may be found in Geoffrey L. Price, "Eric Voegelin: A Classified Bibliography," *Bulletin of the John Rylands University Library of Manchester* 76, no. 2 (Summer 1994): 1–180.

Works by Eric Voegelin

Anamnesis. Trans. and ed. by Gerhart Niemeyer. Notre Dame: University of Notre Dame Press, 1978.

Anamnesis: Zur Theorie der Geschichte und Politik. Munich: R. Piper & Co., 1966.

"Anxiety and Reason." In *The Collected Works of Eric Voegelin*, vol. 28, *What Is History? And Other Late Unpublished Writings*, ed. Thomas A. Hollweck and Paul Caringella. Baton Rouge: Louisiana State University Press, 1990.

Autobiographical Reflections. Ed. Ellis Sandoz. Baton Rouge: Louisiana State University Press, 1989.

"Autobiographical Statement at Age Eighty-Two." In *The Beginning and the Beyond: Papers from the Gadamer and Voegelin Conferences, Supplementary Issue of Lonergan Workshop, Volume 4*, ed. Fred Lawrence. Chico, Calif.: Scholars Press, 1984.

"The Beginning and the Beyond: A Meditation on Truth." In *The Collected Works of Eric Voegelin*, vol. 28, *What Is History? And Other Late Unpublished Writings*, ed. Thomas A. Hollweck and Paul Caringella. Baton Rouge: Louisiana State University Press, 1990.

"Brief an Alfred Schütz über Edmund Husserl." In *Anamnesis: Zur Theorie der Geschichte und Politik.* Munich: R. Piper & Co., 1966.

Collected Works of Eric Voegelin. Vol. 2, *Race and State.* Trans. Ruth Hein of *Rasse und Staat* (1933). Ed. Klaus Vondung. Baton Rouge: Louisiana State University Press, 1997.

Collected Works of Eric Voegelin. Vol. 3, *The History of the Race Idea from Ray to Carus.* Trans. Ruth Hein of *Die Rassenidee in der Geistesgeschichte von Ray bis Carus* (1933). Ed. Klaus Vondung. Baton Rouge: Louisiana State University Press, 1998.

Collected Works of Eric Voegelin. Vol. 12, *Published Essays, 1966–1985.* Ed. Ellis Sandoz. Baton Rouge: Louisiana State University Press, 1990.

Collected Works of Eric Voegelin. Vol. 19, *History of Political Ideas, Volume I: Hellenism, Rome, and Early Christianity.* Ed. Athanasios Moulakis. Columbia: University of Missouri Press, 1997.

Collected Works of Eric Voegelin. Vol. 20, *History of Political Ideas, Volume II: The Middle Ages to Aquinas.* Ed. Peter von Sivers. Columbia: University of Missouri Press, 1997.

Collected Works of Eric Voegelin. Vol. 21, *History of Political Ideas, Volume III: The Later Middle Ages.* Ed. David Walsh. Columbia: University of Missouri Press, 1998.

Collected Works of Eric Voegelin. Vol. 22, *History of Political Ideas, Volume IV: Renaissance and Reformation.* Ed. David L. Morse and William M. Thompson. Columbia: University of Missouri Press, 1998.

Collected Works of Eric Voegelin. Vol. 23, *History of Political Ideas, Volume V: Religion and the Rise of Modernity.* Ed. James L. Wiser. Columbia: University of Missouri Press, 1998.

Collected Works of Eric Voegelin. Vol. 27, *The Nature of the Law, and Related Legal Writings.* Ed. Robert Anthony Pascal, James Lee Babin, and John William Corrington. Baton Rouge: Louisiana State University Press, 1991.

Collected Works of Eric Voegelin. Vol. 28, *What Is History? And Other Late Unpublished Writings.* Ed. Thomas A. Hollweck and Paul Caringella. Baton Rouge: Louisiana State University Press, 1990.

"Configurations of History." In *The Collected Works of Eric Voegelin*, vol. 12, *Published Essays, 1966–1985*, ed. Ellis Sandoz. Baton Rouge: Louisiana State University Press, 1990.

"Consciousness and Order: Foreword to 'Anamnesis' (1966)." Trans. the author, of the "Vorwort" to *Anamnesis: Zur Theorie der Geschichte und Politik.* In *The Beginning and the Beyond: Papers from the Gadamer and Voegelin Conferences, Supplementary Issue of Lonergan Workshop, Volume 4*, ed. Fred Lawrence. Chico, Calif.: Scholars Press, 1984.

Conversations with Eric Voegelin. Ed. R. Eric O'Connor. Thomas More Institute Papers/76. Montreal: Perry Printing Limited, 1980.

"The Eclipse of Reality." In *The Collected Works of Eric Voegelin*, vol. 28, *What Is History? And Other Late Unpublished Writings*, ed. Thomas A. Hollweck and Paul Caringella. Baton Rouge: Louisiana State University Press, 1990.

"Epilogue." In *Eric Voegelin's Thought: A Critical Appraisal*, ed. Ellis Sandoz. Durham, N.C.: Duke University Press, 1982.

"Equivalences of Experience and Symbolization in History." In *The Collected Works of Eric Voegelin*, vol. 12, *Published Essays, 1966–1985*, ed. Ellis Sandoz. Baton Rouge: Louisiana State University Press, 1990.

"Ersatz Religion." In *Science, Politics, and Gnosticism*. Chicago: Henry Regnery Co., 1968.

From Enlightenment to Revolution. Ed. John H. Hallowell. Durham, N.C.: Duke University Press, 1975.

"The German University and the Order of German Society." In *The Collected Works of Eric Voegelin*, vol. 12, *Published Essays, 1966–1985*, ed. Ellis Sandoz. Baton Rouge: Louisiana State University Press, 1990.

"The Gospel and Culture." In *The Collected Works of Eric Voegelin*, vol. 12, *Published Essays, 1966–1985*, ed. Ellis Sandoz. Baton Rouge: Louisiana State University Press, 1990.

"Henry James's *The Turn of the Screw*." In *The Collected Works of Eric Voegelin*, vol. 12, *Published Essays, 1966–1985*, ed. Ellis Sandoz. Baton Rouge: Louisiana State University Press, 1990.

"History and Gnosis." In *The Old Testament and Christian Faith*, ed. Bernhard Anderson. New York: Herder and Herder, 1969.

"Immortality: Experience and Symbol." In *The Collected Works of Eric Voegelin*, vol. 12, *Published Essays, 1966–1985*, ed. Ellis Sandoz. Baton Rouge: Louisiana State University Press, 1990.

"In Search of the Ground." In *Conversations with Eric Voegelin*, ed. R. Eric O'Connor. Thomas More Institute Papers/76. Montreal: Perry Printing Limited, 1980.

"Industrial Society in Search of Reason." In *World Technology and Human Destiny*, ed. Raymond Aron. Ann Arbor: University of Michigan Press, 1963.

"Letter from Voegelin to Alfred Schütz on Edmund Husserl." (Letter to Alfred Schütz, September 17–20, 1943.) Translation of "Brief an Alfred Schütz über Edmund Husserl," in *Anamnesis* (1966). In *Faith and Political Philosophy: The Correspondence Between Leo Strauss and Eric Voegelin, 1934–1964*, trans. and ed. Peter Emberley and Barry Cooper. University Park: Pennsylvania State University Press, 1993.

"Letters to Leo Strauss." In *Faith and Political Philosophy: The Correspondence Between Leo Strauss and Eric Voegelin, 1934–1964*, trans. and ed. Peter Emberley and Barry Cooper. University Park: Pennsylvania State University Press, 1993.

"Liberalism and Its History." *Review of Politics* 36 (1974): 504–20.

"The Meditative Origin of the Philosophical Knowledge of Order." Trans. Frederick G. Lawrence of "Der meditative Ursprung philosophischen Ordnungswissens." In *The Beginning and the Beyond: Papers from the Gadamer and Voegelin Conferences, Supplementary Issue of Lonergan Workshop, Volume 4*, ed. Fred Lawrence. Chico, Calif.: Scholars Press, 1984.

"The Mongol Orders of Submission to European Powers." *Byzantion* 15 (1940–41): 378–413.

"The Moving Soul." In *The Collected Works of Eric Voegelin*, vol. 28, *What Is History? And Other Late Unpublished Writings*, ed. Thomas A. Hollweck and Paul Caringella. Baton Rouge: Louisiana State University Press, 1990.

"Myth as Environment." In *Conversations with Eric Voegelin*, ed. R. Eric O'Connor. Thomas More Institute Papers/76. Montreal: Perry Printing Limited, 1980.

"The Nature of the Law." In *The Collected Works of Eric Voegelin*, vol. 27, *The Nature of the Law, and Related Legal Writings*, ed. Robert Anthony Pascal, James Lee Babin, and John William Corrington. Baton Rouge: Louisiana State University Press, 1991.

"Necessary Moral Bases for Communication in a Democracy." In *Problems of Communication in a Pluralistic Society*. Milwaukee: Marquette University Press, 1956.

The New Science of Politics: An Introduction. Chicago: University of Chicago Press, 1952.

"Nietzsche, The Crisis and the War." *Journal of Politics* 6 (1944): 177–212.

"On Christianity." (Letter to Alfred Schütz, January 1, 1953.) In *The Philosophy of Order: Essays on History, Consciousness and Politics*, ed. Peter J. Opitz and Gregor Sebba. Stuttgart: Klett-Cotta, 1981.

"On Classical Studies." In *The Collected Works of Eric Voegelin*, vol. 12, *Published Essays, 1966–1985*, ed. Ellis Sandoz. Baton Rouge: Louisiana State University Press, 1990.

"On Debate and Existence." In *The Collected Works of Eric Voegelin*, vol. 12, *Published Essays, 1966–1985*, ed. Ellis Sandoz. Baton Rouge: Louisiana State University Press, 1990.

"On Gnosticism." (Letter to Alfred Schütz, January 10, 1953.) In *The Philosophy of Order: Essays on History, Consciousness and Politics*, ed. Peter J. Opitz and Gregor Sebba. Stuttgart: Klett-Cotta, 1981.

"On Hegel: A Study in Sorcery." In *The Collected Works of Eric Voegelin*, vol. 12, *Published Essays, 1966–1985*, ed. Ellis Sandoz. Baton Rouge: Louisiana State University Press, 1990.

"On Readiness to Rational Discussion." In *Freedom and Serfdom*, ed. Albert Hunold. Dordrecht: D. Reidel, 1961.

Order and History. Vol. 1, *Israel and Revelation*. Baton Rouge: Louisiana State University Press, 1956.

Order and History. Vol. 2, *The World of the Polis*. Baton Rouge: Louisiana State University Press, 1957.

Order and History. Vol. 3, *Plato and Aristotle*. Baton Rouge: Louisiana State University Press, 1957.

Order and History. Vol. 4, *The Ecumenic Age*. Baton Rouge: Louisiana State University Press, 1974.

Order and History. Vol. 5, *In Search of Order*. Baton Rouge: Louisiana State University Press, 1987.

"The Origins of Scientism." *Social Research* 15 (1948): 462–94.

"The Origins of Totalitarianism." Review of *The Origins of Totalitarianism*, by Hannah Arendt. With "A Reply" by Arendt and "Concluding Remark" by Voegelin. *Review of Politics* 15 (1953): 68–85.

"The Oxford Political Philosophers." *Philosophical Quarterly* 3 (April 1953): 97–114.

"Philosophies of History: An Interview with Eric Voegelin." *New Orleans Review* 2 (1973): 135–39.

Political Religions. Trans. T. J. DiNapoli and E. S. Easterly, III, of *Die Politischen Religionen* (1939). Toronto Studies in Theology 23. Lewistown, N.Y.: Edwin Mellen Press, 1986.

Die Politischen Religionen. 2d ed. Ausblicke, Stockholm: Berman-Fischer, 1939.

"Political Theory and the Pattern of General History." *American Political Science Review* 38 (1944): 746–54.

"Questions Up." In *Conversations with Eric Voegelin,* ed. R. Eric O'Connor. Thomas More Institute Papers/76. Montreal: Perry Printing Limited, 1980.

"Quod Deus Dicitur." In *The Collected Works of Eric Voegelin,* vol. 12, *Published Essays, 1966–1985,* ed. Ellis Sandoz. Baton Rouge: Louisiana State University Press, 1990.

Rasse und Staat. Tübingen: J. C. B. Mohr (Paul Siebeck), 1933.

"Reason: The Classic Experience." In *The Collected Works of Eric Voegelin,* vol. 12, *Published Essays, 1966–1985,* ed. Ellis Sandoz. Baton Rouge: Louisiana State University Press, 1990.

"Remembrance of Things Past." In *The Collected Works of Eric Voegelin,* vol. 12, *Published Essays, 1966–1985,* ed. Ellis Sandoz. Baton Rouge: Louisiana State University Press, 1990.

"Response to Professor Altizer's 'A New History and a New but Ancient God?'" In *The Collected Works of Eric Voegelin,* vol. 12, *Published Essays, 1966–1985,* ed. Ellis Sandoz. Baton Rouge: Louisiana State University Press, 1990.

Science, Politics, and Gnosticism. Chicago: Henry Regnery Co., 1968.

"Science, Politics, and Gnosticism," trans. William J. Fitzpatrick. In *Science, Politics, and Gnosticism.* Chicago: Henry Regnery Co., 1968.

"Das Sollen im System Kants." In *Gesellschaft, Staat und Recht,* ed. Alfred Verdross. Vienna: Verlag Julius Springer, 1931.

"Theology Confronting World Religions?" In *Conversations with Eric Voegelin,* ed. R. Eric O'Connor. Thomas More Institute Papers/76. Montreal: Perry Printing Limited, 1980.

"Toynbee's History As a Search for Truth." In *The Intent of Toynbee's History,* ed. Edward T. Gargan. Chicago: Loyola University Press, 1961.

"What Is History?" In *The Collected Works of Eric Voegelin,* vol. 28, *What Is History? And Other Late Unpublished Writings,* ed. Thomas A. Hollweck and Paul Caringella. Baton Rouge: Louisiana State University Press, 1990.

"Wisdom and the Magic of the Extreme: A Meditation." In *The Collected Works of Eric Voegelin,* vol. 12, *Published Essays, 1966–1985,* ed. Ellis Sandoz. Baton Rouge: Louisiana State University Press, 1990.

"World Empire and the Unity of Mankind." *International Affairs* 38 (1962): 170–83.

Selected Works on Voegelin and Religious Experience

Altizer, Thomas J. J. "A New History and a New But Ancient God? Voegelin's *The Ecumenic Age.*" In *Eric Voegelin's Thought: A Critical Appraisal,* ed. Ellis Sandoz. Durham, N.C.: Duke University Press, 1982.

———. "The Theological Conflict Between Strauss and Voegelin." In *Faith and Political Philosophy: The Correspondence Between Leo Strauss and Eric Voegelin, 1934–1964*, trans. and ed. Peter Emberley and Barry Cooper. University Park: Pennsylvania State University Press, 1993.

Anderson, Bernhard W. "Politics and the Transcendent: Voegelin's Philosophical and Theological Exposition of the Old Testament in the Context of the Ancient Near East." In *Eric Voegelin's Search for Order in History*, ed. Stephen A. McKnight. Baton Rouge: Louisiana State University Press, 1978.

Babin, James. "Eric Voegelin's Recovery of the Remembering Story." *Southern Review* 34 (Spring 1998): 341–66.

Bueno, Anibal A. "Consciousness, Time and Transcendence in Eric Voegelin's Philosophy." In *The Philosophy of Order: Essays on History, Consciousness and Politics*, ed. Peter J. Opitz and Gregor Sebba. Stuttgart: Klett-Cotta, 1981.

Caringella, Paul. "Voegelin: Philosopher of Divine Presence." In *Eric Voegelin's Significance for the Modern Mind*, ed. Ellis Sandoz. Baton Rouge: Louisiana State University Press, 1991.

Carmody, Denise Lardner, and John Tully Carmody. "Voegelin and the Restoration of Order: A Meditation." *Horizons* 14 (1987): 82–96.

Carmody, John T. "Eric Voegelin's Revelation." *Religion and Intellectual Life* 6 (1989): 44–54.

———. "Noetic Differentiation: Religious Implications." In *Voegelin and the Theologian: Ten Studies in Interpretation*, ed. John Kirby and William M. Thompson. Toronto Studies in Theology, Vol. 10. New York: Edwin Mellen Press, 1983.

Cooper, Barry. "An Introduction to Voegelin's Account of Western Civil Theologies." In *Voegelin and the Theologian: Ten Studies in Interpretation*, ed. John Kirby and William M. Thompson. Toronto Studies in Theology, Vol. 10. New York: Edwin Mellen Press, 1983.

———. *The Political Theory of Eric Voegelin*. Toronto Studies in Theology, Vol. 27. Lewiston, N.Y.: Edwin Mellen Press, 1986.

Corrington, John William. "Order and Consciousness/Consciousness and History: The New Program of Voegelin." In *Eric Voegelin's Search for Order in History*, ed. Stephen A. McKnight. Baton Rouge: Louisiana State University Press, 1978.

Dallmayr, Fred. "Voegelin's Search for Order." *Journal of Politics* 51 (May 1989): 411–30. Reprinted in Fred Dallmayr, *Margins of Political Discourse*. Albany: State University of New York Press, 1989.

Doran, Robert M. *Theology and the Dialectics of History*. Toronto: University of Toronto Press, 1990.

———. "Theology's Situation: Questions to Eric Voegelin." In *The Beginning and the Beyond: Papers from the Gadamer and Lonergan Conferences, Supplementary Issue of Lonergan Workshop, Vol. 4*, ed. Fred Lawrence. Chico, Calif.: Scholars Press, 1984.

Douglass, Bruce. "A Diminished Gospel: A Critique of Voegelin's Interpretation of Christianity." In *Eric Voegelin's Search for Order in History*, ed. Stephen A. McKnight. Baton Rouge: Louisiana State University Press, 1978.

———. "The Gospel and Political Order: Eric Voegelin on the Political Role of Christianity." *Journal of Politics* 38 (1976): 25–45.

Emberley, Peter, and Barry Cooper, trans. and eds. *Faith and Political Philosophy: The Correspondence Between Leo Strauss and Eric Voegelin, 1934–1964.* University Park: Pennsylvania State University Press, 1993.

Federici, Michael P. "Voegelin's Christian Critics." *Modern Age* 36 (1994): 331–40.

Fortin, Ernest L., and Glenn Hughes. "The Strauss-Voegelin Correspondence: Two Reflections and Two Comments." *Review of Politics* 56 (Spring 1994): 337–57.

Franz, Michael. *Eric Voegelin and the Politics of Spiritual Revolt: The Roots of Modern Ideology.* Baton Rouge: Louisiana State University Press, 1992.

Fuller, Timothy. "Philosophy, Faith, and the Question of Progress." In *Faith and Political Philosophy: The Correspondence Between Leo Strauss and Eric Voegelin, 1934–1964*, trans. and ed. Peter Emberley and Barry Cooper. University Park: Pennsylvania State University Press, 1993.

Gebhardt, Jürgen. "Toward the Process of Universal Mankind: The Formation of Voegelin's Philosophy of History." In *Eric Voegelin's Thought: A Critical Appraisal*, ed. Ellis Sandoz. Durham, N.C.: Duke University Press, 1982.

Germino, Dante. "Eric Voegelin: The In-Between of Human Life." In *Contemporary Political Philosophers*, ed. A. de Crespigny and Kenneth Minogue. London: Methuen, 1975.

———. "Eric Voegelin's *Anamnesis*." *Southern Review* 7 (1971): 68–88.

———. *Political Philosophy and the Open Society.* Baton Rouge: Louisiana State University Press, 1982.

———. "Voegelin, Christianity and Political Theory: *The New Science of Politics* Reconsidered." *Rivista Internazionale di Filosofia del Diritto* 4, no. 6 (1985): 40–84.

Granfield, David. *Heightened Consciousness: The Mystical Difference.* New York: Paulist Press, 1991.

Hallowell, John H. "Existence in Tension: Man In Search of His Humanity." *Political Science Reviewer* 2 (1972): 162–84.

Havard, William C. "Voegelin's Changing Conception of History and Consciousness." In *Eric Voegelin's Search for Order in History*, ed. Stephen A. McKnight. Baton Rouge: Louisiana State University Press, 1978.

Heilke, Thomas W. "Anamnetic Tales: The Place of Narrative in Eric Voegelin's Account of Consciousness." *Review of Politics* 58 (1966): 761–92.

Hughes, Glenn. "Eric Voegelin, Ezra Pound, and the Balance of Consciousness." *The Modern Schoolman* 75 (November 1997): 1–21.

———. "Eric Voegelin's View of History as a Drama of Transfiguration." *International Philosophical Quarterly* 30 (1990): 449–64.

———. "The Line That Runs from Time into Eternity: Transcendence and History in Eric Voegelin's *The Ecumenic Age*." *Political Science Reviewer* 27 (1998): 116–54.

———. *Mystery and Myth in the Philosophy of Eric Voegelin.* Columbia: University of Missouri Press, 1993.

Hughes, Glenn, and Frederick Lawrence. "The Challenge of Eric Voegelin." Review of *Collected Works of Eric Voegelin*, Vol. 12, *Published Essays, 1966–1985*, ed. Ellis Sandoz; Vol. 27, *The Nature of the Law, and Related Legal Writings*, ed. Robert Anthony Pascal, James Lee Babin, and John William Corrington; and Vol. 28, *What Is History? And Other Late Unpublished Writings*, ed. Thomas A. Hollweck and Paul Caringella. *The Political Science Reviewer* 24 (1995): 399–452.

Keulman, Kenneth. "The Tension of Consciousness: The Pneumatic Differentiation." In *Voegelin and the Theologian: Ten Studies in Interpretation*, ed. John Kirby and William M. Thompson. Toronto Studies in Theology, Vol. 10. New York: Edwin Mellen Press, 1983.

Kirby, John S. "On Reading Eric Voegelin: A Note on the Critical Literature." In *Voegelin and the Theologian: Ten Studies in Interpretation*, ed. John Kirby and William M. Thompson. Toronto Studies in Theology, Vol. 10. New York: Edwin Mellen Press, 1983.

———. "Symbolism and Dogmatism: Voegelin's Distinction." *Ecumenist* 12 (1975): 26–31.

Kirby, John, and William M. Thompson, eds. *Voegelin and the Theologian: Ten Studies in Interpretation*. Toronto Studies in Theology, Vol. 10. New York: Edwin Mellen Press, 1983.

Kuntz, Paul G. "Voegelin's Experiences of Disorder out of Order and Vision of Order out of Disorder: A Philosophic Meditation on His Theory of Order-Disorder." In *Eric Voegelin's Significance for the Modern Mind*, ed. Ellis Sandoz. Baton Rouge: Louisiana State University Press, 1991.

Lawrence, Frederick. "On 'The Meditative Origin of the Philosophical Knowledge of Order.'" In *The Beginning and the Beyond: Papers from the Gadamer and Lonergan Conferences, Supplementary Issue of Lonergan Workshop, Vol. 4*, ed. Fred Lawrence. Chico, Calif.: Scholars Press, 1984.

———. "Voegelin and Theology as Hermeneutical and Political." In *Voegelin and the Theologian: Ten Studies in Interpretation*, ed. John Kirby and William M. Thompson. Toronto Studies in Theology, Vol. 10. New York: Edwin Mellen Press, 1983.

———, ed. *The Beginning and the Beyond: Papers from the Gadamer and Lonergan Conferences, Supplementary Issue of Lonergan Workshop, Vol. 4*. Chico, Calif.: Scholars Press, 1984.

Levy, David. *The Measure of Man: Incursions in Philosophical and Political Anthropology*. Columbia: University of Missouri Press, 1993.

———. *Political Order: Philosophical Anthropology, Modernity, and the Challenge of Ideology*. Baton Rouge: Louisiana State University Press, 1987.

Lonergan, Bernard J. F. "Theology and Praxis." *Proceedings of the Catholic Theological Society of America* 32 (1977): 1–16.

McAllister, Ted V. *Revolt against Modernity: Leo Strauss, Eric Voegelin, and the Search for a Postliberal Order*. Lawrence: University Press of Kansas, 1996.

McCarroll, Joseph. "Man in Search of Divine Order in History." *Philosophical Studies* (National University of Ireland) 28 (1981): 15–45.

McKnight, Stephen A. "Eric Voegelin, The Renaissance *Prisca Theologia* Tradition, and Changing Perspectives on the Gnostic Features of Modernity." In *International and Interdisciplinary Perspectives on Eric Voegelin*, ed. Stephen A. McKnight and Geoffrey L. Price. Columbia: University of Missouri Press, 1997.

———. "The Evolution of Voegelin's Theory of Politics and History, 1944–1975." In *Eric Voegelin's Search for Order in History*, ed. Stephen A. McKnight. Baton Rouge: Louisiana State University Press, 1978.

———. "Voegelin's New Science of History." In *Eric Voegelin's Significance for the Modern Mind*, ed. Ellis Sandoz. Baton Rouge: Louisiana State University Press, 1991.

———, ed. *Eric Voegelin's Search for Order in History*. Baton Rouge: Louisiana State University Press, 1978.

McKnight, Stephen A., and Geoffrey L. Price, eds. *International and Interdisciplinary Perspectives on Eric Voegelin*. Columbia: University of Missouri Press, 1997.

Montgomery, Marion. *The Men I Have Chosen for Fathers: Literary and Philosophical Passages*. Columbia: University of Missouri Press, 1990.

Morrissey, Michael P. *Consciousness and Transcendence: The Theology of Eric Voegelin*. Notre Dame, Ind.: University of Notre Dame Press, 1994.

Nieli, Russell. "Eric Voegelin: An Eschatological Direction to History?" *Fides et Historia* 22 (1990): 3–15.

———. "Eric Voegelin's Evolving Ideas on Gnosticism, Mysticism, and Modern Radical Politics." *Independent Journal of Philosophy* 5–6 (1988): 93–102.

Niemeyer, Gerhart. "Christian Faith, and Religion, in Eric Voegelin's Work." *Review of Politics* 57 (1995): 91–104.

———. "Eric Voegelin's Philosophy and the Drama of Mankind." *Modern Age* 20 (Winter 1976): 28–39.

———. "God and Man, World and Society: The Last Work of Eric Voegelin." *Review of Politics* 51 (1989): 107–23.

Opitz, Peter J., and Gregor Sebba, eds. *The Philosophy of Order: Essays on History, Consciousness and Politics*. Stuttgart: Klett-Cotta, 1981.

Pangle, Thomas L. "Platonic Political Science in Strauss and Voegelin." In *Faith and Political Philosophy: The Correspondence Between Leo Strauss and Eric Voegelin, 1934–1964*, trans. and ed. Peter Emberley and Barry Cooper. University Park: Pennsylvania State University Press, 1993.

Perkins, Pheme. "Gnosis and the Life of the Spirit: The Price of Pneumatic Order." In *Voegelin and the Theologian: Ten Studies in Interpretation*, ed. John Kirby and William M. Thompson. Toronto Studies in Theology, Vol. 10. New York: Edwin Mellen Press, 1983.

Peters, Ted. "Voegelin for the Theologian." *Dialog: A Journal of Theology* 28 (1989): 210–22.

Porter, J. M. "A Philosophy of History as a Philosophy of Consciousness." *Denver Quarterly* 10 (1975): 96–104.

Ranieri, John J. *Eric Voegelin and the Good Society*. Columbia: University of Missouri Press, 1995.

Rhodes, James M. "Philosophy, Revelation, and Political Theory: Leo Strauss and Eric Voegelin." *Journal of Politics* 49 (1987): 1036–60.

———. "Voegelin and Christian Faith." *Center Journal* 2 (Summer 1983): 55–105.

Rosen, Stanley. "Politics or Transcendence? Responding to Historicism." In *Faith and Political Philosophy: The Correspondence Between Leo Strauss and Eric Voegelin, 1934–1964*, trans. and ed. Peter Emberley and Barry Cooper. University Park: Pennsylvania State University Press, 1993.

Russell, Greg. "Eric Voegelin on the Truth of In-Between Life: A Meditation on Existential Unrest." *Interpretation: A Journal of Bible and Theology* 16 (1989): 415–25.

Sandoz, Ellis. "Eric Voegelin and the Nature of Philosophy." *Modern Age* 13 (1969): 152–68.

———. "Medieval Rationalism or Mystic Philosophy? Reflections on the Strauss-Voegelin Correspondence." In *Faith and Political Philosophy: The Correspondence Between Leo Strauss and Eric Voegelin, 1934–1964*, trans. and ed. Peter Emberley and Barry Cooper. University Park: Pennsylvania State University Press, 1993.

———. *The Voegelinian Revolution: A Biographical Introduction.* Baton Rouge: Louisiana State University Press, 1981.

———. "Voegelin's Philosophy of History and Human Affairs, with Particular Attention to *Israel and Revelation* and Its Systematic Importance." *Canadian Journal of Political Science/Revue Canadienne de Science Politique* 31 (1998): 61–90.

———, ed. *Eric Voegelin's Significance for the Modern Mind.* Baton Rouge: Louisiana State University Press, 1991.

———, *Eric Voegelin's Thought: A Critical Appraisal.* Durham, N.C.: Duke University Press, 1982.

Schmidt, Larry. "Eric Voegelin's Contribution to a Theology of History." In *Voegelin and the Theologian: Ten Studies in Interpretation*, ed. John Kirby and William M. Thompson. Toronto Studies in Theology, Vol. 10. New York: Edwin Mellen Press, 1983.

Schram, Glenn N. "Eric Voegelin, Christian Faith and the American University." *Dialog: A Journal of Theology* 16 (1977): 130–35.

Sebba, Gregor. "History, Modernity and Gnosticism." In *The Philosophy of Order: Essays on History, Consciousness and Politics*, ed. Peter J. Opitz and Gregor Sebba. Stuttgart: Klett-Cotta, 1981.

———. "Orders and Disorders of the Soul." *Southern Review*, n.s., 3 (1967): 282–310.

———. "Prelude and Variations on the Theme of Eric Voegelin." *Southern Review*, n.s., 13 (1977): 646–76.

Simpson, Lewis P. "Voegelin and the Story of the Clerks." In *Eric Voegelin's Significance for the Modern Mind*, ed. Ellis Sandoz. Baton Rouge: Louisiana State University Press, 1991.

Srigley, Ronald D. *Eric Voegelin's Platonic Theology: Philosophy of Consciousness and Symbolization in a New Perspective.* Lewiston, N.Y.: Edwin Mellen Press, 1991.

Thompson, William M. "Voegelin and the Religious Scholar: An Introduction."

In *Voegelin and the Theologian: Ten Studies in Interpretation*, ed. John Kirby and William M. Thompson. Toronto Studies in Theology, Vol. 10. New York: Edwin Mellen Press, 1983.

———. "Voegelin on Jesus Christ." In *Voegelin and the Theologian: Ten Studies in Interpretation*, ed. John Kirby and William M. Thompson. Toronto Studies in Theology, Vol. 10. New York: Edwin Mellen Press, 1983.

Walsh, David. *After Ideology: Recovering the Spiritual Foundations of Freedom.* San Francisco: Harper and Row, 1990.

———. "The Reason-Revelation Tension in Strauss and Voegelin." In *Faith and Political Philosophy: The Correspondence Between Leo Strauss and Eric Voegelin, 1934–1964*, trans. and ed. Peter Emberley and Barry Cooper. University Park: Pennsylvania State University Press, 1993.

———. "The Scope of Voegelin's Philosophy of Consciousness." *Philosophical Studies* (National University of Ireland) 28 (1981): 45–63.

———. "Voegelin's Response to the Disorder of the Age." *Review of Politics* 46 (1984): 266–87.

Weatherby, Harold. "Myth, Fact and History: Voegelin on Christianity." *Modern Age* 12 (1978): 144–50.

Webb, Eugene. *Eric Voegelin: Philosopher of History.* Seattle: University of Washington Press, 1981.

———. "Eric Voegelin's Theory of Revelation." In *Eric Voegelin's Thought: A Critical Appraisal*, ed. Ellis Sandoz. Durham, N.C.: Duke University Press, 1982.

———. "Faith, Truth and Persuasion in the Work of Eric Voegelin." In *Voegelin and the Theologian: Ten Studies in Interpretation*, ed. John Kirby and William M. Thompson. Toronto Studies in Theology, Vol. 10. New York: Edwin Mellen Press, 1983.

———. "Metaphysics or *Existenzerhellung*: A Comparison of Lonergan and Voegelin." *Religious Studies and Theology* 7 (May/September 1987): 36–47.

———. *Philosophers of Consciousness: Polanyi, Lonergan, Voegelin, Ricoeur, Girard, Kierkegaard.* Seattle: University of Washington Press, 1988.

Weiss, Raymond L. "Voegelin's Biblical Hermeneutics." *Independent Journal of Philosophy* 5–6 (1988): 81–84.

Wilhelmsen, Frederick D. " 'Eric Voegelin and the Christian Tradition.' Review of Eric Voegelin, *The Ecumenic Age, Order and History*, vol. 4. 1974." In *Christianity and Political Philosophy*, ed. Frederick Wilhelmsen. Athens: University of Georgia Press, 1978.

Wiser, James. "From Cultural Analysis to Philosophical Anthropology: An Examination of Voegelin's Concept of Gnosticism." *Review of Politics* 42 (1980): 92–104.

———. "Reason and Revelation as Search and Response: A Comparison of Eric Voegelin and Leo Strauss." In *Faith and Political Philosophy: The Correspondence Between Leo Strauss and Eric Voegelin, 1934–1964*, trans. and ed. Peter Emberley and Barry Cooper. University Park: Pennsylvania State University Press, 1993.

Other Works Consulted

Anselm, Saint. "Meditation on Human Redemption." In *The Prayers and Meditations of St. Anselm, with the Proslogion*, trans. Benedicta Ward. New York: Penguin Books, 1953.

Augustine, Saint. *Confessions*, trans. R. S. Pine-Coffin. Baltimore: Penguin Books, 1961.

Bacon, Francis. *The Great Instauration*. Arlington Heights, Ill.: Harlan Davidson, 1980.

———. *Philosophical Works of Francis Bacon*. Ed. J. M. Robertson. Reprint of 1905 ed. Freeport, N.Y.: Books for Libraries Press, 1970.

———. *Works*. 14 vols. Ed. James Spedding, R. L. Ellis, and D. D. Heath. Reprint of 1857–74 ed. Stuttgart: Friedrich Fromann, 1963.

Barr, James. *The Garden of Eden and the Hope of Immortality*. Minneapolis: Fortress Press, 1992.

Bernstein, Richard. "The Meaning of Public Life." In *Religion and American Public Life*, ed. Robin W. Lovin. New York: Paulist Press, 1986.

Blumenberg, Hans. *The Legitimacy of the Modern Age*. Trans. R. M. Wallace. Cambridge, Mass.: MIT Press, 1983.

Carmody, John, and Denise Lardner Carmody. *Interpreting the Religious Experience: A Worldview*. Englewood Cliffs, N.J.: Prentice-Hall, 1987.

Cohn, Norman. *The Pursuit of the Millennium*. Rev. ed. New York: Oxford University Press, 1970.

Copenhaver, Brian P. *Hermetica*. Cambridge: Cambridge University Press, 1992.

Descartes, René. *Discourse on Method and Meditations*. Trans. Lawrence J. Lafleur. Indianapolis, Ind.: Bobbs-Merrill, 1960.

Elshtain, Jean Bethke. *Democracy on Trial*. New York: Basic Books, 1995.

Heiler, Friedrich. "The History of Religions as a Preparation for the Co-operation of Religions." In *The History of Religions*, ed. Mircea Eliade and Joseph M. Kitegawa. Chicago: University of Chicago Press, 1959.

Hobbes, Thomas. *Leviathan*. Harmondsworth, England: Penguin, 1968.

Jonas, Hans. *The Gnostic Religion: The Message of the Alien God and the Beginnings of Christianity*. 2d ed. Boston: Beacon Press, 1963.

Lonergan, Bernard J. F. *Insight: An Essay in Human Understanding*. New York: Harper and Row, 1957.

Manuel, Frank E. *Utopian Thought in the Western World*. Cambridge, Mass.: Harvard University Press, 1979.

Marx, Karl. *Selected Writings*. Ed. David McLellan. Oxford: Oxford University Press, 1977.

McKnight, Stephen A., ed. *Science, Pseudo-Science, and Utopianism*. Columbia: University of Missouri Press, 1992.

Plato. *The Collected Dialogues of Plato*. Ed. Edith Hamilton and Huntington Cairns. Princeton: Princeton University Press, 1961.

———. *Complete Works*. Ed. John M. Cooper. Indianapolis, Ind.: Hackett Publishing Company, 1997.

Pritchard, J. B., ed. *Ancient Near Eastern Texts Relating to the Old Testament*. Princeton: Princeton University Press, 1950.

Rahner, Karl. *Theological Investigations*, vol. 3. Trans. Karl-H. and Boniface Kruger. Baltimore: Helicon Press, 1967.

Scheler, Max. *Man's Place in the Cosmos*. Trans. Hans Meyerhoff of *Die Stellung des Menschen im Kosmos*. New York: Farrar, Straus and Giroux, 1981.

———. *On the Eternal in Man*. Trans. Bernard Noble of *Vom Ewigen im Menschen*. London: SCM Press, 1960.

Shankman, Steven. *In Search of the Classic*. University Park: Pennsylvania State University Press, 1994.

Taylor, Charles. "Comparison, History, Truth." In *Myth and Philosophy*, ed. Frank E. Reynolds and David Tracy. Albany: State University of New York Press, 1990.

———. *Multiculturalism*, ed. Amy Gutmann. Princeton: Princeton University Press, 1994.

———. *Sources of the Self: The Making of the Modern Identity*. Cambridge, Mass.: Harvard University Press, 1989.

Teresa of Avila. *The Interior Castle*, trans. Kieran Kavanaugh and Otilio Rodriguez. New York: Paulist Press, 1979.

Thompson, William M. *Christology and Spirituality*. New York: Crossroad, 1991.

Tracy, David. *The Analogical Imagination*. New York: Crossroad, 1981.

———. "Catholic Classics in American Liberal Culture." In *Catholicism and Liberalism*, ed. R. Bruce Douglass and David Hollenbach. Cambridge: Cambridge University Press, 1994.

———. "Particular Classics, Public Religion, and the American Tradition." In *Religion and American Public Life*, ed. Robin W. Lovin. New York: Paulist Press, 1986.

Walker, D. P. *The Ancient Theology*. Ithaca, N.Y.: Cornell University Press, 1972.

———. *Spiritual and Demonic Magic: From Ficino to Campanella*. London: Warburg Institute, 1958.

Whitney, Charles. "Bacon's *Instauratio*." *Journal of the History of Ideas* 50 (1989): 371–90.

———. *Francis Bacon and Modernity*. New Haven: Yale University Press, 1986.

Index

Abraham, 78–79
absurdism, imbalanced consciousness and, 171, 179
Aeschylus, 151, 177
afterlife, 18, 20, 29n17. *See also* immortality
anamnesis, 126, 127, 129, 130
Anglo-American political tradition, universalisms and, 44, 61n35
Anselm: immortality and, 24; *Proslogion,* 24
apocalyptic consciousness, 75–76, 79–80
apocalypticism, 151, 152; instauration and, 196, 200
apocalyptic pronouncements of New Age, loss of balanced consciousness and, 22
Aquinas, 144, 155
Arendt, Hannah, 51–52
Aristotle, 80, 147–48, 151, 154, 155; commonalities and, 39; contemplation and, 121–22; experience and, 58n9; immortality and, 18, 21, 22–23; Marx and, 145, 146; meditation and, 111; *Metaphysics,* 13, 31n51; myth and, 26, 31n51; *Politics,* 13; virtues and, 120
Asclepius, 190–92
athanatizein, 18, 24, 77, 78, 80
atheist materialism, 177–78
attunement, meditation and, 117, 118, 122, 127

Augustine: balanced consciousness and, 142; *Confessions,* 24, 89, 92, 93, 94, 95, 96–97, 99–101, 106, 108, 109, 110, 112, 122, 123, 124, 125, 126; immortality and, 24

Bacon, Francis, 149, 195–202, 202nn23, 26, 204n35
balance of consciousness, 163–83, 180n3; Augustine and, 142; Christianity and, 152–54, 161n39; existential difficulties and, 166–67; experiences and, 143–44, 151; historical difficulties and, 167–68; human role in, 169–70; loss of, *see* imbalanced consciousness; love and, 169–70, 181n10; *metaxy* and, 155, 168–69, 170, 180; Plato and, 142; as precarious, 151–56; as rarity, 180; spiritual disorder and, 141–51; tension of existence and, 163; transcendence and, 164–69. *See also* ideologies
Bensalem's conversion, 200; Bacon and, 198–99;
Bergson, Henri, 14
biologism, 150
Blumemberg, Hans, 187
Brahman, immanence as illusory and, 173–74, 182n17
Brunner, August, 90
Buddhism, 27n1; meditation and, 134n37

221

and, 69–74, 75, 77, 78–79, 81; immortality and, 19, 21, 25; love and,
16–17; *Symposium,* 19
Solomon's House, Bacon and, 198, 199
Spann, Othmar, 89–90, 92
spiritual disorder, 141–51, 156. *See also*
balance of consciousness; order and
disorder
spiritual horizon, expansion of and
contemporary theology, 25–26
Stalin, Joseph, 154
Stoics, 151
Strauss, Leo, 53–54
symbols: constants and, 45, 62nn42, 43;
equivalence and, 37–38, 59n13; of
immortality, 17–25, 28, 29; meditative exegesis of, 56; shattering of
idols and, 106–8

Taoism, 27n1, 125
Taylor, Charles, 34, 43, 44–45, 46,
61nn40, 41
technology, public role for reason in,
35
tension, reflective, 117–18
tension of existence, balance of consciousness and, 163
theology: expansion of historical and
spiritual horizon and, 25–26;
Voegelin and contemporary, 25–27
toleration, 48–53
totalitarianism, liberalism and, 51–52
Tracy, David, 46, 63n45
transcendence: balance of consciousness and, 164–69; loss of, *see* imbalanced consciousness
Trismegistus, Hermes, 188, 190
Turgot, Anne Robert Jacques, 149–50

uncertainty: ideologies and, 151; ordering and disordering of consciousness and, 143–46
universal humanity, epiphany of,
65–83; Abraham and, 78–79; apocalyptic consciousness and, 75–76,
79–80; decline of philosophy and
civilization and, 65–66; "Dispute of
a Man, Who Contemplates Suicide,
With His Soul" and, 66, 67–69, 70,
71, 72, 74, 75, 76, 78, 79; epiphany
of man and, 67–69; Paul and, 76–78,
79–80; Pauline vision of history
and, 76–78; philosophy in presence
of death and, 69–74; Socrates and,
69–74, 75, 77, 78–79, 81; universal
divine presence in the soul and,
80–81; vision of, 74–82
universalism, reason in public discourse and, 43–45, 61nn35, 39
universities, 156n1; people formed in
life of reason and, 42–43
Upanishads, meditation and, 125, 126,
134n37
utopianism, 202

Vedantic tradition, immanence as illusory and, 173–74, 182n17
virtues, 120; meditation and, 120, 122
vision, meditation and, 121
Voltaire, 149

wars, toleration and, 48–49
Weber, Max, 15
Webster, Charles, 195–96
Whitney, Charles, 196

xynon, 39

Zoroastrianism, 27n1, 194

About the Contributors

Michael Franz is the author of *Eric Voegelin and the Politics of Spiritual Revolt: The Roots of Modern Ideology* (Louisiana State University Press, 1992). He is presently associate professor and chair of the Department of Political Science at Loyola College, Maryland.

Glenn Hughes is the author of *Mystery and Myth in the Philosophy of Eric Voegelin* (University of Missouri Press, 1993) and "The Line That Runs from Time into Eternity: Transcendence and History in Eric Voegelin's *The Ecumenic Age*" (*The Political Science Reviewer*, 1998). He is associate professor of philosophy at St. Mary's University, San Antonio, Texas.

Stephen A. McKnight is the editor of *Eric Voegelin's Search for Order in History* (Louisiana State University Press, 1978) and coeditor of *International and Interdisciplinary Perspectives on Eric Voegelin* (University of Missouri Press, 1997). He is professor of European intellectual and cultural history at the University of Florida in Gainesville.

Michael P. Morrissey is the author of *Consciousness and Transcendence: The Theology of Eric Voegelin* (University of Notre Dame Press, 1994). Formerly assistant professor of theology at the University of St. Thomas in St. Paul, Minnesota, he is presently research assistant for the Institute of Reading Development in Novato, California.

William Petropulos has taught at the Geschwister-Scholl Institute for Political Science at the University of Munich where he is secretary of the Eric-Voegelin-Archiv-Gesellschaft e. V. He is the author of "Eric Voegelin and German Sociology," *Manchester Sociology Occasional Papers*, Number 50, University of Manchester, 1998.

Geoffrey L. Price is the coeditor of *International and Interdisciplinary Perspectives on Eric Voegelin* (University of Missouri Press, 1997). He is the founder and current director of the Centre for Voegelin Studies at the University of Manchester, where he holds the position of senior lecturer in theological studies.

John J. Ranieri is the author of *Eric Voegelin and the Good Society* (University of Missouri Press, 1995) and "Question and Imagination: Eric Voegelin's Approach" (*Lonergan Workshop, Volume 11*, 1995). He is presently assistant professor of philosophy at Seton Hall University in South Orange, New Jersey.

William M. Thompson is the coeditor of *Voegelin and the Theologian: Ten Studies in Interpretation* (Edwin Mellen Press, 1983), and the author of numerous books and articles including *Christology and Spirituality* (Crossroads, 1991). He is professor of theology at Duquesne University and currently is president of the Catholic Society of America.